May 25.

FRIEDRICH DÜRRENMATT

FOUR PLAYS
(1957–62)

FRIEDRICH DÜRRENMATT

FOUR PLAYS

1957-62

JONATHAN CAPE
THIRTY BEDFORD SQUARE
LONDON

PRINTED IN GREAT BRITAIN
BY EBENEZER BAYLIS AND SON, LIMITED
THE TRINITY PRESS, WORCESTER, AND LONDON
ON PAPER MADE BY JOHN DICKINSON AND CO. LTD
BOUND BY A. W. BAIN AND CO. LTD, LONDON

CONTENTS

PREFACE: PROBLEMS OF THE THEATRE   7

ROMULUS THE GREAT   43

THE MARRIAGE OF MR MISSISSIPPI   125

AN ANGEL COMES TO BABYLON   207

THE PHYSICISTS   295

PROBLEMS
OF THE
THEATRE

Translated from the German by
GERHARD NELLHAUS

PREFACE: PROBLEMS OF THE THEATRE

BEHOLD the drive for purity in art as art is practised these days. Behold this writer striving for the purely poetic, another for the purely lyrical, the purely epic, the purely dramatic. The painter ardently seeks to create the pure painting, the musician pure music, and someone even told me, pure radio represents the synthesis between Dionysus and Logos. Even more remarkable for our time, not otherwise renowned for its purity, is that each and everyone believes he has found his unique and the only true purity. Each vestal of the arts has, if you think of it, her own kind of chastity. Likewise, too numerous to count, are all the theories of the theatre, of what is pure theatre, pure tragedy, pure comedy. There are so many modern theories of the drama, what with each playwright keeping three or four at hand, that for this reason, if no other, I am a bit embarrassed to come along now with my theories of the problems of the theatre.

Furthermore, I would ask you not to look upon me as the spokesman of some specific movement in the theatre or of a certain dramatic technique, nor to believe that I knock at your door as the travelling salesman of one of the philosophies current on our stages today, whether as existentialist, nihilist, expressionist or satirist, or any other label put on the compote dished up by literary criticism. For me, the stage is not a battlefield for theories, philosophies and manifestoes, but rather an instrument whose possibilities I seek to know by playing with it. Of course, in my plays there are people and they hold to some belief or philosophy – a lot of blockheads would make for a dull piece – but my plays are not for what people have to say: what is said is there because my plays deal with people, and thinking and believing and philo-

9

sophizing are all, to some extent at least, a part of human nature. The problems I face as playwright are practical, working problems, problems I face not before, but during the writing. To be quite accurate about it, these problems usually come up after the writing is done, arising out of a certain curiosity to know how I did it. So what I would like to talk about now are these problems, even though I risk disappointing the general longing for something profound and creating the impression that an amateur is talking. I haven't the faintest notion of how else I should go about it, of how not to talk about art like an amateur. Consequently I speak only to those who fall asleep listening to Heidegger.

What I am concerned with are empirical rules, the possibilities of the theatre. But since we live in an age when literary scholarship and criticism flourish, I cannot quite resist the temptation of casting a few side glances at some of the theories of the art and practice of the theatre. The artist indeed has no need of scholarship. Scholarship derives laws from what exists already; otherwise it would not be scholarship. But the laws thus established have no value for the artist, even when they are true. The artist cannot accept a law he has not discovered for himself. If he cannot find such a law, scholarship cannot help him with one it has established; and when the artist does find one, then it does not matter that the same law was also discovered by scholarship. But scholarship, thus denied, stands behind the artist like a threatening ogre, ready to leap forth whenever the artist wants to talk about art. And so it is here. To talk about problems of the theatre is to enter into competition with literary scholarship. I undertake this with some misgivings. Literary scholarship looks on the theatre as an object; for the dramatist it is never something purely objective, something separate from him. He participates in it. It is true that the playwright's activity makes drama into something objective (that is exactly his job), but he destroys the object he has created again and again, forgets it, rejects it, scorns it, overestimates it, all in order to make room for something new. Scholarship sees only the result; the process, which led to this result, is what the playwright cannot forget. What he says has to be taken with a grain of salt. What he thinks about his art changes as he creates his art; his thoughts are always subject to his mood and the moment. What alone really counts for him is what he is doing at a given moment; for its sake he can betray what he did just a little while ago. Perhaps a writer should not talk about his art, but once he starts, then it is not altogether a waste of time to listen to him. Literary scholars who have not the faintest notion of the difficulties of writing and of the hidden rocks that force the stream of art into oft unsuspected channels run the danger of merely asserting and stupidly proclaiming laws that do not exist.

Doubtless the unities of time, place and action which Aristotle – so it was supposed for a long time – derived from Greek tragedy constitute the ideal of drama. From a logical and hence also aesthetic point of view, this thesis is incontestable, so incontestable indeed, that the question arises if it does not set up the framework once and for all within which each dramatist must work. Aristotle's three unities demand the greatest precision, the greatest economy and the greatest simplicity in the handling of the dramatic material. The unities of time, place and action ought to be a basic dictate put to the dramatist by literary scholarship, and the only reason scholarship does not hold the artist to them is that Aristotle's unities have not been obeyed by anyone for ages. Nor can they be obeyed, for reasons which best illustrate the relationship of the art of writing plays to the theories about that art.

The unities of time, place and action in essence presuppose Greek tragedy. Aristotle's unities do not make Greek tragedy possible; rather, Greek tragedy allows his unities. No matter how abstract an aesthetic law may appear to be, the work of art from which it was derived is contained in that law. If I want to set about writing a dramatic action which is to unfold and run its course in the same place within two hours, for instance, then this action must have a history behind it, and that history will be the more extensive the fewer the number of stage characters there are at my disposal. This is simply an experience of how the theatre works, an empirical rule. For me a history is the story which took place before the stage action commenced, a story which alone makes the action on the stage possible. Thus the history behind Hamlet is, of course, the murder of his father; the drama lies in the discovery of that murder. As a rule, too, the stage action is much shorter in time than the event depicted; it often starts out right in the middle of the event, or indeed towards the end of it. Before Sophocles' tragedy could begin, Oedipus had to have killed his father and married his mother, activities that take a little time. The stage action must compress an event to the same degree in which it fulfils the demands of Aristotle's unities. And the closer a playwright adheres to the three unities, the more important is the background history of the action.

It is, of course, possible to invent a history and hence a dramatic action that would seem particularly favourable for keeping to Aristotle's unities. But this brings into force the rule that the more invented a story is and the more unknown it is to the audience, the more careful must its exposition, the unfolding of the background be. Greek tragedy was possible only because it did not have to invent its historical background because, it already possessed one. The spectators knew the myths with which each drama dealt; and because these myths were public, ready coin, part of religion, they made the feats of the Greek tragedians possible, feats never to be attained again; they made possible their abbreviations, their straightforwardness, their stichomythy and choruses, and hence also Aristotle's unities. The audience knew what the play was all about; its curiosity was not focused on the story so much as on its treatment. Aristotle's unities presupposed the general appreciation of the subject matter – a genial exception in more recent times is Kleist's *The Broken Jug* – presupposed a religious theatre based on myths. Therefore as soon as the theatre lost its religious, its mythical significance, the unities had to be reinterpreted or discarded. An audience facing an unknown story will pay more attention to the story than to its treatment, and by necessity then such a play has to be richer in detail and circumstances than one with a known action. The feats of one playwright cannot be the feats of another. Each art exploits the chances offered by its time, and it is hard to imagine a time without chances. Like every other form of art, drama creates its world; but not every world can be created in the same fashion. This is the natural limitation of every aesthetic rule, no matter how self-evident such a rule may be. This does not mean that Aristotle's unities are obsolete; what was once a rule has become an exception, a case that may occur again at any time. The one-act play obeys the unities still, even though under a different condition. Instead of the history, the situation now dominates the plot, and thus unity is once again achieved.

But what is true for Aristotle's theory of drama, namely its dependency upon a certain world and hence its validity relative to that world, is also true of every other theory of drama. Brecht is consistent only when he incorporates into his dramaturgy that *Weltanschauung*, the communist philosophy, to which he – so he seems to think – is committed; but in doing so he often cuts off his own nose. Sometimes his plays say the very opposite of what they claim they say, but this lack of agreement cannot always be blamed on the capitalistic audience. Often it is simply a case where Brecht, the poet, gets the better of Brecht, the dramatic theorist, a situation that is wholly legitimate and ominous only were it not to happen again.

Let us speak plainly. My introducing the audience as a factor in the making of a play may have seemed strange to many. But just as it is impossible to have theatre without spectators, so it is senseless to consider and treat a play as if it were a kind of ode, divided into parts and delivered in a vacuum. A piece written for the theatre becomes living theatre when it is played, when it can be seen, heard, felt, and thus experienced immediately. This immediacy is one of the most essential aspects of the theatre, a fact so often overlooked in those sacred halls where a play by Hofmannsthal counts for more than one by Nestroy, and a Richard Strauss opera more than one by Offenbach. A play is an event, is something that happens. In the theatre everything must be transformed into something immediate, something visible and sensible; the corollary to this thought, however, is that not every-thing can be translated into something immediate and corporeal. Kafka, for example, really does not belong on the stage. The bread offered there gives no nourishment; it lies undigested in the iron stomachs of the theatre-going public and the regular sub-scribers. As luck would have it, many think of the heaviness they feel not as a stomach ache, but as the heaviness of soul which Kafka's true works emanate, so that by error all is put right.

The immediacy sought by every play, the spectacle into which it would be transformed, presupposes an audience, a theatre, a stage. Hence we would also do well to examine the theatres for which we have to write today. We all know these money-losing enterprises. They can, like so many other institutions today, be justified only on an idealistic basis: in reality, not at all. The architecture of our theatres, their seating arrangements and their stages, came down from the court theatre or, to be more precise, never got beyond it. For this reason alone, our so-called contem-porary theatre is not really contemporary. In contrast to the primitive Shakespearean stage, in contrast to this 'scaffold', the court theatre made every effort to satisfy a craving for natural-ness, even though this resulted in much greater unnaturalness. No longer was the audience satisfied to imagine the royal chamber behind the 'green curtain'; every attempt was made to show the chamber. Characteristic of such theatre is its tendency to separate audience and stage, by means both of the curtain and of having the spectators sit in the dark facing a well-lit stage. This latter in-novation was perhaps the most treacherous of all, for it alone made possible the solemn atmosphere in which our theatres suffo-cate. The stage became a peep-show. Better lighting was con-stantly invented, then a revolving stage, and it is said they have even invented a revolving house! The courts went, but the court theatre stayed on. Now to be sure, our time has discovered its own form of theatre, the cinema. But no matter how much we may emphasize the differences, and how important it may be to emphasize them, still it must be pointed out that the cinema grew out of the theatre, and that it can at last achieve what the court theatre with all its machinery, revolving stages and other effects only dreamed of doing: simulate reality.

The cinema, then, is nothing more nor less than the democratic form of the court theatre. It intensifies our sense of intimacy immeasurably, so much so that the films easily risk becoming the genuinely pornographic art. For the spectator is forced into being a 'voyeur', and film stars enjoy their immense popularity because those who see them come also to feel that they have slept with them; that is how well film stars are photographed. A larger-than-life picture is an indecency.

Just what, then, is our present-day theatre? If the cinema is the modern form of the old court theatre, what is the theatre? There is no use in pretending that the theatre today is anything much more than a museum in which the art treasures of former golden ages of the drama are put on exhibition. There is no way of changing that. It is only too natural at a time like ours – a time which, always looking towards the past, seems to possess everything but a living present. In Goethe's time the ancients were rarely performed, Schiller occasionally, but mostly Kotzebue and whoever else they were. It is worthwhile to point out that the cinema pre-empts the theatre of its Kotzebues and Birch-Pfeiffers, and it is hard to imagine what sort of plays would have to be put on today, if there were no films and if all the script-writers wrote for the legitimate stage.

If the contemporary theatre is to a large extent a museum, then this has definite effects on the actors whom it employs. They have become civil servants, usually even entitled to their pensions, permitted to act in the theatre when not kept busy making films.

The members of this once despised estate have settled down now as solid citizens – a human gain, an artistic loss. And today actors fit into the order of professional rank somewhere between the physicians and small industrialists, surpassed within the realm of art only by the winners of the Nobel prize, by pianists and conductors. Some actors are visiting professors of sorts, or independent scholars, who take their turn appearing in the museums or arranging exhibitions. The management, of course, takes this into account when it arranges its playbill more or less with an eye to its guest stars; says the management: what play should we put on when this or that authority in this or that field is available to us at such and such a date? Moreover, actors are forced to move about in many different acting styles, now in a baroque style, now in a classical one, today acting naturalism, tomorrow Claudel. An actor in Molière's day did not have to do that. The director, too, is more important, more dominant than ever, like the conductor of an orchestra. Historical works demand, and ought to demand, proper interpretation; but directors as yet dare not be as true to the works they put on as some conductors are, quite naturally, to theirs. The classics often are not interpreted but executed, and the curtain falls upon a mutilated corpse. But then, where is the danger in it all? There is always the saving convention by which all classical things are accepted as perfection, as a kind of gold standard in our cultural life, with all things looked upon as gold that shine in de luxe editions of the classics. The theatre-going public goes to see the classics, whether they be performed well or not; applause is assured, indeed is the duty of the educated man. And thus the public has legitimately been relieved of the task of thinking and of passing judgments other than those learned by rote in school.

Yet there is a good side to the many styles the present-day theatre must master, although it may at first glance appear bad. Every great age of the theatre was possible because of the discovery of a unique form of theatre, of a particular style, which determined the way plays were written. This is easily demonstrable in the English or Spanish theatre, or the Vienna National Theatre, the most remarkable phenomenon in the German-speaking theatre. This alone can explain the astounding number of plays written by Lope de Vega. Stylistically a play was no problem for him. But to the degree that a uniform style of theatre does not exist today, indeed can no longer exist, to that extent is writing for the theatre now a problem and thus more difficult. Therefore our contemporary theatre is two things: on one hand it is a museum, on the other an experimental field, each play confronting the author with new challenges, new questions of style. Yes, style today is no longer a common property, but highly private, even particularized from case to case. We have no style, only styles, which puts the situation in art today in a nutshell. For contemporary art is a series of experiments, nothing more nor less, just like all of our modern world.

If there are only styles, then, too, we have only theories of the art and practice of the theatre, and no longer one dramaturgy. We now have Brecht's and Eliot's, Claudel's and that of Frisch or of Hochwälder: always a new theory of drama for each dramatic offering. Nevertheless one can conceive of a single theory of drama, a theory that would cover all particular instances, much in the same way that we have worked out a geometry which embraces all dimensions. Aristotle's theory of drama would be only one of many possible theories in this dramaturgy. It would have to be a new *poetics*, which would examine the possibilities not of a certain stage, but of the stage, a dramaturgy of the experiment itself.

What, finally, might we say about the audience without which, as we have said before, no theatre is possible? The audience has become anonymous, just 'the paying public', a matter far worse than is at first apparent. The modern author no longer knows his public, unless he writes for some village stage or some festival of drama, neither of which is much fun. A playwright has to imagine his audience; but in truth the audience is he himself – and this

17

is a danger which can neither be altered now nor circumvented. All the dubious, well-worn, politically misused notions which attach themselves to the concepts of 'a people' and 'society', to say nothing of 'a community', have perforce also crept into the theatre. What points is an author to make? How is he to find his subjects, what solutions should he reach? All these are questions for which we may perhaps find an answer once we have gained a clearer notion as to what possibilities still exist in the theatre today.

In undertaking to write a play I must first make clear to myself just where it is to take place. At first glance that does not seem much of a problem. A play takes place in London or Berlin, in the mountains, a hospital or on a battlefield, wherever the action demands. But it does not work out quite that way. A play, after all, takes place upon a stage which in turn must represent London, the mountains or a battlefield. This distinction need not, but can be made. It depends entirely on how much the author takes the stage into account, how strongly he wants to create the illusion without which no theatre can exist, and whether he wants it smeared on thickly with gobs of paint heaped upon the canvas, or transparent, diaphanous and fragile. A playwright can be deadly serious about the place: Madrid, the Rütli, the Russian steppe, or he can think of it as just a stage, the world, his world.

How the stage is to represent a given place is, of course, the task of the scene designer. Since designing scenes is a form of painting, the developments which have taken place in painting in our time have not failed to touch the theatre. But the theatre can really neither abstract man nor language, which is in itself both abstract and concrete, and scenery, no matter how abstract it would pretend to be, must still represent something concrete to make sense, and for both of these reasons, abstraction in scenic design has essentially failed. Nevertheless the 'green curtain' behind which the spectators have to imagine the place, the royal chamber, was reinstituted. The fact was recalled that the dramatic place and the stage were not one and the same, no matter how elaborate, how verisimilar the stage setting might be. The fact is the place has to be created by the play. One word: we are in Venice; another, in the Tower of London. The imagination of the audience needs but little support. Scenery is to suggest, point out, intensify, but not describe the place. Once more it has become transparent, immaterialized. And similarly the place of the drama to be shown on the stage can be made immaterial.

Two fairly recent plays which most clearly illustrate the possibility referred to as immaterializing the scenery and the dramatic place are Wilder's *Our Town* and *The Skin of Our Teeth*. The immaterializing of the stage in *Our Town* consists of this: the stage is nearly empty; only a few objects needed for rehearsals stand about – some chairs, tables, ladders and so on; and out of these everyday objects the place is created, the dramatic place, the town, all out of the word, the play, the wakened imagination of the spectators. In his other play Wilder, that great fanatic of the theatre, immaterializes the dramatic place: where the Antrobus family really lives, in what age and what stage of civilization, is never wholly clear; now it is the ice age, now a world war. This sort of experiment may be met quite often in modern drama; thus it is indefinite where in Frisch's play, *Graf Öderland*, the strange Count Wasteland abides; no man knows where to wait for Godot, and in *The Marriage of Mr Mississippi* (*Die Ehe des Herrn Mississippi*) I expressed the indefiniteness of the locale (in order to give the play its spirit of wit, of comedy) by having the right window of a room look out upon a northern landscape with a Gothic cathedral and an apple tree, while the left window of the same room opens on a southern scene with an ancient ruin, a touch of the Mediterranean and a cypress. The really decisive point in all this is that, to quote Max Frisch, the playwright is making poetry with the stage, a possibility which has always entertained and occupied me and which is one of the reasons, if not the main one, why I write plays. But then – and I am thinking of the comedies of Aristophanes and the comic plays of Nestroy –

in every age poetry has been written not only *for*, but *with* the stage.

Let us turn from these incidental problems to more basic ones. What do the particular problems look like, which I – to cite an author whom I know at least partially, though not fully – have faced? In *The Blind Man* (*Der Blinde*) I wanted to juxtapose the word against the dramatic place, to turn the word against the scene. The blind duke believes he is living in his well-preserved castle whereas he is living in a ruin; he thinks he is humbling himself before Wallenstein, but sinks to his knees before a negro. The dramatic place is one and the same, but by means of the pretence carried on before the blind man, it plays a dual role: the place seen by the audience and the place in which the blind man fancies himself to be. So also, when in my comedy, *An Angel comes to Babylon* (*Ein Engel kommt nach Babylon*), I picked for my dramatic locale the city in which the Tower was built, I had essentially to solve two problems. In the first place the stage had to express the fact that there were two places of action in my comedy, heaven and the city of Babylon; heaven, which was the secret point of origin of the action, and Babylon the locale, where that action ran its course.

Well, I suppose heaven could have been simply represented by a dark background to suggest its infinity, but since I wanted to convey in my comedy the idea that heaven was not something infinite, but something incomprehensible and altogether different, I asked for the stage background, the heaven above the city of Babylon, to be occupied entirely by the Great Nebula in Andromeda, just as we might see it through the telescope on Mount Palomar. What I hoped to achieve thereby was that heaven, the incomprehensible and inscrutable, would take on form, gain, as it were, its own stage presence. In this wise also heaven's rapprochement with the earth was to be brought out, reiterating the coming together of the two that is expressed in the action through the angel's visiting Babylon. Thus, too, a world was constructed

20

in which the result of the action, namely the building of the Tower of Babylon, became possible.

In the second place I had to think of how to make the stage represent Babylon, the place in which the action unfolds. I found the idea of Babylon challenging because of its timeliness, its Cyclopean big-city character, its New York look with skyscrapers and slums, and by having the first two acts take place along the banks of the Euphrates I wished to hint at Paris. Babylon, in brief, stands for the metropolis. It is a Babylon of the imagination, having a few typically Babylonian features, but in a modernized parodied version, with its modernities – for instance the convenience of electric street-lights. Of course the execution of the scenery, the building of the stage itself, is a job for the scene designer, but the playwright must always decide himself just what kind of stage he wants.

I love a colourful stage setting, a colourful theatre, like the stage of Theo Otto, to mention an admirable example. I have little use for a theatre that uses black curtains as was the fashion once upon a time, or for the tendency to glory in threadbare poverty which some stage designers seem to aim for. To be sure the word is important above all else in the theatre; but note: above all else. For after the word there are many other things, which also rightfully belong to the theatre, even a certain wantonness. Thus when someone asked me quite thoughtfully with respect to my play *Mississippi*, where one of the characters enters through a grandfather clock, whether or not I thought a four-dimensional theatre possible, I could only remark that I had not thought of Einstein when I did it. It is just that in my daily life it would give me great pleasure if I could join a gathering and astonish those present by coming into the room through a grandfather clock or by floating in through a window. No one should deny us playwrights the opportunity to satisfy such desires now and then at least on the stage, where such whims can be fulfilled. The old argument as to which came first, the chicken or the egg, can be transformed in art into the question of whether the egg or the chicken, the world as potential or as rich harvest, is to be presented. Artists might very well be divided then into those favouring the egg and those favouring the chicken. The argument is a lively one. Alfred Polgar once said to me, it was odd that while in contemporary Anglo-Saxon drama everything came out in the dialogue, there was always much too much happening on the stage in my plays and that he, Polgar, would sometimes like to see a simple Dürrenmatt play. Behind this truth, however, lies my refusal to say that the egg came before the chicken, and my personal prejudice of preferring the chicken to the egg. It happens to be my passion, not always a happy one perhaps, to want to put on the stage the richness, the manifold diversity of the world. As a result my theatre is open to many interpretations and appears to confuse some. Misunderstandings creep in, as when someone looks around desperately in the chicken coop of my plays, hoping to find the egg of Columbus which I stubbornly refuse to lay.

But a play is bound not only to a place, but also to a time. Just as the stage represents a place, so it also represents a time, the time *during* which the action takes place as well as the time *in* which it occurs. If Aristotle had really demanded the unity of time, place and action, he would have limited the duration of a tragedy to the time it took for the action to be carried out (a feat which the Greek tragedians nearly achieved), for which reasons, of course, everything would have to be concentrated upon that action. Time would pass 'naturally', everything coming one after the other without breaks. But this does not always have to be the case. In general the actions on the stage follow one another but, to cite an example, in Nestroy's magical farce, *Death on the Wedding Day (Der Tod am Hochzeitstag)*, there are two acts taking place simultaneously and the illusion of simultaneity is skilfully achieved by having the action of the second act form the background noise for the first, and the action of the first act the background noise for the second. Other examples of how time is used as a theatrical device could be easily recalled. Time can be shortened, stretched, intensified, arrested, repeated; the dramatist can, like Joshua, call to his heaven's orbits, 'Theatre-Sun, stand thou still upon Gibeon! And thou, Theatre-Moon, in the valley of Ajalon!'

It may be noted further that the unities ascribed to Aristotle were not wholly kept in Greek tragedy either. The action is interrupted by the choruses, and by this means time is spaced. When the chorus interrupts the action, it achieves as regards time – to elucidate the obvious like an amateur – the very same thing the curtain does today. The curtain cuts up and spreads out the time of an action. I have nothing against such an honourable device. The good thing about a curtain is that it so clearly defines an act, that it clears the table, so to speak. Moreover, it is psychologically often extremely necessary to give the exhausted and frightened audience a rest. But a new way of binding language and time has evolved in our day.

If I cite Wilder's *Our Town* once again, I do so because I assume that this fine play is widely known. You may recall that in it different characters turn towards the audience and talk of the worries and needs of their small town. In this way Wilder is able to dispense with the curtain. The curtain has been replaced by the direct address to the audience. The epic element of description has been added to the drama. For this reason, of course, this form of theatre has been called the epic theatre.

Yet when looked at quite closely, Shakespeare's plays or Goethe's *Götz von Berlichingen* are in a certain sense also epic theatre. Only in a different, less obvious manner. Since Shakespeare's histories often extend over a considerable period of time, this time-span is divided into different actions, different episodes, each of which is treated dramatically. *Henry IV*, Part I, consists of nineteen such episodes, while by the end of the fourth act of *Götz* there are already no less than forty-one tableaux. I stopped counting after that. If one looks at the way the overall action has been built up, then, with respect to time, it is quite close to the epic, like a film that is run too slowly, so that the individual shots can be seen. The condensation of everything into a certain time has been given up in favour of an episodic form of drama.

Thus when an author in some of our modern plays turns towards the audience, he attempts to give the play a greater continuity than is otherwise possible in an episodic form. The void between the acts is to be filled; the time-gap is to be bridged, not by a pause, but by words, by a description of what has gone on in the meanwhile, or by having some new character introduce himself. In other words, the expositions are handled in an epic manner, not the actions to which these expositions lead. This represents an advance of the word in the theatre, the attempt of the word to reconquer territory lost a long time ago. Let us emphasize that it is but an attempt; for all too often the direct address to the audience is used to explain the play, an undertaking that makes no sense whatever. If the audience is moved by the play, it will not need prodding by explanations; if the audience is not moved, all the prodding in the world will not be of help.

In contrast to the epic, which can describe human beings as they are, the drama unavoidably limits and therefore stylizes them. This limitation is inherent in the art form itself. The human being of the drama is, after all, a talking individual, and speech is his limitation. The action only serves to force this human being on the stage to talk in a certain way. The action is the crucible in which the human being is molten into words, must become words. This, of course, means that I, as the playwright, have to get the people in my drama into situations which force them to speak. If I merely show two people sitting together and drinking coffee while they talk about the weather, politics or the latest fashions, then I provide neither a dramatic situation nor dramatic dialogue, no matter how clever their talk. Some other ingredient must be added to their conversation, something to add pique, drama, double meaning. If the audience knows that there is some poison in one of the coffee cups, or perhaps even in both, so that the conversation is really one between two poisoners, then this little coffee-for-two idyll becomes through this artistic device a dramatic situation, out of which and on the basis of which dramatic dialogue can develop. Without the addition of some special tension or special condition, dramatic dialogue cannot develop.

Just as dialogue must develop out of a situation, so it must also lead into some situation, that is to say, of course, a new situation. Dramatic dialogue effects some action, some suffering, some new situation, out of which in turn new dialogue can again develop, and so on and so forth.

However, a human being does more than just talk. The fact that a man also thinks, or at least should think, that he feels, yes, more than anything feels, and that he does not always wish to show others what he is thinking or feeling, has led to the use of another artistic device, the monologue. It is true, of course, that a person standing on a stage and carrying on a conversation with himself out loud is not exactly natural; and the same thing can be said, only more so, of an operatic aria. But the monologue (like the aria) proves that an artistic trick, which really ought not to be played, can achieve an unexpected effect, to which, and rightly so, the public succumbs time and again; so much so that Hamlet's monologue, 'To be or not to be', or Faust's, are among the most beloved and most famous passages in the theatre.

But not everything that sounds like a monologue is monologue. The purpose of dialogue is not only to lead a human being to a point where he must act or suffer; at times it also leads into a major speech, to the explanation of some point of view. Many people have lost the appreciation of rhetoric since, as Hilpert maintains, some actor who was not sure of his lines discovered naturalism. That loss is rather sad. A speech can win its way across the footlights more effectively than any other artistic device. But many of our critics no longer know what to make of a speech. An author who today dares a speech will suffer the same fate as the peasant Dicaeopolis; he will have to lay his head upon the executioner's block. Except that instead of the Acharnians of Aristophanes, it will be the majority of critics who descend on the author – the most normal thing in the world. Nobody is more anxious to bash out someone's brains than those who haven't any.

Moreover, the drama has always embodied some narrative elements; epic drama did not introduce this. So, for instance, the background of an action has always had to be related, or an event announced in the form of a messenger's report. But narration on the stage is not without its dangers, for it does not live in the same manner, is not tangible the way an action taking place on the stage is. Attempts have been made to overcome this, as by dramatizing the messenger, by letting him appear at a crucial moment, or by making him a blockhead from whom a report can only be extracted with great difficulties. Yet certain elements of rhetoric must still be present if narration is to succeed on the stage. Stage narratives cannot exist without some exaggeration. Observe, for instance, how Shakespeare elaborates on Plutarch's description of Cleopatra's barge. This exaggeration is not just a characteristic of the baroque style, but a means of launching Cleopatra's barge upon the stage, of making it visible there. But while the speech of the theatre cannot exist without exaggeration, it is important to know when to exaggerate and above all, how.

Furthermore, just as stage characters can suffer a certain fate, so also can their language. The angel that came to Babylon, for example, grows more and more enthusiastic about the earth's beauty from act to act, and hence his language must parallel this rising enthusiasm until it grows into a veritable hymn. In the same comedy the beggar Akki relates his life in a series of *makamat*, passages of a rich and stately prose interspersed with rhymes, refined in grammar, rhetoric, poetic idiom and tradition, that come from the Arabic and flourished a thousand years ago. In this way I try to convey the Arabic character of this personage, his joy in inventing stories and in duelling and playing with words, without at the same time wandering off into another

26

form, the chanson. The *makamat* or anecdotes of Akki are nothing less than the most extreme possibilities offered by his language, and therefore they intensify his being. Through the *makamat* Akki has become all language, and this is just what an author must always strive for, so that there are moments in his plays in which the characters he has created with the written word become living language and nothing less.

A danger lurks here, too, of course. Language can lead a writer astray. The joy of being able all of a sudden to write, of possessing language, as it came over me, for instance, while I was writing *The Blind Man*, can make an author talk too much, can make him escape from his subject into language. To keep close to the subject is itself a great art, achieved only by masterful control of the impetus to talk. Dialogue, like playing on words, can also lead an author into byways, take him unawares away from his subject. Yet ideas flash into his mind again and again, ideas which he ought not resist, even if they disrupt his carefully laid plans. For in addition to being on guard against some of these tempting flashes of ideas, a writer must also have the courage to follow some of them.

These elements and problems of place, time, and action, which are all, of course, interwoven and are but hinted at here, belong to the basic material, to the artistic devices and tools of the craft of the drama. But let me make it clear here and now that I make war upon the notion of 'the craft of the drama'. The very idea that anyone who makes a sufficiently diligent and steadfast endeavour to achieve something in that art will succeed in the end, or even that this craft can be learned, is a notion we thought discarded long ago. Yet it is still frequently met with in critical writings about the art of play-writing. This art is supposed to be a sound and solid, respectable and well-mannered affair. Thus, too, the relationship between a playwright and his art is considered by some to be like a marriage in which everything is quite legal when blessed with the sacraments of aesthetics. For

27

these reasons, perhaps, critics often refer to the theatre, much more than to any other form of art, as a craft which, depending on the particular case, has been more or less mastered. If we investigate closely what the critics really mean by 'the craft of the drama', then it becomes obvious that it is little else but the sum of their prejudices. There is no craft of the theatre; there is only the mastery of the material through language and the stage or, to be more exact, it is an overpowering of the material, for any creative writing is a kind of warfare with its victories, defeats and indecisive battles. Perfect plays do not exist except as a fiction of aesthetics in which, as in the films, perfect heroes may alone be found. Never yet has a playwright left this battle without his wounds; each one has his Achilles' heel, and the playwright's antagonist, his material, never fights fairly. It is cunning stuff, often not to be drawn out of its lair, and it employs highly secret and low-down tricks. This forces the playwright to fight back with every permissible and even non-permissible means, no matter what the wise exhortations, rules and adages of the masters of this craft and their most honoured trade may say. Best foot forward won't get an author anywhere in the drama, not even his foot in the doorway. The difficulties in writing for the drama lie where no one suspects them; sometimes it is no more than the problem of how to have two people say hello, or the difficulty in writing an opening sentence. What is sometimes considered to be the craft of the drama can be easily learned in half an hour. But how difficult it is to divide a given material into five acts, and how few subjects there are which can be divided that way, how nearly impossible it is to write today in iambic pentameter, those things are hardly ever suspected by the hack writers who can slap a play together any time and without trouble, who can always divide any subject into five acts, and who have always written and still write with facility in iambic pentameter. They really pick their material and their language in the way some critics think this is done. They are not so much amateurs when they talk about art as when they tailor art to their talk. No matter what the material

28

is like, they always fashion the same bath-robe to be sure the audience will not catch cold and that it will sleep comfortably. There is nothing more idiotic than the opinion that only a genius does not have to obey those rules prescribed for writers of talent. In that case I should like to be counted among the geniuses. What I want to emphasize strongly is that the art of writing a play does not necessarily start out with the planning of a certain child, or however else a eunuch thinks love is made; but it starts out with love-making, of which a eunuch is incapable. Though really the difficulties, pains and also fortunes of writing do not lie within the realm of things we mean to talk about or even can talk about. We can only talk about the craft of the drama, a craft that exists only when one *talks* of drama, but not when one writes plays. The craft of the drama is an optical illusion. To talk about plays, about art, is a much more utopian undertaking than is ever appreciated by those who talk the most.

Employing this – really non-existent – craft, let us try and give shape to a certain material. Usually there is a central point of reference, the hero. In theories of the drama a difference is made between a tragic hero, the hero of tragedy, and a comic hero, the hero of comedy. The qualities a tragic hero must possess are well known. He must be capable of rousing our sympathy. His guilt and his innocence, his virtues and his vices must be mixed in the most pleasant and yet exact manner, and administered in doses according to well-defined rules. If, for example, I make my tragic hero an evil man, then I must endow him with a portion of intellect equal to his malevolence. As a result of this rule, the most sympathetic stage character in German literature has turned out to be the devil. The role of the hero in the play has not changed. The only thing that has changed is the social position of the character who awakens our sympathy.

In ancient tragedy and in Shakespeare the hero belongs to the highest class in society, to the nobility. The spectators watch a suffering, acting, raving hero who occupies a social position far higher than their own. This still continues to impress audiences today.

Then when Lessing and Schiller introduced the bourgeois drama, the audience saw itself as the suffering hero on the stage. But the evolution of the hero continued. Büchner's Wozzeck is a primitive proletarian who represents far less socially than the average spectator. But it is precisely in this extreme form of human existence, in this last, most miserable form, that the audience is to see the human being also, indeed itself.

And finally we might mention Pirandello who was the first, as far as I know, to render the hero, the character on the stage, immaterial and transparent just as Wilder did the dramatic place. The audience watching this sort of presentation attends, as it were, its own dissection, its own psycho-analysis, and the stage becomes man's internal milieu, the inner space of the world.

Of course, the theatre has never dealt only with kings and generals; in comedy the hero has always been the peasant, the beggar, the ordinary citizen – but this was always in comedy. Nowhere in Shakespeare do we find a comic king; in his day a ruler could appear as a bloody monster but never as a fool. In Shakespeare the courtiers, the artisans, the working people are comic. Hence, in the evolution of the tragic hero we see a trend towards comedy. Analogously the fool becomes more and more of a tragic figure. This fact is by no means without significance. The hero of a play not only propels an action on, he not only suffers a certain fate, but he also represents a world. Therefore we have to ask ourselves how we should present our own questionable world and with what sort of heroes. We have to ask ourselves how the mirrors which catch and reflect this world should be ground and set.

Can our present-day world, to ask a concrete question, be represented by Schiller's dramatic art? Some writers claim it can be, since Schiller still holds audiences in his grip. To be sure, in art everything is possible when the art is right. But the question is if an art valid for its time could possibly be so even for our day.

Art can never be repeated. If it were repeatable, it would be foolish not just to write according to the rules of Schiller.

Schiller wrote as he did because the world in which he lived could still be mirrored in the world his writing created, a world he could build as an historian. But just barely. For was not Napoleon perhaps the last hero in the old sense? The world today as it appears to us could hardly be encompassed in the form of the historical drama as Schiller wrote it, for the reason alone that we no longer have any tragic heroes, but only vast tragedies staged by world butchers and produced by slaughtering machines. Hitler and Stalin cannot be made into Wallensteins. Their power was so enormous that they themselves were no more than incidental, corporeal and easily replaceable expressions of this power; and the misfortune associated with the former and to a considerable extent also with the latter is too vast, too complex, too horrible, too mechanical and usually simply too devoid of all sense. Wallenstein's power can still be envisioned; power as we know it today can only be seen in its smallest part for, like an iceberg, the largest part is submerged in anonymity and abstraction. Schiller's drama presupposes a world that the eye can take in, that takes for granted genuine actions of state, just as Greek tragedy did. For only what the eye can take in can be made visible in art. The state today, however, cannot be envisioned, for it is anonymous and bureaucratic; and not only in Moscow and Washington, but also in Berne. Actions of state today have become *post-hoc* satyric dramas which follow the tragedies executed in secret earlier. True representatives of our world are missing; the tragic heroes are nameless. Any small-time crook, petty government official or policeman better represents our world than a senator or president. Today art can only embrace the victims, if it can reach men at all; it can no longer come close to the mighty. Creon's secretaries close Antigone's case. The state has lost its physical reality, and just as physics can now only cope with the world in mathematical formulae, so the state can only be expressed in statistics. Power today becomes visible, material only when it explodes as in the atom bomb, in this marvellous mushroom which rises and spreads immaculate as the sun and in which mass murder and beauty have become one. The atom bomb cannot be reproduced artistically since it is mass-produced. In its face all man's art that would recreate it must fail, since it is itself a creation of man. Two mirrors which reflect one another remain empty.

But the task of art, in so far as art can have a task at all, and hence also the task of drama today, is to create something concrete, something that has form. This can be accomplished best by comedy. Tragedy, the strictest genre in art, presupposes a formed world. Comedy – in so far as it is not just satire of a particular society as in Molière – supposes an unformed world, a world being made and turned upside down, a world about to fold like ours. Tragedy overcomes distance; it can make myths originating in times immemorial seem like the present to the Athenians. But comedy creates distance; the attempt of the Athenians to gain a foothold in Sicily is translated by comedy into the birds undertaking to create their own empire before which the gods and men will have to capitulate. How comedy works can be seen in the most primitive kind of joke, in the dirty story, which, though it is of very dubious value, I bring up only because it is the best illustration of what I mean by creating distance. The subject of the dirty story is the purely sexual, which because it is purely sexual, is formless and without objective distance. To give form the purely sexual is transmuted, as I have already mentioned, into the dirty joke. Therefore this type of joke is a kind of original comedy, a transposition of the sexual on to the plain of the comical. In this way it is possible today, in a society dominated by John Doe, to talk in an accepted way about the purely sexual. In the dirty story it becomes clear that the comical exists in forming what is formless, in creating order out of chaos.

The means by which comedy creates distance is the conceit.

Tragedy is without conceit. Hence there are few tragedies whose subjects were invented. By this I do not mean to imply that the ancient tragedians lacked inventive ideas of the sort that are written today, but the marvel of their art was that they had no need of these inventions, of conceits. That makes all the difference. Aristophanes, on the other hand, lives by conceits. The stuff of his plays are not myths but inventions, which take place not in the past but the present. They drop into their world like bomb-shells which, by throwing up huge craters of dirt, change the present into the comic and thus scatter the dirt for everyone to see. This, of course, does not mean that drama today can only be comical. Tragedy and comedy are but formal concepts, dramatic attitudes, figments of the aesthetic imagination which can embrace one and the same thing. Only the conditions under which each is created are different, and these conditions have their basis only in small part in art.

Tragedy presupposes guilt, despair, moderation, lucidity, vision, a sense of responsibility. In the Punch-and-Judy show of our century, in this back-sliding of the white race, there are no more guilty and also, no responsible men. It is always, 'We couldn't help it' and 'We didn't really want that to happen.' And indeed, things happen without anyone in particular being responsible for them. Everything is dragged along and everyone gets caught somewhere in the sweep of events. We are all collectively guilty, collectively bogged down in the sins of our fathers and of our forefathers. We are the offspring of children. That is our misfortune, but not our guilt: guilt can exist only as a personal achievement, as a religious deed. Comedy alone is suitable for us. Our world has led to the grotesque as well as to the atom bomb, and so it is a world like that of Hieronymus Bosch whose apocalyptic paintings are also grotesque. But the grotesque is only a way of expressing in a tangible manner, of making us perceive physically the paradoxical, the form of the unformed, the face of a world without face; and just as in our thinking today we seem to be unable to do without the concept of the paradox, so also in art, and in our world which at times seems still to exist only because the atom bomb exists: out of fear of the bomb.

But the tragic is still possible even if pure tragedy is not. We can achieve the tragic out of comedy. We can bring it forth as a frightening moment, as an abyss that opens suddenly; indeed, many of Shakespeare's tragedies are already really comedies out of which the tragic arises.

After all this the conclusion might easily be drawn that comedy is the expression of despair, but this conclusion is not inevitable. To be sure, whoever realizes the senselessness, the hopelessness of this world might well despair, but this despair is not a result of this world. Rather it is an answer given by an individual to this world; another answer would be not to despair, would be an individual's decision to endure this world in which we live like Gulliver among the giants. He also achieves distance, he also steps back a pace or two who takes measure of his opponent, who prepares himself to fight his opponent or to escape him. It is still possible to show man as a courageous being.

In truth this is a principal concern of mine. The blind man, Romulus, Übelohe, Akki, are all men of courage. The lost world-order is restored within them; the universal escapes my grasp. I refuse to find the universal in a doctrine. The universal for me is chaos. The world (hence the stage which represents this world) is for me something monstrous, a riddle of misfortunes which must be accepted but before which one must not capitulate. The world is far bigger than any man, and perforce threatens him constantly. If one could but stand outside the world, it would no longer be threatening. But I have neither the right nor the ability to be an outsider to this world. To find solace in poetry can also be all too cheap; it is more honest to retain one's human point of view. Brecht's thesis, that the world is an accident, which he developed in his *Street Scene* where he shows how this accident happened, may yield – as it in fact did – some magnificent theatre; but he did it by concealing most of the evidence!

34

Brecht's thinking is inexorable, because inexorably there are many things he will not think about.

And lastly it is through the conceit, through comedy, that the anonymous audience becomes possible as an audience, becomes a reality to be counted on, and also one to be taken into account. The conceit easily transforms the crowd of theatre-goers into a mass which can be attacked, deceived, outsmarted into listening to things it would otherwise not so readily listen to. Comedy is a mouse-trap in which the public is easily caught and in which it will get caught over and over again. Tragedy, on the other hand, predicated a true community, a kind of community whose existence in our day is but an embarrassing fiction. Nothing is more ludicrous, for instance, than to sit and watch the mystery plays of the Anthroposophists when one is not a participant.

Granting all this, there is still one more question to be asked: is it permissible to go from a generality to a particular form of art, to do what I just did when I went from my assertion that the world was formless to the particular possibility for writing comedies today. I doubt that this is permissible. Art is something personal, and something personal should never be explained with generalities. The value of a work of art does not depend on whether more or less good reasons for its existence can be found. Hence I have also tried to avoid certain problems, as for example the argument which is quite lively today, whether or not plays ought to be written in verse or in prose. My own answer lies simply in writing prose, without any intention of thereby deciding the issue. A man has to choose to go one way, after all, and why should one way always be worse than another? As far as my concepts of comedy are concerned, I believe that here, too, personal reasons are more important than more general ones that are always open to argument. What logic in matters of art could not be refuted! One talks best about art when one talks of one's own art. The art one chooses is an expression of freedom without which no art can exist, and at the same time also of necessity without which art cannot exist either. The artist always represents his world and himself. If at one time philosophy taught men to arrive at the particular from the general, then – unlike Schiller, who started out believing in general conclusions – I cannot construct a play as he did when I doubt that the particular can ever be reached from the general. But my doubt is mine and only mine, and not the doubt and problems of a Catholic for whom drama holds possibilities non-Catholics do not share. This is so even if, on the other hand, a Catholic who takes his religion seriously, is denied those possibilities which other men possess. The danger inherent in this thesis lies in the fact that there are always those artists who for the sake of finding some generalities to believe in accept conversion, taking a step which is the more to be wondered at for the sad fact that it really will not help them. The difficulties experienced by a Protestant in writing a drama are just the same difficulties he has with his faith. Thus it is my way to mistrust what is ordinarily called the building of the drama, and to arrive at my plays from the unique, the sudden idea or conceit, rather than from some general concept or plan. Speaking for myself, I need to write off into the blue, as I like to put it so that I might give critics a catchword to hang on to. They use it often enough, too, without really understanding what I mean by it.

But these matters are my own concerns and hence it is not necessary to invoke the whole world and to make out that what are my concerns are the concerns of art in general (lest I be like the drunk who goes back to Noah, the Flood, original sin and the beginning of the world to explain what is, after all, only his own weakness). As in everything and everywhere, and not just in the field of art, the rule is: No excuses, please!

Nevertheless the fact remains (always keeping in mind, of course, the reservations just made) that we now stand in a different relationship to what we have called our material. Our unformed, amorphous present is characterized by being surrounded by figures and forms that reduce our time to a mere result, even less,

36

to a mere transitional state, and which give excessive weight to the past as something finished and to the future as something possible. This applies equally well to politics. Related to art it means that the artist is surrounded by all sort of opinions about art and by demands on him which are based not upon his capacities, but upon the historical past and present forms. He is surrounded therefore by materials which are no longer materials, that is possibilities, but by materials which have already taken on shape, that is some definitive form. Caesar is no longer pure subject matter for us; he has become the Caesar whom scholarship made the object of its researches. And so it happened that scholars, having thrown themselves with increasing energy not only upon nature but also upon intellectual life and upon art, establishing in the process intellectual history, literary scholarship, philology and goodness knows what else, have created a body of factual information which cannot be ignored (for one cannot be conscious of these facts and at the same time pretend to be so naïve that one need pay no attention to the results of scholarship). In this way, however, scholars have deprived the artist of materials by doing what was really the artist's task. The mastery of Richard Feller's *History of Berne* precludes the possibility of an historical drama about the city of Berne; the history of Berne was thus given shape before some literary artist could do it. True, it is a scholastic form (and not a mythical one which would leave the way open for a tragedian), a form that severely limits the field for the artist, leaving to art only psychology which, of course, has also become a science. To rewrite such a history in a creative literary manner would now be a tautology, a repetition by means which are not suitable or fitting, a mere illustration of scholarly insights; in short, it would be the very thing science often claims literature to be. It was still possible for Shakespeare to base his Caesar upon Plutarch, for the Roman was not an historian in our sense of the word but a story-teller, the author of biographical sketches. Had Shakespeare read Mommsen he could not have written his Caesar because he would of necessity

37

have lost the supremacy over his materials. And this holds true now in all things, even the myths of the Greeks which, since we no longer live them but only study, evaluate, investigate them, recognizing them to be mere myths and as such destroying them, have become mummies; and these, bound tightly round with philosophy and theology, are all too often substituted for the living thing.

Therefore the artist must reduce the subjects he finds and runs into everywhere if he wants to turn them once more into real materials, hoping always that he will succeed. He parodies his materials, contrasts them consciously with what they have actually been turned into. By this means, by this act of parody, the artist regains his freedom and hence his material; and thus material is no longer found but invented. For every parody presupposes a conceit and an invention. In laughter man's freedom becomes manifest, in crying his necessity. Our task today is to demonstrate freedom. The tyrants of this planet are not moved by the works of the poets. They yawn at a poet's threnodies. For them heroic epics are silly fairy-tales and religious poetry puts them to sleep. Tyrants fear only one thing: a poet's mockery. For this reason, then, parody has crept into all literary genres, into the novel, the drama, into lyrical poetry. Much of painting, even of music, has been conquered by parody, and the grotesque has followed, often well camouflaged, on the heels of parody: all of a sudden the grotesque is there.

But our times, up to every imaginable trick there is, can handle all that and nothing can intimidate it: the public has been educated to see in art something solemn, hallowed and even pathetic. The comic is considered inferior, dubious, unseemly; it is accepted only when it makes people feel as bestially happy as a bunch of pigs. But the very moment people recognize the comic to be dangerous, an art that exposes, demands, moralizes, it is dropped like a hot potato, for art may be everything it wants to be so long as it remains *gemütlich*.

38

We writers are often accused of art that is nihilistic. Today, of course, there exists a nihilistic art, but not every art that seems nihilistic is so. True nihilistic art does not appear to be nihilistic at all; usually it is considered to be especially humane and supremely worthy of being read by our more mature young people. A man must be a pretty bungling sort of nihilist to be recognized as such by the world at large. People call nihilistic what is merely uncomfortable. Then also people say, the artist is supposed to create, not to talk; to give shape to things, not to preach. To be sure. But it becomes more and more difficult to create 'purely' or however people imagine the creative mind should work. Mankind today is like a reckless driver racing ever faster, ever more heedlessly along the highway. And he does not like it when the frightened passengers cry out, 'Watch out' and 'There's a warning sign! Slow down', or 'Don't kill that child!' What is more, the driver hates it even worse when he is asked, 'Who is paying for the car?' or 'Who's providing the petrol and oil for this mad journey?', to say nothing of what happens when he is asked for his driver's licence. What unpleasant facts might then come to light! Maybe the car was stolen from some relatives, the petrol and oil squeezed from the passengers, and really not petrol and oil but the blood and sweat of us all; and most likely he wouldn't even have a driver's licence and it would turn out that this was his first time driving. Of course, it would be embarrassing if such personal questions were to be asked. The driver would much prefer the passengers to praise the beauty of the countryside through which they are travelling, the silver of the river and the brilliant reflection of the ice-capped mountains in the far distance, would even prefer to have amusing stories whispered into his ear. Today's author, however, can no longer confine himself with good conscience to whispering pleasant stories and praising the beautiful landscape. Unfortunately, too, he cannot get out of this mad race in order to sit by the wayside, writing the pure poetry demanded of him by all the non-poets. Fear, worry, and above all anger open his mouth wide.

How very nice it would be if we could end now on this emphatic note. It would be a conclusion that could be considered at least partially safe and not wholly impossible. But in all honesty we must ask ourselves at this point if any of this makes sense today, if it were not better if we practised silence. I have tried to show that the theatre today is, in the best sense of the word to be sure, in part a museum, and in part a field of experimentation. I have also tried to show here and there what these experiments are. Is the theatre capable of fulfilling this, its latter destiny? Not only has the writing of plays become more difficult today but also the rehearsing and performing of these plays is harder. The very lack of time results at best in only a decent attempt, a first probing, a slight advance in what might be the right direction. A play that is to be more than a merely conventional piece, that is really to be an experiment, can no longer be solved at the writing desk. Giraudoux's fortune was that he had Jouvet. Unhappily this happens only once or twice. The repertory theatre of Germany can afford less and less to experiment. A new play must be got rid of as quickly as possible. The museum's treasures weigh too heavily in the scales. The theatre, our whole culture, lives on the interest of the well invested intellect, to which nothing can happen any more and for which not even royalties have to be paid. Assured of having a Goethe, Schiller or Sophocles at hand, the theatres are willing now and then to put on a modern piece – but preferably only for a premiere performance. Heroically this duty is discharged, and sighs of relief are breathed all round when Shakespeare is performed next time. What can we say or do? Clear the stages completely! Make room for the classics! The world of the museum is growing and bursts with its treasures. The cultures of the cave-dwellers have not yet been investigated to the nth degree. Let the custodians of the future concern themselves with our art when it is our turn. It does not make much difference then if something new is added, something new is written. The demands made of the artist by aesthetics increase from day to day. What is wanted is the perfection which is read

40

into the classics. And let the artist even be suspected of having taken one step backwards, of having made a mistake, just watch how quickly he is dropped. Thus a climate is created in which literature can be studied but not made. How can the artist exist in a world of educated and literate people? This question oppresses me, and I know no answer. Perhaps the writer can best exist by writing detective stories, by creating art where it is least suspected. Literature must become so light that it will weigh nothing upon the scale of today's literary criticism: only in this way will it regain its true worth.

[This version of *Problems of the Theatre* was prepared for publication from the manuscript of a lecture delivered by Friedrich Dürrenmatt in the autumn of 1954 and the spring of 1955 in different cities of Switzerland and West Germany.]

ROMULUS THE GREAT

An Historical Comedy
without historic basis
In four Acts
Second version . 1957

Translated from the German by
GERHARD NELLHAUS

CHARACTERS

ROMULUS AUGUSTUS	Emperor of the Western Roman Empire
JULIA	His Wife
REA	His Daughter
ZENO, THE ISAURIAN	Emperor of the Eastern Roman Empire
EMILIAN	Roman Patrician
MARES	Minister of War
TULLIUS ROTUNDUS	Minister of State
SPURIUS TITUS MAMMA	Captain of Cavalry
ACHILLES	Chamberlain to Romulus
PYRAMUS	Chamberlain to Romulus
APOLLONIUS	Antique Dealer
CAESAR RUPF	Industrialist
PHYLAX	Actor
ODOAKER	Ruler of the Teutons
THEODORIC	His Nephew
PHOSPHORIDES	Chamberlain to Zeno
SULPHURIDES	Chamberlain to Zeno
COOK, PORTERS, TEUTONS	

The Time: The morning of March 15th to the morning of March 16th, A.D. 476.

The Place: The Country Residence of Emperor Romulus.

The great artistic trick of taking small deviations from the truth for truth itself upon which the entire system of differential equation is built, is also the basis for our wittiest thinking which might all collapse if the deviations were taken with philosophic strictness.

LICHTENBERG

ACT ONE

It is the year four hundred and seventy-six. One early March morning the Cavalry officer, SPURIUS TITUS MAMMA, *arrives on his dying horse in Campania at the imperial summer residence in which the Emperor of Rome lives the whole year round. The* CAPTAIN, *soiled and with his left arm in a bloody bandage, dismounts, moving with difficulty; he stumbles, stirring up a huge flock of cackling chickens; hurries, finding no one, through the villa and finally enters the Emperor's study. Here, too, everything seems to him at first empty and deserted. There are a few wobbly, half-broken chairs and up on the walls the venerable busts of Rome's statesmen, thinkers and poets, all of a somewhat exaggeratedly solemn mien ...*

SPURIUS TITUS MAMMA. Hallo, hallo, anybody here?
    (*Silence. At last the* CAVALRY OFFICER *notices two ancient, grey and immovable chamberlains, standing like statues, at each side of a door in the middle of the background.* PYRAMUS *and* ACHILLES *have been in the service of the Emperor for years. The* CAVALRY OFFICER *stares at them in amazement and, impressed by their dignified appearance, becomes quite timid.*)
    Hallo!
PYRAMUS. Silence, young man.
SPURIUS TITUS MAMMA. It's about time. I was beginning to think this place was dead to the world. I am dog-tired.
    (*Panting for breath, he throws himself into a chair.*)
ACHILLES. And who are you?
SPURIUS TITUS MAMMA. Spurius Titus Mamma, Captain of Cavalry.
PYRAMUS. And what do you want?

47

SPURIUS TITUS MAMMA. I have to speak to the Emperor.

ACHILLES. Have you an appointment?

SPURIUS TITUS MAMMA. No time for formalities. I bring urgent news.

PYRAMUS. Nothing is urgent at the Court of a Roman Emperor, Spurius Titus Mamma.

(*The* CAPTAIN *jumps up angrily.*)

SPURIUS TITUS MAMMA. But I come from Pavia, from the Imperial Commander, Orestes, with bad news!

(*The two chamberlains look at each other thoughtfully.*)

PYRAMUS. Bad news from Pavia?

ACHILLES (*shakes his head*). News from Pavia cannot really be bad. Pavia is too insignificant for that!

SPURIUS TITUS MAMMA. But the Roman Empire is collapsing!

(*He is simply speechless at the composure of the two chamberlains.*)

PYRAMUS. Impossible.

ACHILLES. An organization as immense as the Roman Empire simply cannot totally collapse.

SPURIUS TITUS MAMMA. But the Teutons are coming.

ACHILLES. They have been coming for the past five hundred years, Spurius Titus Mamma.

(*The* CAVALRY OFFICER *grabs* ACHILLES *by the shoulders and shakes him as if he were a rotten column.*)

SPURIUS TITUS MAMMA. As a patriot, it is my duty to speak to the Emperor! At once!

ACHILLES. Patriotism which conflicts with cultivated behaviour is undesirable.

SPURIUS TITUS MAMMA. For the love of the gods!

(*Discouraged, he lets go of* ACHILLES *and now* PYRAMUS *tries to appease him.*)

PYRAMUS. Let me give you some good advice, young man. Take it and you will gain your objective swiftly. First go to the Lord High Steward. At ten o'clock sharp, two hours from now, he will hold audience. Add your name to the list of new arrivals. Request permission from the Minister of State to deliver an important message to the Imperial Court and perhaps then, in the course of the next few days, you may be able to deliver your news personally to the Emperor.

(*The* CAVALRY OFFICER *no longer knows what to think.*)

SPURIUS TITUS MAMMA. To the Lord High Steward!

PYRAMUS. Right round the corner, third door on the left.

SPURIUS TITUS MAMMA. To the Minister of State!

PYRAMUS. Seventh door on the right.

SPURIUS TITUS MAMMA (*still speechless*). To deliver my news in the course of the next few days!

ACHILLES. In the course of the next few weeks.

SPURIUS TITUS MAMMA. Unhappy Rome! Two chamberlains are your downfall! (*He runs desperately out to the left. The two chamberlains again freeze into immobility.*)

ACHILLES. Most regrettably I note that as our century progresses, its manners decline.

PYRAMUS. He who misjudges our worth digs Rome's grave.

(*The* EMPEROR, ROMULUS AUGUSTUS, *appears in the door where the chamberlains are standing. He is wearing a purple toga and a golden wreath. His Majesty is past fifty, calm, at ease and sure of himself.*)

PYRAMUS AND ACHILLES. Hail, Caesar.

ROMULUS. Hail. Are today the Ides of March?

ACHILLES. Yes, my Emperor, the Ides of March. (*He bows.*)

ROMULUS. An historic date. According to Roman Law all officials and civil servants of my empire are to be paid today. An ancient rite to keep emperors from being assassinated. Get me the Minister of Finance.

ACHILLES. The Minister of Finance has fled, my Emperor.

ROMULUS. Fled?

PYRAMUS. With the imperial cash-box.

ROMULUS. Why? There was nothing in it.

ACHILLES. He did it in the hope of covering up the general bankruptcy of the imperial finances.

ROMULUS. Clever, that man. If you want to hide a great scandal, it's best to stage a little one. Let him henceforth be called 'The Saviour of his Country'. Where is he now?

ACHILLES. They say in Syracuse – as head clerk of a wine export business.

ROMULUS. Let us hope that in business this loyal official will succeed in recovering the losses he incurred serving the state. Let's see now! (*He takes his wreath off his head, breaks off two golden leaves and hands one to each of the chamberlains.*) Let each of you turn his golden leaf into sesterces. But after deducting what I owe you, give me back any money left. I still have to pay my cook; he's the most important man in my empire.

PYRAMUS AND ACHILLES. Yes, Your Majesty.

ROMULUS. When I began to reign there were thirty-six leaves in my wreath, this symbol of imperial power. Now there are only five. (*Thoughtfully he looks at the wreath before putting it back on.*) My morning repast.

PYRAMUS. Your breakfast.

ROMULUS. My morning repast. In my house I decide what is classical Latin.

(*The old man brings in a small table; on it stands the* EMPEROR'*s breakfast. There is ham, bread, asparagus wine, a small bowl of milk, an egg in its cup.* ACHILLES *brings in a chair. The* EMPEROR *sits down and opens the egg.*)

ROMULUS. Did Augustus lay?

PYRAMUS. No, my Emperor.

ROMULUS. Tiberius?

PYRAMUS. Julian, nothing.

ROMULUS. Flavius?

PYRAMUS. Domitian did, but Your Majesty expressly did not wish to eat even one of Domitian's eggs.

ROMULUS. Domitian was a bad emperor. No matter how many eggs that bird lays, I shall not eat them.

PYRAMUS. Yes, my Emperor.

(*The* EMPEROR *eats up the egg.*)

ROMULUS. And who laid this egg?

PYRAMUS. Marcus Aurelius, as usual.

ROMULUS. A fine bird. Compared to him, the other emperors are worthless. Did anybody else lay anything?

PYRAMUS. Odoaker. (*He is somewhat embarrassed.*)

ROMULUS. I declare!

PYRAMUS. Two eggs.

ROMULUS. Marvellous. And Orestes, my Commander-in-Chief, who is supposed to conquer this Teutonic chieftain?

PYRAMUS. Nothing.

ROMULUS. Nothing? I never did think much of him. Let that one be served for supper tonight, stuffed with chestnuts.

PYRAMUS. Yes, Your Majesty.

(*The* EMPEROR *eats ham and bread.*)

ROMULUS. And what news of the bird bearing my name?

PYRAMUS. She is the noblest, most gifted fowl we possess, the blue-ribbon product of Roman poultry raising.

ROMULUS. Did she lay, this noble bird?

(PYRAMUS *looks at* ACHILLES, *pleading for help.*)

ACHILLES. Almost, my Emperor.

ROMULUS. Almost? What does that mean? A hen either lays or she does not.

ACHILLES. Not yet, my Emperor.

(*The* EMPEROR *makes a decisive gesture.*)

ROMULUS. If a hen lays not, she's still good for the pot. Let the cook prepare my namesake along with Orestes and Caligula.

PYRAMUS. But, Your Majesty, the day before yesterday you ate Caligula together with Philippus Arabus, served with asparagus.

ROMULUS. Then let him take my predecessor, Julius Nepos. He was not good for anything either. And in future, I desire that the eggs of the hen Odoaker be served for my morning repast. This fine animal has my fullest admiration. What enormous talent. Let us take from the Teutons whatever good they produce; they seem to be coming anyhow.

(*The Minister of State,* TULLIUS ROTUNDUS, *pale as death, rushes in from the left.*)

TULLIUS ROTUNDUS. My Emperor!

ROMULUS. What do you wish of your Emperor, Tullius Rotundus?

TULLIUS ROTUNDUS. It is terrible, simply frightful.

ROMULUS. I know, my dear Minister. For two years now I have not paid you, and today, when I meant to do it, the Minister of Finance ran away with the imperial cash-box.

TULLIUS ROTUNDUS. Our position is so catastrophic that nobody, but nobody, thinks of money any more, my Emperor.

(*The* EMPEROR *drinks his bowl of milk.*)

ROMULUS. Well, I am in luck again.

TULLIUS ROTUNDUS. A cavalry captain, Spurius Titus Mamma, rode his horse at the gallop two days and two nights to bring Your Majesty news from Pavia.

ROMULUS. Two days and two nights! Now that is really something. He shall be made a Centurion for his athletic prowess.

TULLIUS ROTUNDUS. I will lead the Centurion, Spurius Titus Mamma, to Your Majesty right away.

ROMULUS. But, my dear Minister of State, isn't he tired?

TULLIUS ROTUNDUS. Of course, he is exhausted in mind and body.

ROMULUS. In that case, my dear Tullius Rotundus, you had better lead him to the quietest guest chamber in my house. Even athletes must sleep.

(*The* MINISTER OF STATE *is taken aback.*)

TULLIUS ROTUNDUS. But his news, Your Majesty.

ROMULUS. Precisely. Even the worst news sounds quite acceptable from the mouth of a person who is well rested, freshly bathed, shaved, and well fed. Let him come tomorrow.

(*The* MINISTER OF STATE *is speechless.*)

TULLIUS ROTUNDUS. Your Majesty! But this is world-shaking news.

ROMULUS. News never shakes the world. Events do that, but

52

once we get news of them, they're past altering. News only agitates the world: it's best to do without news.

(TULLIUS ROTUNDUS *bows in confusion and goes off to the left.* PYRAMUS *sets a large joint of roast beef before* ROMULUS.)

ACHILLES. The art dealer, Apollonius.

(APOLLONIUS, *the art dealer, enters from the left. He is dressed elegantly in the Greek manner. He bows.*)

APOLLONIUS. My Emperor.

ROMULUS. For three weeks I have been waiting for you.

APOLLONIUS. I beg your forgiveness, my Emperor. I have been at an auction in Alexandria.

ROMULUS. You prefer an auction in Alexandria to the meeting of creditors of the Roman Empire?

APOLLONIUS. Business is business, my Emperor.

ROMULUS. Well, were you not delighted with the busts I sold you? Cicero, especially, was a valuable piece.

APOLLONIUS. An exception, my Emperor. I was able to send off five hundred plaster casts to the academies which are being founded everywhere in the ancient Teutonic forests.

ROMULUS. For heaven's sake, Apollonius, is Germania being civilized?

APOLLONIUS. The light of reason cannot be stopped. When the Teutons become civilized at home, they will no longer invade the Roman Empire.

(*The* EMPEROR *carves the beef.*)

ROMULUS. When the Teutons come to Italia or Gaul, we will civilize them. But if they remain in Germania, they will civilize themselves and that will be ghastly. Do you wish to buy the remaining busts or not?

(*The art dealer looks around.*)

APOLLONIUS. I had better look them over once more. There is little call for busts these days; quite frankly, the only ones that sell are those of famous pugilists and buxom courtesans. Besides, some of these busts seem of rather dubious style.

ROMULUS. Each bust has the style it deserves. Achilles, hand Apollonius a ladder.

(ACHILLES *hands a ladder to the art dealer. The Greek climbs the ladder and keeps himself occupied examining the busts, now climbing up the ladder, now down, moving the ladder from place to place. The* EMPRESS JULIA *enters from the right.*)

JULIA. Romulus.

ROMULUS. My dear wife.

JULIA. How can you eat at a time like this?

(*The* EMPEROR *puts down his knife and fork.*)

ROMULUS. As you wish, my dear Julia.

JULIA. I'm deeply troubled, Romulus. The Lord High Steward, Ebius, gave me to understand that we have had terrible news. Now I don't quite always believe Ebius, since he is a Teuton and his real name is Ebi –

ROMULUS. Ebius is the only man fluent in all five world-languages: Latin, Greek, Hebrew, German, and Chinese, though I must admit German sounds Chinese to me. But no matter, Ebius is better educated than any Roman will ever be.

JULIA. You are a real Germanophile, Romulus.

ROMULUS. Nonsense. I do not like them half as much as I like my chickens.

JULIA. Romulus!

ROMULUS. Pyramus, set a place for the Empress and bring Odoaker's first egg.

JULIA. Remember my weak heart!

ROMULUS. Precisely. Sit down and eat.

(*The* EMPRESS *sits down at the left of the table with a sigh.*)

JULIA. Now will you tell me at last what terrible news came this morning?

ROMULUS. I don't know. The courier who brought it is sleeping.

JULIA. Then have him awakened, Romulus!

ROMULUS. Think of your heart, my dear wife.

JULIA. As the mother of my country ...

ROMULUS. As the father of my country, I will probably be

Rome's last emperor. For that reason alone, I occupy a rather forlorn position in world history. No matter what happens I shall end up with a bad reputation. But there is one bit of fame no one shall take from me: no one shall ever say that I had wilfully disturbed the sleep of any man unnecessarily.

(*The* PRINCESS REA *enters from the right.*)

REA. Good day, Father.

ROMULUS. Good day, dear daughter.

REA. Did you sleep well?

ROMULUS. Since I am the Emperor I always sleep well.

(REA *sits down at the right of the table.*)

ROMULUS. Pyramus, set a place for the Princess, too, and bring Odoaker's second egg.

REA. Oh, did Odoaker lay two eggs today?

ROMULUS. These Teutons are highly productive. Would you like some ham?

REA. No, thank you.

ROMULUS. Cold roast beef?

REA. No, thank you.

ROMULUS. A little fish?

REA. No, thank you.

ROMULUS. Some asparagus wine?

(*He frowns.*)

REA. No, thank you, Father.

ROMULUS. Ever since you have been taking dramatic lessons from this actor, Phylax, you have no appetite. Just what are you studying?

REA. Antigone's elegy before her death.

ROMULUS. Why study that old tragic text? Why not comedy? It's more fitting for our time.

(*The* EMPRESS *is enraged.*)

JULIA. Romulus, you know very well this would not be fitting for a young maiden whose betrothed has been languishing for more than three years in a Teutonic dungeon,

55

ROMULUS. Calm yourself, my dear wife; people whose number is up, like us, can only understand comedy.

ACHILLES. His Excellency, the Minister of War, wishes to speak to His Majesty. He says it is urgent.

ROMULUS. Strange, but the Minister of War always comes when I am discussing literature. Let him come after my morning repast.

JULIA. Will you tell the Minister that the Emperor's family will be delighted to see him, Achilles.

(ACHILLES *bows and goes off to the left. The* EMPEROR *wipes his mouth with his napkin.*)

ROMULUS. You are being excessively martial again, my dear wife.

(*The* MINISTER OF WAR *enters, bowing, from the left.*)

MARES. My Emperor.

ROMULUS. Odd, how pale all my officials are today. I had noticed it earlier in the Minister of State. What do you wish, Mares?

MARES. As the Minister responsible for the conduct of the war against the Teutons, I must demand that Your Majesty receive the Captain of Cavalry, Spurius Titus Mamma, now.

ROMULUS. But isn't our athlete asleep yet?

MARES. It is unworthy of a soldier to sleep when he knows his Emperor is in need.

ROMULUS. My officers' sense of duty is beginning to annoy me.

(*The* EMPRESS *rises.*)

JULIA. Romulus!

ROMULUS. My dearest Julia?

JULIA. You are going to receive Spurius Titus Mamma immediately.

(PYRAMUS *whispers something into the* EMPEROR'*s ear.*)

ROMULUS. That is quite unnecessary, my dear wife. Pyramus just now announced that Odoaker has laid a third egg.

JULIA. Romulus, your empire is tottering, your soldiers are sacrificing themselves and you do nothing but speak of your feathered flock!

ROMULUS. Precisely. And this is entirely legitimate ever since the geese saved the Capitol. I no longer need Spurius Titus Mamma. The ruler of the Teutons, Odoaker, has conquered Pavia. I know this is so because the hen bearing his name has just laid three eggs, and all things come in threes. You see how it all fits; without this natural harmony, there would be no order in the world.

(*Great consternation.*)

REA. My dear Father!

JULIA. That cannot be true.

MARES. Unfortunately, it is the truth, Your Majesty. Pavia has fallen. Rome has suffered the bitterest defeat of its history. The captain brought us the last words of the Commander, Orestes. He and his entire army fell into Teutonic hands.

ROMULUS. I know the last words of my generals even before they fall into Teutonic hands: As long as there is a drop of blood in our veins, no one will give up. Every one of them said that. Now, my dear Minister of War, will you please go and tell the Centurion of Cavalry that he is to go to bed.

(MARES *bows in silence and goes off to the left.*)

JULIA. You must do something, Romulus. You must do something immediately or else we shall be lost!

ROMULUS. This afternoon I will issue a proclamation to my soldiers.

JULIA. Your legions, to the very last man, have deserted to the Teutons.

ROMULUS. In that case I will proclaim Mares, Imperial Marshal.

JULIA. Mares is a silly fool.

ROMULUS. Precisely. There is not a sensible man left today who would become Minister of War of the Roman Empire. I will issue a communiqué that I am in good health.

JULIA. What good will that do?

ROMULUS. I'm reigning as always. You cannot possibly ask more of me than that, my dear wife.

(APOLLONIUS, *who has been busy looking at busts, descends*

57

from his ladder, approaches the EMPEROR *and shows him a bust.*)

APOLLONIUS. Three gold pieces for this Ovid, my Emperor.

ROMULUS. Four pieces. Ovid was a great poet.

JULIA. And who is this, Romulus?

ROMULUS. The art dealer Apollonius, from Syracuse. I am selling him my busts.

JULIA. But you cannot possibly squander the famous poets, thinkers, and statesmen of Rome's great past!

ROMULUS. We are having a closing-down sale.

JULIA. Do bear in mind that these busts are the only things my father, Valentian, left you.

ROMULUS. But I still have you, my dear wife.

REA. I simply cannot stand it any more.

(*She rises.*)

JULIA. Rea!

REA. I'm going to study Antigone.

(*She goes off to the right.*)

JULIA. You see, even your daughter no longer understands you!

ROMULUS. That's only because of her drama lessons.

APOLLONIUS. Three gold pieces and six sesterces. My final offer, Your Majesty.

ROMULUS. Why don't you take a few more busts? Then we will settle the whole thing in a lump sum.

(APOLLONIUS *starts climbing up his ladder again. The* MINISTER OF STATE *rushes in from the left.*)

TULLIUS ROTUNDUS. My Emperor!

ROMULUS. Now what do you want, Tullius Rotundus?

TULLIUS ROTUNDUS. Zeno the Isaurian, Emperor of East Rome, begs for asylum.

ROMULUS. Zeno the Isaurian? But is he not safe in Constantinople?

TULLIUS ROTUNDUS. No one is safe in this world any more.

ROMULUS. Well, where is he?

TULLIUS ROTUNDUS. In the ante-room.

ROMULUS. Did he bring along his chamberlains, Sulphurides and Phosphoridos?

TULLIUS ROTUNDUS. They were the only ones who could flee with him.

ROMULUS. If he will leave Sulphurides and Phosphoridos outside, then Zeno may come in. Byzantine chamberlains are too strict to suit me.

TULLIUS ROTUNDUS. Very well, Your Majesty.

> (*The* EMPEROR ZENO, *the Isaurian, rushes in from the left. He is dressed considerably more expensively and more elegantly than his West Roman colleague.*)

ZENO. Hail to you, my exalted Imperial Brother!

ROMULUS. Hail to you.

ZENO. Hail to you, exalted Imperial Sister!

JULIA. Hail to you, exalted Imperial Brother!

> (*They all embrace.* ZENO *strikes the attitude of an East Roman emperor seeking political asylum.*)

ZENO. I plead for help.

ROMULUS. I won't insist on your reciting all the numerous verses the Byzantine ceremonial demands of an emperor seeking asylum, my dear Zeno.

ZENO. I cannot cheat my chamberlains.

ROMULUS. But if I will not let them in?

ZENO. Well, in that case, I won't recite the prescribed formalities this time, that is as long as my chamberlains don't see. I'm exhausted. Ever since we left Constantinople they've made me recite the innumerable verses of 'I plead for help' at least three times a day in front of all sorts of political personalities. My voice is simply ruined.

ROMULUS. Sit down.

ZENO. Thank you.

> (*Relieved, he sits down at the table, but at that very moment his two* CHAMBERLAINS *rush in, both dressed in severe black clothes.*)

THE TWO CHAMBERLAINS. Your Majesty!

ZENO. By Zeus! How did my chamberlains manage to get in?

SULPHURIDES. Your elegiac verses, Your Majesty.

ZENO. I have already recited them, my dear Sulphurides and Phosphoridos.

SULPHURIDES. Impossible, Your Majesty. I appeal to your pride. You are not some private person running away. You are the East Roman Emperor in emigration and as such you must submit gladly to all the ceremonial rules of the Byzantine Court, no matter how incomprehensible they may be. Now, if you please?

ZENO. If it absolutely has to be?

PHOSPHORIDES. It has to be, Your Majesty. The Byzantine Court ceremonial is not only a symbol of world order, indeed it is the world order itself. You should have understood that a long time ago. Commence, Your Majesty. Do not shame your chamberlains any longer.

ZENO. But I'm going to.

SULPHURIDES. Step back three paces, Your Majesty.

PHOSPHORIDOS. On your knees, with head bent, Your Majesty.

ZENO. Pleading mercy, I approach you. May the moon ...

PHOSPHORIDOS. The sun.

ROMULUS. Achilles! Pyramus!

PYRAMUS. Yes, Majesty?

ACHILLES. Your Majesty?

ROMULUS. Throw out those two Byzantine chamberlains and lock them up in the chicken yard.

ACHILLES. Very well, my Emperor.

SULPHURIDES. We protest!

PHOSPHORIDOS. Respectfully but emphatically!

(*At last the two are pushed out of the door by* ACHILLES *and* PYRAMUS; *they disappear with* ACHILLES. PYRAMUS *exhaustedly wipes the sweat off his brow.*)

ZENO. The gods be thanked, my chamberlains are gone. Under their mountain of formalities and rules they bury me alive. I must walk according to style, speak according to style, even eat and drink according to style. I cannot stand all that style.

But the moment they're gone I feel the ancient strength of my Isaurian forefathers rise in me. The old faith, firm as a rock – is the fence to your chicken yard good and firm?

ROMULUS. You can depend on it. Pyramus, set a place for Zeno and bring an egg.

PYRAMUS. But we only have Domitian's egg.

ROMULUS. In this case it will do.

ZENO (*embarrassed*). As a matter of fact, you know, you and I have been at war these past seven years. Only the common Teutonic menace kept our armies from any major engagements.

ROMULUS. We? At war? I didn't know that.

ZENO. But I took Dalmatia from you.

ROMULUS. Did it ever belong to me?

ZENO. At the last division of the empire it was assigned to you.

ROMULUS. Speaking between us emperors, it has been quite some time since I've had a comprehensive view of world politics. Why did you have to leave Constantinople?

ZENO. Verina, my mother-in-law, formed an alliance with the Teutons and drove me out.

ROMULUS. Odd. And you have such excellent relations with the Teutons.

ZENO. Romulus! (*His feelings are hurt.*)

ROMULUS. You had entered into an alliance with them in order to depose your own son as emperor – if my information about the complicated situation at the Byzantine Court is correct.

JULIA. Romulus!

ZENO. The Teutons are overrunning our empires. All our defences have been more or less breached. We can no longer march separately. We cannot afford the luxury of petty suspicions between our two empires. We must save our culture.

ROMULUS. Why? Is culture something anyone can save?

JULIA. Romulus!

(*In the meantime the antique dealer has approached the* EMPEROR *with several busts.*)

61

APOLLONIUS. For the two Gracchi, Pompeius, Scipio, and Cato, two gold pieces and eight sesterces.

ROMULUS. Three gold pieces.

APOLLONIUS. All right, but in that case I will take Marius and Scilla also.

(*He climbs back up the ladder.*)

JULIA. Romulus, I demand that you send this antique dealer away immediately.

ROMULUS. We cannot possibly afford that, dear Julia. We have not paid for the chicken feed.

ZENO. Amazing. A world goes up in flames and you make silly jokes. Every day thousands of human beings are dying and here you muddle along. What does chicken feed have to do with the approach of the Barbarians?

ROMULUS. I have my worries, too, after all.

ZENO. It seems you have not recognized the full extent of the Teutonic threat to the world. (*He drums with his fingers on the table.*)

JULIA. That is exactly what I have been saying, over and over again.

ZENO. But the success of the Teutons cannot merely be explained on material grounds. We must look deeper than that. Our cities surrender, our soldiers defect, our peoples no longer believe in us because we doubt ourselves. We must pull ourselves together, Romulus, we must think of our ancient greatness, we must recall Caesar, Augustus, Trajan, and Constantine. There is no other way; without belief in ourselves and in our political mission, we are lost.

ROMULUS. All right then, let us believe.

(*Silence. Everyone sits in an attitude of devotion.*)

ZENO. You really believe? (*He seems somewhat unsure.*)

ROMULUS. Firm as a rock.

ZENO. In our ancient greatness?

ROMULUS. In our ancient greatness.

ZENO. In our historic mission?

ROMULUS. In our historic mission.

ZENO. And you, Empress Julia?

JULIA. My belief has always been firm.

(ZENO *feels easier.*)

ZENO. A marvellous feeling, is it not? One can positively feel the positive power charging these rooms. High time, too.

(*All three continue in an attitude of great belief.*)

ROMULUS. And now?

ZENO. What do you mean?

ROMULUS. Well, now that we believe?

ZENO. That is the main thing.

ROMULUS. But what is to happen now?

ZENO. Unimportant.

ROMULUS. But we must do something now that we think positively.

ZENO. Everything else will happen all by itself. All we have to do is find an idea to set against the slogan of the Teutons: 'For freedom and liberty.' I propose 'For slavery and God.'

ROMULUS. I don't know whether God is on our side. Information on that is rather vague.

ZENO. 'For order against anarchy.'

ROMULUS. No, not that. Personally, I'm more in favour of a practical slogan, a proposition that can be realized. For example: 'For better agriculture and bigger chickens.'

JULIA. Romulus!

(MARES *rushes in from the left. He is beside himself.*)

MARES. The Teutons are marching on Rome!

(ZENO *and* JULIA *jump frightened to their feet.*)

ZENO. When is the next boat for Alexandria?

ROMULUS. Tomorrow morning, half past eight. What do you want there?

ZENO. To plead for asylum with the Emperor of Abyssinia. Even from there I shall continue my indefatigable fight against the Teutonic menace. Though at times it seems to me

63

it would be better to fall into the hands of the Teutons than into the clutches of my chamberlains.

(*The* EMPRESS *gathers composure.*)

JULIA. The Teutons are marching on Rome and you are still eating your breakfast.

(*The* EMPEROR *rises with dignity.*)

ROMULUS. A politician's prerogative. Mares, I appoint you Field-Marshal of the Empire.

MARES. I will save Rome, my Emperor! (*He falls upon his knees and swings his sword about.*)

ROMULUS. That is just what I needed! (*He sits down again.*)

MARES. Only one thing can save us: total mobilization. (*He rises determinedly.*)

ROMULUS. And what do these words mean?

MARES. I just thought of them. Total mobilization means the most absolute and complete employment of all the forces of a nation for military purposes.

ROMULUS. Purely stylistically, I do not like that.

MARES. Total mobilization must be established in all those parts of the empire not yet occupied by the enemy.

ZENO. The Field-Marshal is right. Only total mobilization can save us. That is the very idea we were looking for. 'Total mobilization' is something everyone will understand.

ROMULUS. Ever since men clubbed each other, war has been a crime; total mobilization will make it lunacy. I put the fifty members of my personal guard at your disposal, Marshal.

MARES. Your Majesty! Odoaker has an army of one hundred thousand Teutons, all well armed.

ROMULUS. The greater the general, the fewer troops he needs.

MARES. Never in history has a Roman general been so insulted.

(*He salutes and goes off to the left. In the meantime* APOLLONIUS *has taken down several busts, leaving only the one in the centre.*)

APOLLONIUS. Ten gold pieces for all that useless trash.

ROMULUS. I would prefer you to speak in more respectful tones of Rome's great past, Apollonius.

APOLLONIUS. The expression 'trash' refers only to your legacy's worth as antiques. It really does not represent an historic judgment.

ROMULUS. But you must give me the ten gold pieces immediately.

APOLLONIUS. Haven't I always, Your Majesty? I will leave one bust: that of King Romulus. (*He counts out ten gold pieces.*)

ROMULUS. But my namesake founded Rome!

APOLLONIUS. A beginner's effort. That is why it is already falling apart.

(*The* EMPEROR *of the Eastern Roman Empire is growing increasingly embarrassed.*)

ZENO. You failed to introduce me to this gentleman, Romulus.

ROMULUS. The Emperor of the Eastern Roman Empire, Zeno the Isaurian – Apollonius.

APOLLONIUS. Your Majesty. (*He bows coolly.*)

ZENO. You really should visit the Island of Patmos some time. It has remained loyal to me, my dear Apollonius, and there I own many unique pieces of Greek antiquity.

APOLLONIUS. Quite possibly I can arrange a visit some day, Your Majesty.

ZENO. Perhaps, then, since I shall be embarking for Alexandria tomorrow, you would grant me a small advance ...

APOLLONIUS. I am sorry. On principle I never pay imperial houses in advance. Times are too turbulent, and political institutions too unstable. And lately, the interest of my clients has turned from antiquity towards Teutonic handicraft. Primitive art is all the rage now. A horror, but de gustibus non est disputandum. May I take my leave of Your Majesties?

ROMULUS. I am sorry, Apollonius, that you were caught in the midst of the dissolution of my empire.

APOLLONIUS. I don't mind, Your Majesty. That is what I live off, as an antique dealer. I will send some of my porters for the busts I have lined up.

(*He bows once more and goes off to the left. The* EMPEROR *of the Eastern Empire shakes his head.*)

ZENO. I cannot understand it, Romulus. For years I have not been able to get any credit. Every day I see it more clearly: ours is not a profitable occupation.

(*The Minister of State,* TULLIUS ROTUNDUS, *enters from the left.*)

TULLIUS ROTUNDUS. Majesty!

ROMULUS. Is our athlete finally asleep, Tullius Rotundus?

TULLIUS ROTUNDUS. I didn't come to speak to you about Spurius Titus Mamma, but about Caesar Rupf.

ROMULUS. His name is unfamiliar.

TULLIUS ROTUNDUS. A very important person. He wrote Your Majesty a letter.

ROMULUS. Since I was inaugurated as emperor I haven't read letters. Who is he?

TULLIUS ROTUNDUS. A manufacturer of trousers. The producer of those Teutonic garments pulled up over one's legs. They are becoming quite the fashion with us.

ROMULUS. Is he rich?

TULLIUS ROTUNDUS. Incredibly rich.

ROMULUS. At last, a man who makes sense.

JULIA. You had best receive him immediately, Romulus.

ROMULUS. We await the manufacturer of trousers with pleasure.

(CAESAR RUPF *enters from the left. He is powerfully built, and dressed richly. He heads directly for* ZENO, *thinking him the Emperor, but* ZENO, *embarrassed, directs him towards* ROMULUS. CAESAR RUPF *holds a broad-rimmed travel hat of ancient design in his hand. He nods briefly.*)

CAESAR RUPF. Emperor Romulus.

ROMULUS. Welcome to you. This is my wife, the Empress Julia, and this, the Emperor of the Eastern Roman Empire, Zeno the Isaurian.

(CAESAR RUPF *nods very briefly.*)

ROMULUS. What do you wish of me, Caesar Rupf?

CAESAR RUPF. At the time of the Emperor Augustus, my fore-

fathers came from Germania to settle in Rome. Ever since
the first century, we have been the leaders of the garment
industry.

ROMULUS. I am pleased to hear that. (*He hands* CAESAR'*s hat to a
surprised* ZENO.)

CAESAR RUPF. When it comes to manufacturing trousers, Your
Majesty, I go all out.

ROMULUS. Of course.

CAESAR RUPF. And I am, of course, also one hundred per cent
aware that Rome's conservative circles are against trousers,
just as they are against everything else that dawns new on the
horizon.

ROMULUS. Where trousers commence, culture ends.

CAESAR RUPF. As Emperor you can, of course, afford this jest.
But as a man of unclouded realism, I can quite soberly say:
to trousers belongs the future. A modern state whose citizens
do not wear trousers will go to pot. There is a profound
inner connection between the fact that the Teutons wear
trousers and that they are making such incredible progress.
This inner connection may seem a Sphinxian puzzle to men
who are first, last and always statesmen, but who never think
in depth. For a man of business, however, it is as clear as
daylight. Only a Rome that wears trousers will be equipped
to meet the onslaught of the Germanic hordes.

ROMULUS. If I could share your optimism, my dear Caesar
Rupf, I would don one of your fabled garments myself.

CAESAR RUPF. I have sworn, by all that is holy, to wear trousers
only when it has dawned on the very simplest of souls that
without trousers humanity might just as well crawl in a hole.
Professional honour, Your Majesty, no compromising that.
Either all men wear trousers or Caesar Rupf abdicates.

ROMULUS. And what do you propose?

CAESAR RUPF. Your Majesty, on one hand we have the international firm of Caesar Rupf and on the other, the Roman
Empire. Correct?

ROMULUS. Certainly.

CAESAR RUPF. Let us call a diamond a diamond, not tarnished by any sentimentalities. Behind me stand a few million sesterces; behind you, the deluge.

ROMULUS. The difference cannot be put better.

CAESAR RUPF. First I thought I would buy up the whole Roman Empire.

(*The* EMPEROR *can hardly suppress his joyful excitement.*)

ROMULUS. Let us talk about this in all seriousness, Caesar Rupf. In any event, let me ennoble you. Achilles, a sword!

CAESAR RUPF. Thank you, Your Majesty, I have already bought myself every possible title. You see, to tell you the ice-cold truth, I decided against that deal. The Roman Empire is so run-down that to put it back on its feet would be too expensive, even for an international firm like mine. And no one could know if it would turn out to be a profitable deal. We might end up with a state colossus and that, too, would be no good. Either one is an international firm or an empire and I must say, quite frankly, an international firm is much more profitable. Therefore I decided against that purchase, Emperor Romulus, but I am not against an alliance.

ROMULUS. And just how do you imagine an alliance between the empire and your firm?

CAESAR RUPF. Organic, quite organic. As a businessman I am entirely for the organic. Think 'organic' or go broke, is my motto. First we have to put the Teutons out in the cold.

ROMULUS. Precisely that seems a little difficult.

CAESAR RUPF. A businessman of international stature does not know the word 'difficult', especially not when he commands the necessary pocket money. Odoaker, in answer to my direct inquiry, has declared himself ready to evacuate Italy for the sum of ten million.

ROMULUS. Odoaker?

CAESAR RUPF. The Teutonic Chief.

ROMULUS. Odd. Of all people I never thought he could be bought.

CAESAR RUPF. Every man has his price, Your Majesty.

ROMULUS. And what do you ask of me in return for this help?

CAESAR RUPF. I will pay the ten million and subsidize the empire with a few odd millions so that it might just keep its head above water like every other sound and healthy state, on one condition. One condition, I say, aside from the fact, of course, that trousers will be the obligatory dress; and that is, that you give me your daughter, Rea, for my wife. It is as clear as day that only in this way can the alliance be cemented organically.

ROMULUS. My daughter is engaged to an impoverished patrician who for three years has been languishing as a prisoner of the Teutons.

CAESAR RUPF. You see, Your Majesty, I am as cold as ice. You must admit, without batting an eye, that the Roman Empire can only be saved by an unshakeable alliance with an experienced business firm; otherwise the Teutons who lie in readiness before Rome will advance on us in leaps and bounds. This very afternoon you will give me your answer. If it is no, I will marry Odoaker's daughter. The firm of Rupf must have an heir. I am in the best years of my life and the storms and stresses of business life, compared to which your battles are mere child's play, have made it impossible for me till now to seek my happiness in the arms of a beloved spouse. It is not easy to choose between these two possibilities, although it would seem politically more natural to take the Teutonic princess without hesitation. However, my sense of gratitude towards my adopted homeland has swayed me to make this proposal to you. For I do not wish that the firm of Rupf should be suspected of partiality in the forum of history.

(He bows briefly, tears his hat out of ZENO's *hand and goes off to the left. The other three remain sitting at the table. Stunned, they keep silent.)*

JULIA. Romulus, you must speak to Rea immediately.

ROMULUS. And what am I to say to our daughter, my dear wife?

JULIA. Simply that she will have to marry Caesar Rupf immediately.

ROMULUS. I will sell the Roman Empire for a handful of sesterces here and now, but I have not the faintest intention of bargaining away my daughter.

JULIA. Rea will voluntarily sacrifice herself for the empire.

ROMULUS. For centuries, we have sacrificed much to the state. Now it is time for the state to sacrifice itself for us.

JULIA. Romulus!

ZENO. If your daughter does not marry him now, the world will come to an end.

ROMULUS. We will come to an end. That's quite a difference.

ZENO. We are the world.

ROMULUS. We are provincials for whom the world has grown too large. We can no longer comprehend it.

ZENO. A man like you should not be Emperor of Rome. (*He beats his fist on the table and goes off to the right. Five pot-bellied porters enter from the left.*)

FIRST PORTER. We came to get the busts.

ROMULUS. Help yourselves, please. They are all lined up against the walls.

FIRST PORTER. Every one an emperor. Don't drop them. They are likely to crack.

(*The room is filled with porters who are carrying busts out.*)

JULIA. Romulus. They call me Julia, mother of our country. I am proud of this title. Let me speak to you now as the mother of my country. You sit the whole day over your breakfast. You are only interested in your chickens. You do not receive your courier. You refuse total mobilization. You do not advance against your enemy. You will not give your daughter to the one man who can save us. Just what *do* you want?

ROMULUS. I do not want to interfere with the course of history, my dear Julia.

JULIA. Then I'm ashamed to be your wife! (*She goes off to the right.*)

ROMULUS. You may clear the table, Pyramus. I have finished my morning repast. (*He wipes his mouth with a napkin.* PYRAMUS *carries the table out.*)

My finger bowl, Achilles.

(ACHILLES *brings a bowl filled with water.* ROMULUS *washes his hands.* SPURIUS TITUS MAMMA *rushes in from the left.*)

SPURIUS TITUS MAMMA. My Emperor. (*He falls upon his knee.*)

ROMULUS. Who are you?

SPURIUS TITUS MAMMA. Spurius Titus Mamma, Captain of Cavalry.

ROMULUS. What do you wish?

SPURIUS TITUS MAMMA. For two days and two nights, I rode here from Pavia. Seven horses collapsed under me. Three arrows wounded me and when I arrived they would not let me come to you. Here, my Emperor, is the final message from Orestes, your last general, before he fell into the enemy's hands. (*He hands a roll to the* EMPEROR. *The* EMPEROR *remains unmoved.*)

ROMULUS. You are exhausted and wounded. Why this extraordinary effort, Spurius Titus Mamma?

SPURIUS TITUS MAMMA. That Rome may live.

ROMULUS. Rome died long ago. You are sacrificing yourself for a corpse. You are fighting for a shadow. The country you live for is no more than a grave. Go to sleep, Captain, our times have turned your heroism into a pose.

(*He rises majestically and goes out through the door in the centre.* SPURIUS TITUS MAMMA *rises very disturbed, then suddenly throws the message of Orestes on the floor, stamps upon it, and screams.*)

SPURIUS TITUS MAMMA. Emperor, you're a disgrace to Rome!

ACT TWO

The afternoon of the fateful day in March in the year 476. A park, with the EMPEROR'*s villa in the rear. Chickens are clucking, cocks are crowing and now and again a fowl flies across the stage, especially whenever someone comes in. The porch of the dilapidated villa is covered with chicken dirt. A door opens on to the porch, and some steps lead from the porch into the park. On the walls of the villa is inscribed in chalk: 'Long Live Independence, Long Live Liberty!' The impression of the scene is that of a chicken yard, even though in the right foreground there are a few rather elegant garden chairs which have seen better days. From time to time thick dark smoke rises from a low building in the rear. The chancery lies slightly to the left of stage at right angles to the villa. The mood is one of enormous despair, of the sense of the decline of the world, 'après nous le déluge.'*

Characters: TULLIUS ROTUNDUS *sits on one chair; on another the Minister of War,* MARES, *now Rome's Marshal, sits asleep in full armour, a map of Italy spread across his knees, his helmet and baton lying next to him on the ground. His shield is leaning against the wall of the house. It, too, has the Teutonic slogan smeared upon it.* SPURIUS TITUS MAMMA, *who is still very dirty and bandaged, drags himself along the wall, leans against it, then drags himself on.*

SPURIUS TITUS MAMMA. I am tired, so tired, I am dead tired.
    (*A cook dressed in a white apron and tall cook's hat appears in the door of the villa.*)
COOK. I have the honour to announce the menu for tonight's dinner. Tonight, on the Ides of March anno 476, the company

72

shall dine on soup Julienne and three fine hens stuffed with roasted chestnuts à la Campania.

(*Clucking and enticing the chickens, he strides off on to the porch towards the rear. He holds a knife hidden behind him. The chickens scatter in front.*)

COOK. Julius, Nepos, Orestes, Romulus, chick, chick, chick ...

(ZENO *the Isaurian appears from the left. He stops to scrape his sandals on the ground.*)

ZENO. Now I have stepped on another egg! Isn't there anything here but chickens? My sandals are all sticky and yellow.

TULLIUS ROTUNDUS. Raising chickens is the Emperor's sole passion.

(*A courier runs into the palace from the right.*)

COURIER. The Teutons are in Rome! The Teutons are in Rome!

TULLIUS ROTUNDUS. More bad tidings. Nothing but bad news all day long.

ZENO. And all on account of this mania for chickens. Let us hope the Emperor is at least praying right now in the chapel for his people.

TULLIUS ROTUNDUS. The Emperor is sleeping.

ZENO. We're trying feverishly to save civilization and the Emperor is asleep – what's that smell?

TULLIUS ROTUNDUS. We are burning the Emperor's archives.

(ZENO *is thunderstruck.*)

ZENO. You – are – burning the archives! Why, for heaven's sake?

TULLIUS ROTUNDUS. These invaluable documents of the Roman art of government must under no circumstances fall into the hands of the Teutons. To take them to safety costs money – and we lack the financial means.

ZENO. And so you just burn the archives? With a smile on your lips as if you did not believe in the final triumph of right. Your whole western empire is beyond all help – it is rotten to the core. No spirit, no courage ...

(*The two chamberlains appear from the right.*)

73

CHAMBERLAINS. Your Majesty.

ZENO. My chamberlains have escaped from the chicken yard.

(*He is frightened to death. The two take him by the hand.*)

SULPHURIDES. Your Majesty, we must repeat our verses of lamentations. It is of the most urgent necessity.

PHOSPHORIDOS. If you please, Zeno the Isaurian.

ZENO. I plead for help, O Sun ...

SULPHURIDES. O Moon.

ZENO. O Moon in this universe of darkest night. Pleading mercy, I approach you. Be it the moon ...

PHOSPHORIDOS. The sun.

ZENO. The sun – ouch, another egg!

(*He scrapes the egg off his sandals. Then he is led off by his chamberlains.*)

SPURIUS TITUS MAMMA. I've had no sleep for a hundred hours, for a hundred hours.

(*Chickens cackle fearfully. The COOK appears on the right, then disappears into the villa. In each hand he holds a chicken and another one under his right arm. His apron is covered with blood.*)

COOK. Call these things chickens! And I'm supposed to serve things like this! Each one named after an emperor and yet all so skinny. What good is it to be named after an emperor if they're so skinny they'll hardly make a good soup? Fortunately, we'll stuff them with chestnuts. That way at least their lordships will have something to fill their stomachs, even if it's only good for dogs.

SPURIUS TITUS MAMMA. This eternal cackling is driving me crazy. I am so tired, so dog-tired. Riding all the way here at the gallop from Pavia, after such enormous loss of blood.

TULLIUS ROTUNDUS. Go and rest behind the villa, the cackling is not as loud there.

SPURIUS TITUS MAMMA. Tried that already. But the princess is having her drama lessons there, and next to the pond the Emperor of the Eastern Roman Empire is practising ...

MARES. Quiet! (*He goes back to sleep.*)

TULLIUS ROTUNDUS. You really should not speak in such a loud voice or the Imperial Marshal will wake up.

SPURIUS TITUS MAMMA. I'm so unspeakably tired. And then there is all this smoke, this stinking burning smoke!

TULLIUS ROTUNDUS. Why not at least sit down?

SPURIUS TITUS MAMMA. If I sit down I'll fall asleep.

TULLIUS ROTUNDUS. That would be the most natural thing for you to do, being so tired.

SPURIUS TITUS MAMMA. I don't want sleep, I want revenge.

(*The* IMPERIAL MARSHAL *rises in despair.*)

MARES. Who can think and plan with all this noise going on? Strategy is a matter of intuition. Before making the bloody incision it is necessary, as in surgery, to attain a certain inner composure. In the conduct of war nothing is worse than wanton noise-making at headquarters.

(*Angrily, he rolls up his map, takes his helmet, and starts towards the house. Picking up his shield he looks at it, startled.*)

Someone scribbled the enemy's slogan on my shield. Even the walls of the palace have been defaced.

TULLIUS ROTUNDUS. The maidservant from Helvetia.

MARES. That calls for a court martial.

TULLIUS ROTUNDUS. Now really, this is no time for such things, Marshal.

MARES. Sabotage.

TULLIUS ROTUNDUS. Lack of personnel. After all, somebody has to help the Lord High Steward pack.

MARES. But you can help. As Minister of State, what else do you have to do now?

TULLIUS ROTUNDUS. I have to prepare the legal basis upon which the Emperor's residence may be moved to Sicily.

MARES. I shall not be led astray by your defeatism. Our strategic position grows more favourable hour by hour. It improves from defeat to defeat. The farther the Teutons dare to advance into our peninsula, the farther they will find themselves down a blind alley. Then we shall be able to squash them with ease from our bases in Sicily and Corsica.

TULLIUS ROTUNDUS. First squash the Emperor.

MARES. We simply *cannot* lose. The Teutons have no fleet. That makes us unassailable in our islands.

TULLIUS ROTUNDUS. But we have no fleet either! So what good are the islands to us? The Teutons will sit unassailable in Italy.

MARES. Then we shall build a fleet.

SPURIUS TITUS MAMMA. Build one! The empire is bankrupt.

TULLIUS ROTUNDUS. We'll worry about that later. Right now the main problem is how to get to Sicily.

MARES. I shall order a three-masted schooner.

TULLIUS ROTUNDUS. A three-master! We cannot possibly afford one. They're as expensive as sin. Just try to find a galley.

MARES. Now I've been demoted to a shipping agent.

(*He ambles off into the villa.*)

TULLIUS ROTUNDUS. You see, now you've woken the Imperial Marshal.

SPURIUS TITUS MAMMA. I am so tired.

TULLIUS ROTUNDUS. I only hope we'll find a villa in Sicily we can afford to rent.

(*Fearful cackling. From the left appears the ragged figure of* EMILIAN. *He is gaunt and pale. He looks around.*)

EMILIAN. Is this the Emperor's villa in Campania?

(*The* MINISTER OF STATE *looks astonished at the ghostlike figure.*)

TULLIUS ROTUNDUS. Who are you?

EMILIAN. A ghost.

TULLIUS ROTUNDUS. And what do you want?

EMILIAN. The Emperor is father to us all. Isn't that true?

TULLIUS ROTUNDUS. To all patriots.

EMILIAN. I am a patriot. I came to visit the house of my father.

76

(*He looks around again.*) What a filthy chicken yard. What a dilapidated villa. Call this a chancery? Look at that weather-beaten Venus by the pond, the ivy everywhere, the moss, eggs hidden in the weeds – some of them have got under my feet already – and somewhere, I'm sure, the Emperor must lie snoring.

TULLIUS ROTUNDUS. Better take yourself off or I shall whistle for the guards. They're exercising on the lawn in the park.

EMILIAN. They're sleeping on the lawn in the park, hypnotized by the cackling of the chickens. No need to disturb their peaceful slumber.

(*The* EMPRESS *appears in the doorway.*)

JULIA. Ebius! Ebius! Has anyone seen the Lord High Steward, Ebi?

EMILIAN. The mother of her country.

TULLIUS ROTUNDUS. Isn't he helping with the packing, Your Majesty?

JULIA. Since this morning he cannot be found anywhere.

TULLIUS ROTUNDUS. Then he must have fled already.

JULIA. Typically Teuton.

(*The* EMPRESS *exits.*)

SPURIUS TITUS MAMMA. When you come right down to it, it is the Romans who are fleeing!

(*For a moment he has grown extremely angry, but then his anger collapses. However, in order not to fall asleep he walks back and forth desperately.* EMILIAN *sits down in the Marshal's seat.*)

EMILIAN. Are you Tullius Rotundus, Minister of State?

TULLIUS ROTUNDUS. Oh, do you know me?

EMILIAN. In the past you, Tullius Rotundus, and I often sat together. On many summer evenings.

TULLIUS ROTUNDUS. I don't remember at all.

EMILIAN. How should you? In the meantime an empire has fallen.

TULLIUS ROTUNDUS. Tell me at least, where do you come from?

77

EMILIAN. From the world of reality, straight to this farce of an imperial residence.

SPURIUS TITUS MAMMA. I am tired, simply dog-tired.

(*More cackling of chickens.* MARES *comes out of the villa.*)

MARES. I forgot my marshal's baton.

EMILIAN. Here it is, Sir.

(*He gives the baton to the general.* MARES *waddles back into the villa.*)

TULLIUS ROTUNDUS. I understand: you have come from the front. You are a brave man. You have spilled your heart's blood for your country. What can I do for you?

EMILIAN. What can you do against the Teutons?

TULLIUS ROTUNDUS. Nobody can do anything against them directly. Our resistance is calculated on a long-range basis. The mills of God grind slowly.

EMILIAN. Then you cannot do anything for me.

(*Several porters bearing trunks come out of the villa.*)

ONE OF THE PORTERS. Where are we to take the Empress's trunks?

TULLIUS ROTUNDUS. To Naples.

(*The porters carry the trunks away, one by one. They dilly-dally. During the remainder of the scene one or other of the porters reappears now and again.*)

TULLIUS ROTUNDUS. These are bitter times. A tragic epoch. But still such a highly organized legal system as the Roman Empire will survive even the worst crises. Our superior culture, our higher standard of living will win out against the Teutons.

SPURIUS TITUS MAMMA. I'm so incredibly tired.

EMILIAN. Tell me, do you love our poet, Horace? Do you write in our finest classical style?

TULLIUS ROTUNDUS. I am a jurist.

EMILIAN. Once I loved Horace, and wrote in the finest classical style.

TULLIUS ROTUNDUS. Are you a poet, then?

EMILIAN. I was a representative of the highest culture.

TULLIUS ROTUNDUS. Then write again, create anew! Spirit conquers brute matter.

EMILIAN. Where I just came from, the brutes conquered the spirit.

(*Renewed cackling; more chickens flying about. From the right along the villa appears* REA *with* PHYLAX, *an actor.*)

REA. Do you, citizens of my father's land,
See me now go upon my last journey
And see me look upon
The last light of the sun.
And then nevermore?

SPURIUS TITUS MAMMA. If I listen to classical poetry now I'll fall asleep on the spot!

(*He staggers off to the left.*)

PHYLAX. Continue, dear Princess, more forcefully, more dramatically!

REA. The god of death who silences all
Leads me alive
To the shores of hell. Not for me was
The marriage hymn. Nor does a bridegroom
Sing to me, no, not one song, for see
I am betrothed to Acheron.

PHYLAX. For see, I am betrothed to Acheron.

REA. For see, I am betrothed to Acheron.

PHYLAX. More tragically, Princess, more rhythmically. More of a cry from within, more soul, or no one will buy these immortal verses from you. One feels that you do not have any real conception of Acheron, the god of death. You talk as if he were something abstract. You have not experienced him within yourself. He has remained literary for you, not real. Sad, terribly sad. Listen once again: For see, I am betrothed to Acheron.

REA. For see, I am betrothed to Acheron.

PHYLAX. Woe, a fool ...

REA. Woe, a fool you make of me, O my father's land!
Why do you mock me
Though I have not yet perished,
And while I still see the light of day, and why
Do you force me
With your shameful law
Unwept by loved ones into this monstrous grave!
Not one of the living, not one of the dead.

PHYLAX. Not one of the living, not one of the dead. Where is the
tragedy, Princess? Where the feeling of immeasurable grief?
Once again now: Not one of the living ...

REA. Not one of the living, not one of the dead!

(EMILIAN *has risen and stands before the reciting* PRINCESS.
She stares at him in amazement.)

What do you want?

EMILIAN. Who are you?

REA. I should think I have a better right to ask you who you
are.

EMILIAN. I am what comes back when one has been where I
have. Who are you?

REA. I am Rea, the Emperor's daughter.

EMILIAN. Rea, the Emperor's daughter? I did not recognize you.
You are beautiful, but I had forgotten your face.

REA. Did we know each other?

EMILIAN. I believe – yes, I remember – we once did.

REA. Do you come from Ravenna? Did we play together as
children?

EMILIAN. We played together when I was a man.

REA. Won't you tell me who you are?

EMILIAN. My name is written in my left hand.

(*He shows his left hand.*)

REA. Oh, how terrible!

EMILIAN. Shall I withdraw my hand?

REA. I cannot bear to look at it.

(*She turns away.*)

EMILIAN. Then you will never know who I am.
(*He hides his hand.*)

REA. Give me your hand! (*She offers her right hand.* EMILIAN *puts his left into hers.*) This ring! Emilian's ring!

EMILIAN. Your bridegroom's ring, yes.

REA. But he is dead.

EMILIAN. Croaked.

REA. The ring's partly embedded in the flesh.
(*She stares at the hand lying in hers.*)

EMILIAN. This branded flesh and ring are one.

REA. Emilian! You are Emilian!

EMILIAN. I was.

REA. I no longer recognize you, Emilian.
(*She stares at him again.*)

EMILIAN. You will never recognize me again. Though I've come back I've been prisoner of the Teutons.
(*They stand and stare at each other.*)

REA. I waited for you three years.

EMILIAN. In a Teutonic dungeon three years are an eternity, Daughter of the Emperor. No one should wait as long as that for anybody.

REA. But now you are here. Come, come with me into my father's house.

EMILIAN. The Teutons are coming.

REA. We know.

EMILIAN. Then go, get a knife.
(*The* PRINCESS *looks at him, frightened.*)

REA. What do you mean, Emilian?

EMILIAN. I mean, even a woman can fight with a knife.

REA. We must not fight any more. The Roman armies are beaten. We have no more soldiers.

EMILIAN. Soldiers are just human beings and any human being can fight. There are still many people here. Women, slaves, old folks, cripples, children, ministers. Go, get a knife.

REA. That makes no sense, Emilian. We must surrender to the Teutons.

EMILIAN. I had to surrender to the Teutons three years ago. Look at what they made of me, Daughter of the Emperor. Go, get a knife.

REA. I waited for you three years. Day after day, hour after hour. And now I am frightened of you.

EMILIAN. 'For see, I am betrothed to Acheron.' Did you not just recite those verses? They've turned into reality, your verses. Go, get a knife. Hurry! Hurry!

(REA *flees into the house.*)

PHYLAX. But Princess! Your lesson is not over yet. The climax is still to come. A particularly elevated passage about Hades. The most beautiful in all classical literature.

REA. I have no need of literature any more. Now I know what the god of death is like.

(*She disappears into the villa. The actor rushes after her.*)

TULLIUS ROTUNDUS. Marcus Junius Emilian, returned from Teutonic prison. I am profoundly moved.

EMILIAN. Then profoundly move up to the front. Else you are profoundly full of luxury.

TULLIUS ROTUNDUS. My dear friend, surely you suffered much and deserve our respect. But you must not just assume that *we* here at the Emperor's residence have not suffered as well. To sit here and receive sad tidings after sad tidings, without being able to do anything about it all, that, no doubt, is the worst that can happen to a man of politics.

(*A courier runs into the palace from the left.*)

COURIER. The Teutons are marching along the Via Appia towards the south. The Teutons are marching along the Via Appia towards the south.

TULLIUS ROTUNDUS. You see! Towards the south. Directly towards us. We hardly finished mentioning one bad tiding when a new one comes.

(MARES *appears in the door of the villa.*)

82

MARES. No galley to be had far and wide.

TULLIUS ROTUNDUS. But there is one anchored in the harbour at Naples.

MARES. It floated over to the Teutons.

TULLIUS ROTUNDUS. But for heaven's sake, Marshal, we *must* have a ship.

MARES. I'll try to get a fisherman's boat.

(*He disappears again. The* MINISTER OF STATE *is angry.*)

TULLIUS ROTUNDUS. You see, here I was all prepared to re-organize the Empire from Sicily. I have planned social reforms, right down to disability insurance for the dock workers. But, of course, I can only put these plans into effect if we find a vessel!

SPURIUS TITUS MAMMA. This smoke, this eternal acrid smoke.

(*Cackling of hens.* CAESAR RUPF *enters from the left.*)

CAESAR RUPF. Gentlemen, I hope it is crystal clear to you that after the fall of Rome the empire will not be worth a scrap of paper. Bankruptcy has been coupled with a military fiasco; the Roman Empire will never be able to pull itself out of this quagmire.

EMILIAN. Who are you?

CAESAR RUPF. Caesar Rupf, owner of the international firm of Rupf, coats and trousers.

EMILIAN. What do you want?

CAESAR RUPF. It must be as clear as daylight to even a partially informed politician that there is but one way to save Rome: that is, for me to put up a few millions. I demand that, for the honest offer I have made, I receive a decent answer. Yes or No. Wedding feast or world defeat. Either I return home with a bride or the Empire can go to the dogs.

EMILIAN. What's going on here, Minister of State?

TULLIUS ROTUNDUS. Odoaker agreed to evacuate Italy for the sum of ten million. This – manufacturer of trousers – is willing to pay that sum.

EMILIAN. His conditions?

TULLIUS ROTUNDUS. That Princess Rea marry him.

EMILIAN. Go, get the Princess.

TULLIUS ROTUNDUS. You mean ...

EMILIAN. And call the entire court together.

(*The* MINISTER OF STATE *goes into the villa.*)

EMILIAN. You shall have your answer, Sir.

(*The* CAPTAIN OF CAVALRY *staggers from the right to the left of the stage.*)

SPURIUS TITUS MAMMA. For a hundred hours I haven't slept. A hundred hours. I am so tired, so tired. I could drop dead.

(*In the door of the villa there appear* REA, TULLIUS ROTUNDUS, ZENO, MARES, PHOSPHORIDOS, SULPHURIDES, *the* COOK *and the guards.*)

REA. You called me, Emilian?

EMILIAN. Yes, I called you. Come to me.

(REA *slowly approaches* EMILIAN.)

EMILIAN. You waited three years for me, Daughter of the Emperor?

REA. Three years, day after day, night after night, hour after hour.

EMILIAN. You love me?

REA. I love you.

EMILIAN. With all your heart?

REA. With all my heart.

EMILIAN. And would do anything I ask you?

REA. I will do anything.

EMILIAN. Even take a knife?

REA. I will take a knife, if you wish it.

EMILIAN. So great is your love, Daughter of the Emperor?

REA. My love for you is beyond all measure. I no longer know you, but I love you. I am frightened of you, but I love you.

EMILIAN. Then marry this splendid pot-belly and bear him children.

(*He points to* CAESAR RUPF.)

ZENO. At last, a reasonable West Roman.

THE COURT. Marry, Princess, marry!

TULLIUS ROTUNDUS. Make this sacrifice for your country, my girl!

(*All stare at* REA, *full of hope.*)

REA. And leave you?

EMILIAN. You must leave me.

REA. And love another?

EMILIAN. Yes, love him who alone can save your country.

REA. But I love you.

EMILIAN. I cast you off so that Rome may live.

REA. You want to wound me as you have been wounded, Emilian.

EMILIAN. We must do what is necessary. Our shame will nourish Italy; our dishonour renew its strength.

REA. If you really loved me, you would not ask this of me.

EMILIAN. I can ask this of you only because you love me.

(*She looks at him in fright.*)

EMILIAN. You will obey, Daughter of the Emperor. Your love is beyond all measure.

REA. I will obey.

EMILIAN. You will be his wife?

REA. I shall be his wife.

EMILIAN. Then give your hand to this man, this trouser-manufacturer, who knows his own mind, clear and cold as ice. (REA *obeys.*)

Now, Caesar Rupf, the Emperor's only daughter has given you her hand. See, all of you, the golden bull is crowned with an imperial bridal wreath, for in our day, when mankind is being outraged as never before, coupling is a virtue.

(CAESAR RUPF *is deeply moved.*)

CAESAR RUPF. Princess, you must believe me, the tears in my eyes are as genuine as gold. By this union the international firm of Rupf has reached a pinnacle of success never before attained in my line.

(*Huge columns of smoke.*)

MARES. The empire is saved.

COOK. Western culture preserved! To celebrate this day I will roast Flavian.

SULPHURIDES AND PHOSPHORIDOS. Your Majesty, the Ode of Joy!

BOTH TOGETHER WITH ZENO.

O Byzantium, joy be thine!
Your name and fame like flames outshine
The moon and stars and sun.

Yea, our faith and hopes have been
Wondrously fulfilled again.
Salvation is ours, O Byzantium!

TULLIUS ROTUNDUS. Stop the burning of the archives this very instant.

VOICE OF ACHILLES. The Emperor!

(*The smoke clears away. The* EMPEROR, *surrounded by his Court, appears in the doorway.* ACHILLES *and* PYRAMUS *are behind him.* PYRAMUS *is carrying a flat basket. Silence.*)

ROMULUS. You are lively and in high spirits. What is the reason for all these goings-on?

(*Silence.*)

EMILIAN. Welcome, O Caesar of the good dinner-table. Greetings unto you, Emperor of fine fowl. Hail unto you whom your soldiers call Romulus the Little.

(*The* EMPEROR *looks attentively at* EMILIAN.)

ROMULUS. Hail unto you, Emilian, my daughter's bridegroom.

EMILIAN. You are the first to recognize me, Emperor Romulus. Not even your daughter knew me.

ROMULUS. Doubt not her love, though. Old age simply has sharper eyes. Emilian, be welcomed.

EMILIAN. Forgive me, Father of the world, for not responding perhaps to your greeting as is customary. For too long I was a prisoner of the Teutons. Now I no longer know the customs of your court. But knowing Rome's history will help

86

me. There were emperors who were hailed thus: Well won,
O mighty one. And others: Well murdered, Your Majesty,
and thus you shall be hailed: Well slept, Emperor Romulus.
(*The* EMPEROR *sits down on an easy chair in the doorway and
looks for a long time at* EMILIAN.)

ROMULUS. Your body bears witness to great want and tribulation.
You suffered hunger and thirst.

EMILIAN. I went hungry and you ate your meals.

ROMULUS. I see your hands. You were tortured.

EMILIAN. I was tortured while your chickens flourished.

ROMULUS. You are full of despair.

EMILIAN. I escaped from my prison in Germania. I came to you
on foot, Emperor of Rome. I measured the vast expanse of
your dominions, mile after mile, step after step. I saw your
empire, Father of the world …

ROMULUS. Since I've been Emperor I have not left my country
residence. Tell me about my empire, Emilian.

EMILIAN. Wherever I went I saw nothing but immense decay.

ROMULUS. Tell me of my subjects.

EMILIAN. Your people have been robbed by war profiteers,
cheated by black marketeers, oppressed by mercenaries,
jeered at by Teutonic soldiers.

ROMULUS. I'm not ignorant of these things.

EMILIAN. How can you know what you have never seen,
Emperor of Rome?

ROMULUS. I can imagine it, Emilian. Come into my house. My
daughter has been waiting for you these many years.

EMILIAN. I'm no longer worthy of your daughter, Emperor of
Rome.

ROMULUS. You are not unworthy – only unhappy.

EMILIAN. I've been dishonoured. The Teutons forced me to
crawl beneath a blood-smeared yoke. Naked. Like a beast.

MARES. Revenge!

REA. Emilian!
(*She embraces her betrothed.*)

87

EMILIAN. I'm a Roman officer. I've lost my honour. Go to him, Daughter of the Emperor, go to the man you now belong to.

(REA *steps slowly back to* CAESAR RUPF.)

EMILIAN. Your daughter has become the wife of this trouser-manufacturer, Emperor of Rome, and my shame has saved the empire.

(*The* EMPEROR *rises*.)

ROMULUS. The Emperor will not permit this marriage.

(*All stand as if turned to stone*.)

CAESAR RUPF. Papa!

REA. I shall marry him, Father. You cannot keep me from doing the one thing that will save my country.

ROMULUS. My daughter will submit to the Emperor's will. The Emperor knows what he is doing when he throws his empire to the flames, when he lets fall what must break, when he grinds under foot what is doomed.

(REA, *head bowed, goes into the house*.)

ROMULUS. To our duties, Pyramus. The chicken feed! Augustus! Tiberius! Trajan! Hadrian! Marcus Aurelius! Odoaker!

(*He goes off to the right, scattering chicken feed. His chamberlains follow him. The rest of the Court stand without moving*.)

TULLIUS ROTUNDUS. Better start burning the archives again!

(*Everything is again enveloped in heavy smoke*.)

EMILIAN. Down with the Emperor!

ACT THREE

The night of the Ides of March in the year 476 ... The Emperor's bedroom with a row of windows at left and a door at the back. On the right is a bed and another door. In the centre of the room stand two couches forming an angle that opens towards the audience. Between the couches stands a small, low, elegant table. In the foreground, both on the right and left, are two wardrobes. Near midnight. Full moon. The room lies in darkness except for the light which falls through the windows on to the floor and walls. The door at the back opens. PYRAMUS appears with a three-armed candelabra and with it lights a second candelabra standing by the bed. Then he places the candelabra he carries on the low table. The EMPEROR enters by the door on the right, dressed in a rather shabby nightshirt. Behind him ACHILLES.

ROMULUS. My bath tonight did me doubly good: first, because we had a fine supper, and then after such a depressing day nothing helps as much as a good bath. Such days are not for me. I am an untragic human being, Achilles.

ACHILLES. Does Your Majesty wish to don the Emperor's toga or his dressing-gown?

ROMULUS. My dressing-gown. I shall not govern any more today.

ACHILLES. Your Majesty is supposed to sign the proclamation to the Roman people tonight.

ROMULUS. Tomorrow will do.

(ACHILLES *wants to help him put on the dressing-gown. The* EMPEROR *stops him.*)

ROMULUS. Bring me my imperial dressing-gown, Achilles. This one's too shabby.

ACHILLES. The Empress has already packed the imperial dressing-gown. It belonged to her father.

ROMULUS. Indeed. Well then, help me put on this rag.

(*He slips on the gown and takes the wreath off his head.*)

ROMULUS. What? The wreath was on my head all this time? I even forgot to take it off for my bath. Hang it up by my bed, Pyramus.

(*He gives the wreath to* PYRAMUS, *who hangs it up by the bed.*)

ROMULUS. How many leaves are left?

PYRAMUS. Two.

ROMULUS. My expenses today were enormous. (*The* EMPEROR *sighs and goes to the window.*) At last some fresh air. The wind has turned and blown the smoke away. This afternoon was a torture. But at least the archives are ashes. The only sensible order my Minister of State ever gave.

PYRAMUS. Future historians will bemoan this loss, O my Emperor.

ROMULUS. Nonsense. They will invent better sources than our imperial archives.

(*He sits down on the couch on the left.*)

ROMULUS. Hand me Catullus, Pyramus, or has my wife packed that scroll, too, since it belonged to her father's library?

PYRAMUS. It was packed, my Emperor.

ROMULUS. So be it. Then I shall just have to try to remember as much of Catullus as I can. Good verses are never wholly forgotten. A cup of wine, Achilles.

ACHILLES. Does Your Majesty wish to drink wine from Falerone or from Syracuse?

ROMULUS. From Falerone. In days like these one should drink the best.

(ACHILLES *places a large cup in front of the* EMPEROR. PYRAMUS *fills it.*)

PYRAMUS. This bottle of Falerone, vintage year 70, is all that's left, my Emperor.

ROMULUS. Then leave it here.

ACHILLES. The Empress, mother of our country, wishes to speak to Your Majesty.

ROMULUS. The Empress may enter. I shall not need this second candelabra.

(*The chamberlains bow and leave.* PYRAMUS *takes the candelabra standing nearest the bed. The foreground only is now lit. The background is bathed by the growing light of the moon.* JULIA *appears in the back.*)

JULIA. The Lord High Steward has gone over to the Teutons. I always warned you about Ebi.

ROMULUS. Well, should he as a Teuton die for us Romans?

(*Silence.*)

JULIA. I came to speak with you for the last time.

ROMULUS. You're wearing your travelling clothes, my dear wife.

JULIA. I'm leaving for Sicily tonight.

ROMULUS. Is the fishing boat ready?

JULIA. A raft.

ROMULUS. But isn't that a little dangerous?

JULIA. Staying is more dangerous.

(*Silence.*)

ROMULUS. I wish you a safe journey.

JULIA. Perhaps we shall not see each other for a long time.

ROMULUS. We shall never see each other again.

JULIA. I am determined to continue the resistance against the enemy from Sicily. At any price.

ROMULUS. Resistance at any price is the greatest nonsense there is.

JULIA. You are a defeatist.

ROMULUS. I only weigh the odds. If we defend ourselves, our fall will be bloodier. That may look grandiose, but what is the sense? Why burn a world already lost?

(*Silence.*)

JULIA. Then you really don't want Rea to marry this Caesar Rupf?

ROMULUS. No.

JULIA. And you don't wish to go to Sicily?

ROMULUS. The Emperor will not flee.

JULIA. That will cost you your head.

ROMULUS. Quite likely. But should that make me act headless now?

(*Silence.*)

JULIA. We've been married twenty years, Romulus.

ROMULUS. What do you wish to say to me when you remind me of this enormous fact?

JULIA. We once loved each other.

ROMULUS. You know you are lying.

(*Silence.*)

JULIA. Then you only married me in order to become Emperor.

ROMULUS. Precisely.

JULIA. You dare to say this calmly to my face?

ROMULUS. Of course. Our marriage was horrible, but I never committed the crime of keeping you in doubt for a single day why I had married you. I married you in order to become Emperor and you married me to become Empress. You became my wife because I was a descendant of the highest Roman nobility. And you were the daughter of the Emperor Valentian and a slave girl. I made you legitimate and you crowned me.

(*Silence.*)

JULIA. We needed each other.

ROMULUS. Precisely.

JULIA. Then it's your duty now to come with me to Sicily. We belong together.

ROMULUS. I have no more duties towards you. I gave you what you wanted from me. You became Empress.

JULIA. You cannot reproach me for anything. We acted the same way.

ROMULUS. No, we did not act the same way. Between your action and mine is an infinite difference.

JULIA. I cannot see that.

ROMULUS. You married me out of ambition. Everything you have ever done was done out of ambition. Even now, out of ambition, you will not give up this lost war.

JULIA. I'm going to Sicily because I love my country.

ROMULUS. You don't know your country. What you love is the abstract idea of a state which offered you the opportunity of becoming Empress by marriage.

(*The two are again silent.*)

JULIA. All right then, why not speak the truth? Why not be open with one another? I *am* ambitious. For me, there is nothing but the empire. I am the great-granddaughter of Julian, the last great Emperor. And proud of it. And what are you? The son of a bankrupt patrician. But you're ambitious, too, or you would not have become the Emperor of an entire world – you would have remained the nobody you were.

ROMULUS. What I did was dictated not by ambition but by necessity. What was the end for you was for me a means to an end. I became Emperor purely out of political insight.

JULIA. Political insight? When did you ever have any? In the twenty years of your reign you did nothing but eat, drink, sleep, read, and raise chickens. You never left your country estate, never entered your capital, and the financial reserves of the empire were so totally used up that now we must live like common labourers. Your only skill was to defeat with a joke any thought aimed at getting rid of you. But that your attitude is based on political insight is an enormous lie. Nero's megalomania and Caligula's madness were evidence of greater political maturity than your passion for chickens. Yours was no political insight but just plain indolence!

ROMULUS. Precisely. It was my political insight to do nothing.

JULIA. For that you didn't have to become Emperor.

ROMULUS. But that was the only way in which my doing nothing could make sense. To do nothing as a private citizen is completely ineffectual.

JULIA. And to do nothing as Emperor jeopardizes the state.

ROMULUS. Precisely.

JULIA. What do you mean?

ROMULUS. You've discovered the meaning of my doing nothing.

JULIA. But you cannot possibly doubt the necessity of the state.

ROMULUS. I don't doubt the necessity of the state. I merely doubt the necessity of our state. Our state has become a world empire, an institution officially engaged in murder, plunder, suppression, and oppressive taxation at the expense of other people – until I came along.

JULIA. Then I don't understand why, of all things, you had to become Emperor if that is what you thought about the Roman Empire.

ROMULUS. For hundreds of years now the Roman Empire has existed only because there was still an Emperor. Therefore, only by becoming Emperor did I have the opportunity to liquidate the empire.

JULIA. Either you are mad or the world is.

ROMULUS. I think the latter.

JULIA. Then you only married me in order to destroy the empire.

ROMULUS. For no other reason.

JULIA. And from the very beginning you planned for nothing but Rome's fall.

ROMULUS. For nothing else.

JULIA. Then you deliberately sabotaged any attempts to save the Empire?

ROMULUS. Deliberately.

JULIA. You acted the cynic and the perpetual over-stuffed buffoon in order to stab us in the back?

ROMULUS. You can put it that way if you like.

JULIA. You deceived me.

ROMULUS. You deceived yourself about me. You thought I was just as power-mad as you. You had it all figured out, but your calculation was wrong.

94

JULIA. Your calculation is coming out all right.

ROMULUS. Rome is falling.

JULIA. You are Rome's traitor.

ROMULUS. No, Rome's judge.

> (*They are silent. Then* JULIA *cries out in despair.*)

JULIA. Romulus!

ROMULUS. You had better leave for Sicily now. I have nothing more to say to you.

> (*Slowly the* EMPRESS *leaves.* ACHILLES *steps out of the background.*)

ACHILLES. My Emperor.

ROMULUS. My cup is empty. Fill it again.

> (ACHILLES *fills the cup.*)

ROMULUS. You are trembling.

ACHILLES. Indeed, my Emperor.

ROMULUS. What is the matter with you?

ACHILLES. Your Majesty doesn't like me to discuss the military situation.

ROMULUS. You know that I expressly forbade you to do so. I only talk about the military situation with my barber. He is the only one who understands something about it.

ACHILLES. But Capua has fallen.

ROMULUS. That is no excuse whatever to spill good wine.

ACHILLES. I beg your pardon.

> (*He bows.*)

ROMULUS. Now go to sleep.

ACHILLES. The Princess would like to speak to Your Majesty.

ROMULUS. My daughter may enter.

> (ACHILLES *leaves.* REA *comes from behind.*)

REA. Father.

ROMULUS. Come, come, sit down by me.

> (REA *sits down by him.*)

ROMULUS. What do you wish to tell me?

REA. Rome is in danger, Father.

ROMULUS. It is odd that tonight of all nights everyone wants to discuss politics with me. The noon meal is really the proper time for that.

REA. What shall I talk about then?

ROMULUS. About things one talks to one's father about at night. About things closest to your heart, my child.

REA. Rome is closest to my heart.

ROMULUS. Then you no longer love Emilian for whom you waited so long?

REA. But I do, Father.

ROMULUS. But no longer as passionately as before, no longer the way you once loved him?

REA. I love him more than my own life.

ROMULUS. Then talk to me about Emilian. If you love him, then he is more important than our run-down empire.

(*Silence.*)

REA. Father, let me marry Caesar Rupf.

ROMULUS. My dear daughter, I find this Rupf fellow quite congenial because he has money, but his conditions are unacceptable.

REA. He will save Rome.

ROMULUS. Precisely. This is what makes this man so unnatural. A garment manufacturer who wants to save the Roman Empire must be mad.

REA. There's no other way to save our country.

ROMULUS. I admit there is no other way. The country can only be saved with money, or it will surely be lost. But we must choose between a catastrophic capitalism and a capital catastrophe. So my dear child, you simply cannot marry this Caesar Rupf; you love Emilian.

(*Silence.*)

REA. I must leave him to serve my country.

ROMULUS. That is easily said.

REA. My country, above all.

ROMULUS. You see, you studied tragedy too much.

REA. But shouldn't one love one's country more than anything else in the world?

ROMULUS. No, one should never love it as much as one loves other human beings. Above all, always keep an open mind about any country. A country turns killer more easily than any man.

REA. Father.

ROMULUS. Yes, Daughter.

REA. I cannot possibly let my country down.

ROMULUS. You must.

REA. I cannot live without a country.

ROMULUS. Can you live without your beloved? To remain loyal to a human being is greater and much more difficult than to remain loyal to a state.

REA. It is my country, not just a state.

ROMULUS. Every state calls itself 'country', or 'nation', when it is about to commit murder.

REA. Our unconditional love for our country was what made Rome great.

ROMULUS. But our love did not make Rome good. With our virtues we nurtured a beast. We became drunk on the greatness of our country as on wine, but now what we love has turned into gall and wormwood.

REA. You are ungrateful to your country.

ROMULUS. No. Only I am not like that sire of heroes in one of your tragedies who says 'good appetite' to the state when the state wants to devour one of his children. Go, marry Emilian!

REA. Emilian has rejected me, Father.

ROMULUS. If there remains one spark of love in your body, you will not let this separate you from your lover. You will remain with him even when he rejects you. You will stick by him even if he is a criminal. But you can be separated from your country. Shake its dust off your feet when it has become a murderer's den and a place of execution, for then your love for your country is powerless.

(*Silence. A human figure climbs through the window on the left and then hides somewhere in the dark at the back.*)

REA. If I go back to him now he will surely reject me again. He will always reject me.

ROMULUS. Then you must simply keep on going back to him.

REA. He no longer loves me. He loves only Rome.

ROMULUS. Rome will come to an end and then all he will have left is your love.

REA. I am afraid.

ROMULUS. Learn to conquer your fears. That is the only art we must learn to master these days. Learn to look at things fearlessly and fearlessly to do the right thing. I've been trying to practise this all my life. Now, you try it, too. Go to him.

REA. Yes, Father, I will.

ROMULUS. Well said, my child. This is how I love you. Go to Emilian. Take leave of me. You will never see me again, for I shall die.

REA. Father!

ROMULUS. The Teutons will kill me. I have always counted on that death. That is my secret. I sacrifice Rome through sacrificing myself.

(*Silence.*)

REA. My Father.

ROMULUS. But you will live. Now go, my child; go to Emilian.

(REA *slowly leaves.* PYRAMUS *steps out of the background.*)

PYRAMUS. My Emperor.

ROMULUS. What do you wish?

PYRAMUS. The Empress has left.

ROMULUS. That is well.

PYRAMUS. Does Your Majesty wish to go to bed?

ROMULUS. Not yet. First I must have a talk with one other person. Bring me a second cup.

PYRAMUS. Yes, my Emperor.

(*He brings a second cup.*)

ROMULUS. Here, put it next to mine and fill it.
>   (PYRAMUS *fills it.*)
ROMULUS. And now mine, too.
>   (PYRAMUS *fills the* EMPEROR'S *cup.*)
PYRAMUS. The bottle is empty, my Emperor.
ROMULUS. Then you may go to sleep.
>   (PYRAMUS *bows and exits.* ROMULUS *sits without moving till the chamberlain's steps are no longer heard.*)
ROMULUS. Emilian, come forward. We are alone now.
>   (EMILIAN *slowly comes out of the darkness, wrapped in a black cloak.*)
EMILIAN. You knew I was here?
ROMULUS. A few seconds ago you climbed into my room through the window. My wine cup reflected your figure. Sit down.
EMILIAN. I shall stand.
ROMULUS. You came very late. It is midnight.
EMILIAN. Some visits are made only at midnight.
ROMULUS. You see, I was ready to receive you. To welcome you I had this cup filled with excellent wine. Let us touch glasses.
EMILIAN. So be it.
ROMULUS. To your homecoming.
EMILIAN. To that which shall be fulfilled this midnight.
ROMULUS. And what is that?
EMILIAN. Let us toast justice, Emperor Romulus.
ROMULUS. Justice is a terrible thing, Emilian.
EMILIAN. Terrible, like my wounds.
ROMULUS. All right then: To justice.
EMILIAN. We are alone. Only the darkness is witness to this moment when the Emperor of Rome and a man just returned from his Teutonic prison toast justice with cups of blood-red wine.
>   (ROMULUS *rises and they touch glasses. At the same instant someone cries out and from under the couch of the Emperor the head of* TULLIUS ROTUNDUS *appears.*)

99

ROMULUS. For heaven's sake, my dear Minister, has something happened to you?

TULLIUS ROTUNDUS. Your Majesty stepped on my fingers.
(*He moans.*)

ROMULUS. I'm sorry, but I couldn't possibly know you were under there. Every Minister of State cries out when justice is toasted.

TULLIUS ROTUNDUS. I merely wanted to propose to Your Majesty an all-inclusive old age insurance programme for the Roman Empire.
(*He crawls out from under the bed, not without some embarrassment, dressed in a black cloak similar to* EMILIAN's.)

ROMULUS. Your hand is bleeding, Tullius Rotundus.

TULLIUS ROTUNDUS. From fright I scratched myself with my dagger.

ROMULUS. My dear Tullius, one must be very careful with daggers.
(*He walks towards the left.*)

EMILIAN. Are you going to call your chamberlains, Emperor Romulus?
(*They face one another,* EMILIAN *hostile and resolute,* ROMULUS *smiling.*)

ROMULUS. What for, Emilian? You know perfectly well they are asleep by midnight. But I do want to get a bandage for my wounded Minister of State.
(*He goes to the wardrobe on the left and opens it. Inside the wardrobe stands, somewhat bent,* ZENO *the Isaurian.*)

ROMULUS. Forgive me, Emperor of East Rome. I didn't know you were sleeping in my wardrobe.

ZENO. Oh, you are excused. Ever since I fled from Constantinople my insecure life has accustomed me to this sort of thing.

ROMULUS. I'm sincerely sorry you have such troubles.
(ZENO *climbs out of the wardrobe. He, too, is dressed in a black cloak. He looks about astonished.*)

ZENO. Why, is someone else here?

ROMULUS. Don't be disturbed. They came in quite by chance.

(*He takes a cloth from an upper shelf of the wardrobe.*)

ROMULUS. Amazing! There is yet another person in here.

ZENO. My chamberlain, Sulphurides.

(SULPHURIDES *climbs out. He is extremely tall. He is also dressed in a black cloak. He bows ceremoniously before* ROMULUS. ROMULUS *looks at him.*)

ROMULUS. Good evening. You should really have placed him in the other wardrobe, my Imperial Brother. And where did you put your chamberlain Phosphoridos?

ZENO. He's still under your bed, Emperor Romulus.

ROMULUS. He might as well come out, too. He need not be embarrassed.

(PHOSPHORIDOS, *who is a short man, crawls out from under the Emperor's bed. He, too, is dressed in a black cloak.*)

SULPHURIDES. We have come, Your Majesty ...

PHOSPHORIDES. To recite our ode of woe.

SULPHURIDES. The complete recital of which Your Majesty has not yet had the pleasure to hear.

ROMULUS. By all means, only not at this silent midnight hour.

(ROMULUS *sits down and gives the cloth to* TULLIUS ROTUNDUS.)

ROMULUS. Bind your wounds with this cloth, my dear Minister. I don't like to see blood.

(*The door of the wardrobe on the right falls open and* SPURIUS TITUS MAMMA *falls full length to the floor with a crash.*)

ROMULUS. Well, even our athlete is not asleep yet?

SPURIUS TITUS MAMMA. I am tired, simply dead tired.

(*He gets up unsteadily.*)

ROMULUS. You lost your dagger, Spurius Titus Mamma.

(SPURIUS TITUS MAMMA, *with a frown, picks up his dagger, and hastily hides it under his cloak.*)

SPURIUS TITUS MAMMA. I haven't slept for one hundred and ten hours.

ROMULUS. Let anyone else present come forward.

(*From under the couch on the left crawls* MARES, *followed by a soldier. Both are wrapped in black cloaks.*)

MARES. Excuse me, my Emperor. I want to discuss the total mobilization.

ROMULUS. And whom did you bring along for this discussion, Marshal?

MARES. My adjutant.

(*The* COOK *with his tall white hat now crawls forth slowly from under the Emperor's couch. He, too, is wrapped in a black cloak. For the first time the* EMPEROR *is visibly moved.*)

ROMULUS. You, too, Cook? And with the very kitchen knife with which you slaughtered so many emperors?

(*With downcast eyes the* COOK *steps into the half-circle of men around the* EMPEROR.)

ROMULUS. I see you all dressed in black. You crawled forth from under my bed and my couch, and out of my wardrobes, after spending half the night there in very complicated and un-comfortable positions. Why?

(*Deep silence.*)

TULLIUS ROTUNDUS. We want to speak with you, Emperor Romulus.

ROMULUS. The Emperor was not aware that court cere-monial prescribes gymnastics for those wishing to speak with him.

(*He gets up and rings a bell.*)

ROMULUS. Pyramus! Achilles!

(ACHILLES *and* PYRAMUS, *dressed in their nightshirts and caps, rush forth trembling.*)

ACHILLES. My Emperor!

PYRAMUS. Majesty!

ROMULUS. My imperial toga, Achilles! My imperial wreath, Pyramus!

(ACHILLES *places the toga about the* EMPEROR's *shoulders, and* PYRAMUS *the wreath upon his head.*)

ROMULUS. Take the table and cups out, Achilles. This is a solemn moment.

(ACHILLES *and* PYRAMUS *carry the table off to the right.*)

ROMULUS. Now, go back to sleep.

(PYRAMUS *and* ACHILLES *bow and leave, greatly confused and frightened.*)

ROMULUS. The Emperor is ready to hear all of you. What is it you have to say to him?

TULLIUS ROTUNDUS. We demand the provinces back.

MARES. Your legions.

EMILIAN. The Empire.

(*Deep silence.*)

ROMULUS. The Emperor doesn't owe you an accounting.

EMILIAN. You owe Rome an accounting.

ZENO. You must answer before history.

MARES. You depended on our power.

ROMULUS. I did not depend on your power. Had I acquired the world with your help, you would be justified. But I lost a world you never won. I passed it on out of my hands like a bad coin. I am free, I have nothing to do with you. You are but moths dancing about my light, shadows which will fade when I no longer shine.

(*The conspirators inch away from him towards the wall.*)

I owe an accounting to only *one* of you and to this one I shall now speak. Come forward, Emilian.

(EMILIAN *slowly steps forward from the right.*)

I cannot speak to you as to an officer who has lost his honour. I am a civilian and never understood what is meant by an officer's honour. But I will speak to you as to a human being who was tortured and who suffered greatly. I love you like a son, Emilian. For me you represent the final great argument against those who, like myself, refuse to defend themselves; in you I'm willing to see the militant challenge of the people, violated again and again, the victims of power defiled a thousand times. What do you demand of your Emperor, Emilian?

EMILIAN. I demand an answer, Emperor Romulus.

ROMULUS. You shall have your answer.

EMILIAN. What did you do to keep your people from falling into the hands of the Teutons?

ROMULUS. Nothing.

EMILIAN. What have you done to keep Rome from being violated as I was?

ROMULUS. Nothing.

EMILIAN. And how will you justify yourself? You are accused of having betrayed your empire.

ROMULUS. I didn't betray my empire; Rome betrayed herself. Rome knew the truth but chose violence. Rome knew humaneness but chose tyranny. Rome doubly demeaned herself: before her own people and before the other nations in her power. You are standing before an invisible throne, Emilian; before the throne of all the Roman Emperors, of whom I am the last. Shall I touch your eyes that you may see this throne, this pyramid of skulls down whose steps cascade rivers of blood in endless waterfalls, generating Rome's power? What kind of an answer do you expect I can hand down to you, as I sit on top of the colossus that is Roman history? What can be said about your wounds by your Emperor who sits enthroned above the corpses of his own sons and the sons of strangers, above the mound of human sacrifices swept to his feet by the wars of Rome's glory and the gladiatorial games for Rome's amusement? Rome has grown weak, a tottering old hag, but her guilt has not been expiated and her crimes not erased. Over night the new day has dawned. The curses of Rome's victims are being fulfilled. The axe is put to the trunk, the rotten tree is being felled. The Teutons are coming; we have spilled the stranger's blood; we must now pay back with our own. Don't turn away, Emilian, don't retreat before the majesty that is mine, rising before you, covered as it is with the ancient guilt of our history, making it more horrible than your own body. Now we are speaking of justice, the justice to which we drank. Answer my question now: Do we still have the right to defend ourselves? Do we still have the right to be more than victims?

(EMILIAN *is silent.*)

You are silent.

(EMILIAN *slowly retreats to those surrounding the* EMPEROR *in a wide half-circle.*)

You are stepping back among those who came to me like thieves in the night. Let us be honest with one another. Let there be not one hair's breadth of a lie, not one hand's width of deceit between us. I know what all of you are hiding under your black cloaks, I know what your hands are clutching. But you made one mistake. You thought you were coming to a man who could not defend himself, while I now spring upon you with the claws of truth and grip you with the teeth of justice. You aren't attacking me, but I'm attacking you. You aren't accusing me, but I'm accusing you. Defend yourselves! Don't you know before whom you stand? In full knowledge I brought about the fall of the country you wish to defend. I broke the ice on which you stepped and burned the foundation on which you built. Why do you cling so silently to the walls of my chamber? You have only one answer. Kill me if you believe I am in the wrong! But if in truth we no longer have a *right* to defend ourselves, then surrender to the Teutons. Answer me.

(*They remain silent.*)

Answer!

(EMILIAN *lifts his dagger on high.*)

EMILIAN (*shouts*). Long live Rome!

(*All draw their daggers and step towards* ROMULUS *who remains calmly seated. The daggers close in over him. At that moment a horrifying cry of fright can be heard at the back: 'The Teutons are coming!' Gripped by panic everyone rushes away through windows and doors. The* EMPEROR *does*

105

not move. Pale from fright, PYRAMUS *and* ACHILLES *step out of the background.*)

ROMULUS. Well, where are they, the Teutons?

PYRAMUS. In Nola, Your Majesty.

ROMULUS. What is all the shouting about, then? Why, they cannot be here before tomorrow morning. I shall go to bed now.

(*He rises.*)

PYRAMUS. Very well, my Emperor.

(PYRAMUS *takes off the* EMPEROR'*s toga, his wreath, and his robe.* ROMULUS, *going to his bed, suddenly stops.*)

ROMULUS. I see one of them still lying here in front of my bed, Achilles. Who is it?

(*The chamberlain lights up the body with a candelabra.*)

ACHILLES. It is Spurius Titus Mamma, Your Majesty, sound asleep.

ROMULUS. Heavens be thanked. Our athlete is asleep at last. Let him lie.

(ROMULUS *steps over him into his bed.* PYRAMUS *blows out the candles and goes off with* ACHILLES *in the dark.*)

ROMULUS. Pyramus!

PYRAMUS. Yes, my Emperor.

ROMULUS. When the Teutons arrive, let them come in.

ACT FOUR

The morning following the Ides of March in the year 476.

The Emperor's study as in ACT ONE. *Now only the bust of the founder of Rome, King Romulus, sits over the door at the back.* ACHILLES *and* PYRAMUS, *awaiting the* EMPEROR, *are standing by the door.*)

ACHILLES. A beautiful morning, a refreshing morning.

PYRAMUS. I cannot understand it: even on this day when the world's coming to an end the sun still rises.

ACHILLES. There's no depending even on nature.
      (*Silence.*)

PYRAMUS. For sixty years, under eleven emperors, we have served Rome. To me it is historically incomprehensible that Rome should cease to exist during our lifetime.

ACHILLES. I'm washing my hands in innocence. I was always a perfect chamberlain.

PYRAMUS. Indeed. In every respect, we were the only really solid pillars of the empire.

ACHILLES. With our office, antiquity will end.
      (*Silence.*)

PYRAMUS. To think the day is coming when neither Latin nor Greek will be spoken, only an impossible tongue like Teutonic.

ACHILLES. Imagine men at the helm of world politics, Teutonic chieftains, Chinese and Zulus, with not a thousandth of our culture. Arma virumque cano. I know all of Virgil by heart.

PYRAMUS. Mehnin aeide thea, and I, Homer!

107

ACHILLES. From every point of view, the times about to begin
will be frightful.

PYRAMUS. Yes, the darkness of the Middle Ages. Without wishing to be a pessimist, I say mankind will never recover from
the present catastrophe.

(ROMULUS *enters, wearing the imperial toga and wreath.*)

ACHILLES AND PYRAMUS. Hail Caesar!

ROMULUS. Hail: I am late. Yesterday's unexpectedly large number of audiences exhausted me. This morning I was so sleepy
I was hardly able to climb over the athlete still snoring in
front of my bed. Last night I governed more than at any time
in all the twenty years of my reign.

ACHILLES. True, my Emperor.

ROMULUS. How strangely quiet it is here this morning. How
desolate! Has everyone deserted?

(*Silence.*)

ROMULUS. Where is my daughter, Rea?

(*Silence.*)

ACHILLES. The Princess ...

PYRAMUS. And Emilian ...

ACHILLES. And the Empress ...

PYRAMUS. The Secretary of State, the Imperial Marshal, the cook
and all the others ...

ROMULUS. Well?

ACHILLES. Drowned on their raft crossing to Sicily.

PYRAMUS. A fisherman brought the news.

ACHILLES. Only Zeno the Isaurian, together with his chamberlains, escaped on the ferry to Alexandria.

(*Silence.*)

ROMULUS. My daughter, Rea, and my son, Emilian.

(*He looks closely at the two chamberlains.*)

ROMULUS. I have no tears and I see none in your eyes.

ACHILLES. We are old.

ROMULUS. And I will die today. The Teutons will kill me. Yes,
today. No pain can hurt me now. He who is about to die

weeps not for the dead. Never was I more composed. Never more cheerful than now, when it is all over. My morning repast.

PYRAMUS. Your breakfast?

ACHILLES. But the Teutons, Your Majesty. At any moment the Teutons might –

PYRAMUS. And with all the flags in the empire at half-mast –

ROMULUS. Nonsense. There is no more empire to mourn and I shall make my exit as I have lived.

PYRAMUS. Very well, my Emperor.

(ROMULUS *sits down on an easy chair standing in the middle of the foreground.* PYRAMUS *brings a small table to him, laden with the* EMPEROR's *usual breakfast. The* EMPEROR *looks contemplatively at the breakfast dishes.*)

ROMULUS. Why do you serve my last morning meal on this cheap tin plate and this cracked bowl?

PYRAMUS. The Empress took the imperial set of plates away with her. They belonged to her father.

ACHILLES. And now they are at the bottom of the sea.

ROMULUS. Never mind. Indeed, perhaps these old dishes are more fitting for my last meal.

(*He opens a soft-boiled egg.*)

ROMULUS. Augustus, of course, didn't lay again.

(PYRAMUS *looks at* ACHILLES, *pleading for help.*)

PYRAMUS. Nothing, my Emperor.

ROMULUS. Tiberius?

PYRAMUS. Julian, nothing.

ROMULUS. Flavian?

PYRAMUS. Domitian. But Your Majesty expressly did not wish to consume her products.

ROMULUS. Then just who laid this egg? (*He spoons out the egg.*)

PYRAMUS. Marcus Aurelius, as always.

ROMULUS. Anyone else lay?

PYRAMUS. Odoaker.

(*He is somewhat embarrassed.*)

ROMULUS. I declare.

PYRAMUS. Three eggs, Your Majesty.

ROMULUS. Mark my word! Today that one will lay a record.

(*The* EMPEROR *drinks his milk.*)

ROMULUS. You are both so solemn. What's on your minds?

ACHILLES. For twenty years we have served Your Majesty.

PYRAMUS. And for forty years before that we served Your Majesty's ten predecessors.

ACHILLES. For sixty years we accepted the direst poverty to serve our Emperors.

PYRAMUS. Every hackman was paid better than the imperial chamberlains. Let it be said openly this once, Your Majesty.

ROMULUS. True, true. However, you must remember that a hackney driver takes in more than an emperor.

(PYRAMUS *looks at* ACHILLES, *pleading for help.*)

ACHILLES. Caesar Rupf, the industrialist, offered us positions as valets in his house in Rome.

PYRAMUS. Four thousand sesterces a year and three evenings off a week.

ACHILLES. Time enough to write our memoirs.

ROMULUS. A fantastic offer. You are free to go.

(*He takes the imperial wreath off his brow and gives each a leaf.*)

Here, the last two leaves off my wreath. This marks the last financial transaction of my reign.

(*Battle noises are heard.*)

What is that noise?

ACHILLES. The Teutons, my Emperor. The Teutons are here!

ROMULUS. Why, then, I will just have to receive them.

PYRAMUS. Does Your Majesty wish to put on the imperial sword?

ROMULUS. But I thought it was pawned!

(PYRAMUS *looks pleadingly at* ACHILLES.)

ACHILLES. No pawnshop would take it. It is rusty, and Your Majesty had plucked out the imperial jewels a long time ago.

PYRAMUS. Shall I bring it?

ROMULUS. Imperial swords, my dear Pyramus, are best left in their corners.

PYRAMUS. Has Your Majesty finished breakfast?

ROMULUS. A little more asparagus wine, if you please.

(PYRAMUS *pours with a shaking hand.*)

ROMULUS. You both may go now. Your Emperor no longer has need of you. You were always faultless chamberlains.

(*The two chamberlains go off frightened. The* EMPEROR *drinks his glass of asparagus wine. A* TEUTON *enters from the left. He moves about freely and unconcerned. He is quite sure of himself and there is nothing about him except his trousers that is barbarian. He looks at the room as if he were walking through a museum, and indeed, makes notes now and then on a small pad, which he takes out of a leather briefcase. He is wearing trousers, a loose-fitting coat, broad-brimmed travel hat, all of it very unwarlike except for the sword at his side. Behind him comes a young man, wearing a war-like uniform which, however, must not be 'operatic'. The* TEUTON *notices, as if incidentally and among other objects, the* EMPEROR. *They look at each other with astonishment.*)

TEUTON. A Roman!

ROMULUS. Greetings unto you.

(*The young* TEUTON *draws his sword.*)

YOUNG WARRIOR (THEODORIC). Die, Roman dog!

TEUTON. Sheathe your sword, dear Nephew.

YOUNG WARRIOR. As you say, dear Uncle.

TEUTON. I beg your pardon, Roman.

ROMULUS. But, of course. You are a real Teuton, aren't you?

(*He looks at him dubiously.*)

TEUTON. Of ancient lineage.

ROMULUS. I find it hard to imagine: Tacitus describes you people as having huge barbarian bodies, defiant cold blue eyes and reddish hair. But when I look at you, I would easily take you for a disguised Byzantine botanist.

TEUTON. My notions of what you Romans were like were quite

different, too. I had always heard of their bravery, but you were the only one who didn't run away.

ROMULUS. Obviously our ideas about different races and peoples are quite wrong. I suppose those are trousers covering your legs?

TEUTON. Of course.

ROMULUS. A truly remarkable garment. Where do you button it?

TEUTON. In front.

ROMULUS. Most practical.

(*He drinks more asparagus wine.*)

TEUTON. What are you drinking?

ROMULUS. Asparagus wine.

TEUTON. May I have a taste?

ROMULUS. I grew it myself.

(*The* EMPEROR *fills a cup. The* TEUTON *drinks and shudders.*)

TEUTON. Impossible stuff! Soon nobody will drink it. Beer is better.

(*The* TEUTON *sits down at the table next to* ROMULUS *and takes off his hat.*)

I must congratulate you on the Venus standing by the pond in your park.

ROMULUS. Why, is she something special?

TEUTON. A genuine Praxiteles.

ROMULUS. What bad luck! I always believed it was a worthless copy and now the antique dealer has already left.

TEUTON. Permit me.

(*With professional eye, he examines the shell of the egg the* EMPEROR *has eaten.*)

TEUTON. Not bad.

ROMULUS. Are you a chicken fancier?

TEUTON. A very keen one.

ROMULUS. Remarkable! I, too, am a chicken fancier!

TEUTON. You, too?

ROMULUS. Yes, I, too.

TEUTON. At last a human being with whom I can talk about my passion. Do the chickens in the park belong to you?

ROMULUS. Yes. A fine domestic breed. Imported from Gaul.

TEUTON. Do they lay well?

ROMULUS. Why, what do you think?

TEUTON. Be honest now. Judging by this egg they're only average.

ROMULUS. You're right. They are laying less and less. Confidentially, between us chicken fanciers, they worry me. Only one hen is really good.

TEUTON. The grey one with the yellow spots?

ROMULUS. How did you know?

TEUTON. Because I had this hen brought down to Italy. I wanted to know how she would fare in a southern climate.

ROMULUS. Now it is my turn to congratulate you. Truly, an excellent breed.

TEUTON. I developed it myself.

ROMULUS. You seem to be a first-rate chicken breeder.

TEUTON. As the father of my country, it is part of my job.

ROMULUS. The father of your country? Who are you?

TEUTON. Odoaker, ruler of the Teutons.

ROMULUS. I am truly pleased to make your acquaintance.

ODOAKER. And who are you?

ROMULUS. Romulus, Emperor of Rome.

ODOAKER. I, too, am pleased to make your acquaintance. Though, in fact, I knew right off to whom I was speaking.

ROMULUS. You knew it?

ODOAKER. Forgive the pretence. It is somewhat embarrassing for two enemies suddenly to find themselves face to face. That is why I thought it more useful at first to talk chickens rather than politics. May I present my nephew? Bow, Nephew.

YOUNG WARRIOR. Yes, dear Uncle.

ODOAKER. Please leave us, Nephew.

YOUNG WARRIOR. Very well, dear Uncle.

(*He goes off. Silence. The two look at each other.*)

ODOAKER. So you are Romulus. All these years my thoughts were always occupied with you.

ROMULUS. And you are Odoaker. I pictured you as my enemy – and now you are a chicken fancier just like me.

ODOAKER. Now the moment I waited for all these years has come.

(*The* EMPEROR *wipes his mouth with his napkin and rises.*)

ROMULUS. You find me ready.

ODOAKER. Ready for what?

ROMULUS. For death.

ODOAKER. You expected to die?

ROMULUS. The whole world knows how you Teutons deal with your prisoners.

ODOAKER. Have your thoughts about your enemies been so shallow, Emperor Romulus, that you must go by the world's judgment?

ROMULUS. What could you have in mind for me other than death?

ODOAKER. You shall see. Nephew!

(*The* YOUNG WARRIOR *enters from the right.*)

YOUNG WARRIOR. Yes, dear Uncle.

ODOAKER. Bow before the Emperor of Rome, Nephew.

YOUNG WARRIOR. Yes, dear Uncle.

(*He bows.*)

ODOAKER. Lower, Nephew.

YOUNG WARRIOR. Very well, dear Uncle.

ODOAKER. Throw yourself upon your knee before the Emperor of Rome.

YOUNG WARRIOR. As you say, dear Uncle.

(*He throws himself upon his knee.*)

ROMULUS. What does this mean?

ODOAKER. Now rise, Nephew.

YOUNG WARRIOR. Very well, dear Uncle.

ODOAKER. Now you may go again.

YOUNG WARRIOR. As you say, dear Uncle.

(*He goes off.*)

ROMULUS. I don't understand.

ODOAKER. I didn't come to kill you, Emperor of Rome. I came to subject myself and my entire people to you.

(ODOAKER, *too, kneels.* ROMULUS *is frightened to death.*)

ROMULUS. This is madness!

ODOAKER. A Teuton may be guided by reason, too, Emperor of Rome.

ROMULUS. You are mocking me.

(ODOAKER *rises.*)

ODOAKER. Romulus, a moment ago we talked sensibly about chickens. Isn't it possible to talk just as sensibly about nations and people?

ROMULUS. Speak.

ODOAKER. May I sit down again?

ROMULUS. Why do you ask? You are the victor.

ODOAKER. You're forgetting that just now I subjected myself to you.

(*Silence.*)

ROMULUS. Do sit down.

(*Both sit down,* ROMULUS *gloomily,* ODOAKER *watching* ROMULUS *carefully.*)

ODOAKER. You have seen my nephew. His name is Theodoric.

ROMULUS. Of course.

ODOAKER. A polite young man. 'Yes, dear Uncle; very well, dear Uncle,' all day long. His conduct is faultless. He is ruining my people with his way of life. He never touches girls, drinks nothing but water, and sleeps on the bare ground. Every day he practises with his weapons. Even now, while waiting in the ante-room, he is sure to be exercising.

ROMULUS. He is a hero, that is why.

ODOAKER. He is the ideal of the Teutons. He dreams of ruling the world and the people dream with him. That is why I had to undertake this campaign. I, all alone, opposed my nephew, the poets, and our public opinion, but I was forced to give in. I was hoping to conduct this war humanely. The opposition of the Romans was slight. Still, the farther south I advanced, the greater were the misdeeds of my army. Not because my army is any more cruel than any other army, but because *every* war turns men into beasts. I was shocked, I tried to call a halt to the campaign. I was ready to accept the sum offered by the manufacturer of trousers. Because up to now my captains could still be bribed, and because up to now I might still be able to have things my way. But only up to now. Soon I will not be able to do it any more. Then we shall have become, once and for all, a people of heroes. Save me, Romulus, you are my only hope.

ROMULUS. Your hope for what?

ODOAKER. For escaping with my life.

ROMULUS. Are you in danger?

ODOAKER. Right now my nephew is still tame; right now, he is still the polite young man. But one of these days, in a few years, he will kill me. I know this Teutonic loyalty.

ROMULUS. Is that why you wish to subject yourself to me?

ODOAKER. My entire life I have sought the true greatness of man, not that falsely acclaimed greatness of my nephew, who some day shall be called Theodoric the Great, if I know those historians. I am a peasant and I hate war. I sought a human way of life not to be found in the primeval Teutonic forests. I found it in you, Emperor Romulus. Your head steward, Ebius, saw through you.

ROMULUS. Ebi? At my Court? On your orders?

ODOAKER. He was my spy, but he sent good reports: Of a true human being, of a just man, of you, Romulus.

ROMULUS. He sent you reports of a fool, Odoaker. My whole life was aimed at the day when the Roman Empire would collapse. I took it upon myself to be Rome's judge, because I was ready to die. I asked of my country this enormous sacrifice because I, myself, was willing to be sacrificed. By rendering my country defenceless, I allowed its blood to flow because my own blood was ready to be spilled. And now I am to live; my sacrifice is not being accepted. Now I am to be the one who alone was saved. Even worse, just before you came I received the news that my only daughter, whom I loved, died together with her bridegroom, with my wife and the entire Court. I bore this news easily because I thought I was going to die. But now it hits me pitilessly and pitilessly proves me wrong. All I have done has become absurd. Kill me, Odoaker.

(*Silence.*)

ODOAKER. You are speaking in anguish. Conquer your grief and accept my submission.

ROMULUS. You are afraid. Conquer your fear and kill me.

(*Silence.*)

ODOAKER. You thought of your own people, Romulus, but now you must think of your enemies. If you do not accept my submission, if you and I do not make our way together, then the world will fall to my nephew; then a second Rome will rise, a Teutonic empire, as transitory as Rome and as bloody. If that comes to pass your work, the fall of Rome, will become absurd. You cannot escape your own greatness, Romulus. You are the only man who knows how to rule this world. Be merciful, accept my submission, become our Emperor. Protect us from Theodoric's bloody greatness.

(*Silence.*)

ROMULUS. I can do so no more, Odoaker. Even if I wanted to. You've taken from me the very thing that justified my actions.

ODOAKER. Is this your last word?

(ROMULUS *kneels.*)

ROMULUS. Kill me! I beg you on my knees.

ODOAKER. I cannot force you to help us. This is a misfortune for us. But neither can I kill you. For I love you.

ROMULUS. If you will not kill me, there is still a solution. The only man who would still murder me is sleeping in front of my bed. I will go and wake him.

(*As he rises,* ODOAKER *rises also.*)

ODOAKER. That is no solution, Romulus. You are desperate now.

Your death would be senseless. It would only make sense if the world were as you imagine it. But it isn't. Your enemy, too, is a human being who would do what is right, just as you do. You must accept your destiny. There is no other way.

(*Silence.*)

ROMULUS. Shall we sit down?

ODOAKER. What else can we do?

ROMULUS. What are you planning to do with me now?

ODOAKER. I will send you into retirement.

ROMULUS. Into retirement?

ODOAKER. It is the only possibility left to us.

(*Silence.*)

ROMULUS. Of all possible fates, retirement is the worst.

ODOAKER. Do not forget that I, too, am about to face the worst. You will have to proclaim me King of Italy. But it will be the beginning of my end unless I act promptly, here and now. Whether I want to or not, I will have to begin my reign with a murder.

(*He draws his sword and starts to go off to the right.*)

ROMULUS. What are you going to do?

ODOAKER. Kill my nephew. Right now I am still stronger than he.

ROMULUS. Now you are desperate, Odoaker. If you kill your nephew a thousand new Theodorics will rise. Your people feel differently about things than you do. Your people want the heroic life. You cannot change that.

(*Silence.*)

ODOAKER. Let us sit down again. We are caught in a vicious circle.

(*They sit down again.*)

ROMULUS. My dear Odoaker, I wanted to make my destiny and you wanted to avoid yours. Now it is our destiny to be politicians who have foundered on the rock of events. We thought we could drop the world from our hands, you, your

Germania and I, my Rome. Now we must busy ourselves with the pieces that are left. I wanted Rome's end because I feared its past; and you, you wanted the end of Germania because you shuddered at its future. Two spectres ruled us, for we have power neither over what was nor over what will be. Our only power is over the present. But we did not think of the present and now we founder on it. I must now live through the present in retirement, and weighing on my conscience will be a daughter I loved, a son, a wife, and indeed many other unhappy human beings.

ODOAKER. And I shall have to reign.

ROMULUS. Reality has put our ideas right.

ODOAKER. Bitterly right.

ROMULUS. Let us bear this bitterness. Let's try to endow the nonsense with sense! Try in the few years which will still be yours to rule the world faithfully. Give peace to the Teutons and to the Romans alike. To your task then, Ruler of the Teutons. Take up your reign! Maybe there will be a few years which world history will forget because they will be unheroic years – but they will be among the happiest this confused world has ever lived through.

ODOAKER. And then I shall have to die.

ROMULUS. Take comfort. Your nephew will kill me, too. He will never forgive me for having had to kneel before me.

ODOAKER. Then let us do our sad duty.

ROMULUS. Let us do it quickly. Once more and for the last time, let us play this comedy. Let us act *as if* final accounts were settled here on earth, as if the spirit won over the material called man.

ODOAKER. Nephew.

(*The nephew enters from the right.*)

THEODORIC. Yes, dear Uncle?

ODOAKER. Call in our captains, Nephew.

THEODORIC. Yes, dear Uncle.

(*He again goes off to the right. The room fills up with* TEUTONS, *dirty and fatigued from their long marches. They are dressed in monotonous linen clothes and simple helmets.* ODOAKER *rises.*)

ODOAKER. Teutons! Covered with dust and tired from your long marches, burned by the sun, you have now come to the end of your campaign. You are standing before the Emperor of Rome. Show him all honours.

(*The* TEUTONS *stand at attention.*)

Teutons! You have laughed at this man and mocked him in the songs you sang all day on the highways and at night by your campfires. But I discovered his humanity. Never have I seen a greater human being, and never shall you see a greater one, no matter who my successor is. Speak now, O Emperor of Rome.

ROMULUS. The Emperor is dissolving his Empire. Look, all of you, once more upon this tinted globe, this dream of a great empire, floating in space, driven by the slightest breath of my lips. Yes, look once more upon these far-flung lands encircling the blue sea with its dancing dolphins, these rich provinces golden with wheat, these teeming cities overflowing with life; yes, this empire once was a sun warming mankind, but at its zenith it scorched the world; now it is a harmless bubble and in the hands of the Emperor it dissolves into nothing.

(*Solemn silence. The* TEUTONS *stare in amazement at the* EMPEROR *who rises.*)

ROMULUS. I now proclaim Odoaker, Ruler of the Teutons, King of Italy!

TEUTONS. Long live the King of Italy!

ODOAKER. I, for my part, assign to the Emperor of Rome the villa of Lucullus in the Campania. Furthermore, he is to receive a yearly pension of six thousand gold coins.

ROMULUS. The Emperor's years of hunger are over. Take this wreath and the imperial toga. You will find the imperial sword among the garden tools. Will someone fetch me my namesake off the wall, the bust of King Romulus, the founder of Rome?

(*A Teuton brings him the bust.*)

ROMULUS. My thanks to you.

(*He puts the bust under his arm.*)

ROMULUS. Now I shall leave you, Ruler of the Teutons. I'm going into retirement.

TEUTONS. Long live Romulus the Great.

(SPURIUS TITUS MAMMA, *carrying a drawn sword, bursts in from behind.*)

SPURIUS TITUS MAMMA. Where is the Emperor? I shall kill him.

(*The* KING OF ITALY *steps up to him with dignity.*)

ODOAKER. Put down your sword, Captain. There is no emperor any more.

SPURIUS TITUS MAMMA. The empire?

ODOAKER. Is dissolved.

SPURIUS TITUS MAMMA. Then the last imperial officer slept right through the fall of his homeland.

(SPURIUS TITUS MAMMA *sinks down upon the Emperor's seat, downcast and broken-hearted.*)

ROMULUS. Gentlemen, the Roman Empire has ceased to exist.

(*The* EMPEROR *goes off slowly with bent head, carrying the bust under his arm. The* TEUTONS *stand by respectfully.*)

NOTES

Here is a difficult comedy, because it is seemingly a light one! Now what is the devotee of German literature to make of that? Style is what sounds solemn. Such a one will think of *Romulus* as a kind of farce, and will place it somewhere between Theo Lingen and Shaw. Nor is that fate entirely unfitting for Romulus. For twenty years he played the fool, and the world around him did not realize there was a method to his nonsense. That itself is something to think about! My characters must emerge from the way they appear. This applies to the actors and the director. Practically speaking: what should Emilian be like? He has been on the road for days, perhaps weeks, along secret paths, past destroyed cities, and finally he reaches the Emperor's villa which, after all, he knows well. But he asks now: is this the Emperor's villa in Campania? If we do not feel his unbelievable astonishment at seeing the Emperor's villa so dilapidated and looking like a chicken yard, then the question will seem merely rhetorical; this also holds when he asks his beloved, with fear and hesitancy: who are you? For truly, he no longer knows her. Truly he has forgotten her, but still he suspects that he once knew and loved this girl. Emilian is the counterpart to Romulus. His fate must be seen with human eyes, with the eyes, as it were, of the Emperor. For the Emperor can see behind Emilian's façade of the dishonoured officer, 'the victim of power, defiled a thousand times'. Romulus takes Emilian seriously, knowing him to be a human being who was captured and tortured, and who is unhappy. What Romulus will not accept is Emilian's demand that his beloved 'get a knife', nor will Romulus accept that Emilian should couple off his own beloved to save the country. If an actor does not discover the humanity within each of my characters, he cannot represent any of them. This holds for all my plays. But there is an additional difficulty facing the actor playing Romulus, and it is clearly this: he must not allow the audience to feel sympathetic towards Romulus too quickly. That is easily said and perhaps almost impossible to achieve. Still it should be clearly kept in mind as a tactical approach. What the Emperor really stands for should only be revealed in the third Act. In the first Act it should be quite understandable why the Captain of the Cavalry calls him 'a disgrace to Rome'; just as understandable should be Emilian's verdict at the end of Act Two, 'Down with the Emperor.' If Romulus sits in judgment over the world in Act Three, the world sits in judgment over him in Act Four. Look closely at what kind of a human I have sketched here: surely, a witty man, a man at ease and humane, but in the last analysis, a human being who proceeds with the utmost firmness and lack of consideration for others, a man who does not shrink from demanding the same absoluteness of purpose from others. He is indeed a dangerous fellow, a man determined to die. That is the terror lying within this imperial chicken fancier, this judge of the world disguised as a fool. His tragedy lies in the comedy of his end; instead of a sacrificial death he has earned for himself retirement. But then – and this alone is what makes him great – he has the wisdom and the insight to accept his fate.

THE MARRIAGE
OF
MR MISSISSIPPI

Translated from the German by

MICHAEL BULLOCK

FIRST PUBLISHED IN GREAT BRITAIN 1964
TRANSLATED BY MICHAEL BULLOCK FROM THE GERMAN
Die Ehe des Herrn Mississippi

© 1957 BY PETER SCHIFFERLI, VERLAGS AG 'DIE ARCHE', ZÜRICH
ENGLISH VERSION © 1964 BY JONATHAN CAPE

CHARACTERS

ANASTASIA
FLORESTAN MISSISSIPPI
FRÉDÉRIC RENÉ SAINT-CLAUDE
COUNT BODO VON ÜBELOHE-ZABERNSEE
DIEGO, the Minister of Justice
THE MAID
THREE PRIESTS
THREE MEN in raincoats with their right hands in their pockets
TWO WARDERS
PROFESSOR ÜBERHUBER
PSYCHIATRISTS

PART ONE

A room whose late-bourgeois magnificence and splendour will not be altogether easy to describe. Yet since the action takes place in this room and in this room alone, since in fact we may say that the events which follow represent the story of this room, an attempt must be made to describe it. The room stinks to high heaven. In the background are two windows. The view from them is bewildering. To the right the branches of an apple tree, and behind it some northern city with a Gothic cathedral; to the left a cypress, the remains of a classical temple, a bay, a harbour. So much for what lies outside. Between the two windows, but no higher than they are, a grandfather clock. Also Gothic in style. Let us turn to the right-hand wall. Here there are two doors. The door at the back of the stage leads through the veranda into a second room – it isn't important, I really only need it in Part Two; the door front stage right leads to an entrance hall and the front door; the kitchen is also situated there, perhaps round the corner to the right of the entrance hall. Let us not bother about the possible lay-out of the house, we will assume that it is a rambling mansion to which many alterations and additions have been made. Between the doors on the right stands a small sideboard; this time I should like to suggest Louis Quinze. On it is a Venus. Of plaster. Naturally. In the left-hand wall there is only one door. It opens between fin-de-siècle mirrors. The door leads into a boudoir, which in turn leads into the bedroom, rooms which we shall not enter – though many others will. Front stage left the Louis Seize frame of a second mirror dangles in mid-air, of course without a glass, so that anyone looking in it will see the audience. Front stage right there might hang a small, oval, blank picture. In the centre stands a round Biedermeier coffee table; this is really the main character in the play, upon which all the action centres, and the production should make this clear; it is flanked by

E   129

two Louis Quatorze chairs. A bit of Empire furniture can undoubtedly be introduced somewhere – say, left front stage a small sofa and left back stage a folding screen. The producer will have to forgo putting in anything Russian, unless the political situation happens to render this desirable. On the little table stands a Japanese vase containing red roses in Part One. I suggest that Part Two should take place without flowers. The table is laid for coffee for three people. One guesses it is Dresden china. Further objects: to the right three MEN, *looking not unlike good-humoured brewers, wearing raincoats and red armbands, their right hands in their pockets; and in the centre, say between the coffee table and the door on the left, or perhaps slightly to the south of the latter,* SAINT-CLAUDE. *Without going into great detail regarding this character we may think of him as rather squarely built, massive, a man of steel, dressed at the moment in evening dress that obviously doesn't fit, and red socks. In addition, somewhere in the room, preferably coming from the cathedral, the solemn ringing of bells.*

THE FIRST OF THE THREE IN RAINCOATS. You have been condemned to death, Saint-Claude. Put your hands behind your head.

 (SAINT-CLAUDE *obeys.*)

Go and stand between the windows.

 (SAINT-CLAUDE *obeys.*)

Turn your face to the wall. That's the simplest way to die.

 (SAINT-CLAUDE *turns his face to the wall. The ringing dies away. A shot.* SAINT-CLAUDE *stands where he is. The three* MEN *in raincoats – their right hands in their pockets again – go out right.* SAINT-CLAUDE *turns round to the audience and delivers the following speech, like a cross between the director of a rather second-rate theatre and a Mephistopheles.*)

SAINT-CLAUDE. Ladies and gentlemen, as you may have noticed, I have just been shot to the sound of church bells fading into the distance. The bullet struck me somewhere between the shoulder blades, as far as I can judge – it's not easy to be sure – (*he reaches round to feel his back*) shattered my heart on its way through and apparently came out of my chest here, making a hole in my tail coat and buckling the medal 'Pour le Mérite' – which is a bit embarrassing, since neither the coat nor the medal belong to me – and finally damaging the wallpaper. At least, that is what I imagine happened. My present condition is a pleasant one. Apart from my very natural surprise at finding myself still here, I feel fine; in particular, my liver has suddenly ceased to bother me. It used to be the seat of an insidious disease which in my life before death I was always trying to conceal, but which, as I must now admit, was largely responsible for my rather extreme views – although at the time I thought I was governed solely by moral considerations. My death, which you have just witnessed – this exceedingly trivial but, sad to relate, not by any means unusual death – really takes place at the end of the play, as you may have guessed, because once men with armbands appear on the scene the game's up, it's the end of everything. But for what I might call therapeutic reasons we have shifted my murder to the beginning; this enables us to get one of the worst scenes over quickly. Moreover – and I can't hide this from you either – at the painful moment when my death takes place there will be other bodies lying around here, a fact which at this juncture would only confuse you, although it is not really surprising, since this comedy deals, among other things, with the marriage of my friend Mr Mississippi. Among other things, I say, because it concerns the somewhat regrettable fate of three men (*three over-dramatic busts, portraying from left to right Saint-Claude, Übelohe and Mississippi, the two outside ones encircled by black crape, descend from above and remain suspended in the air back stage*) who, for various reasons, had taken it into their heads to change and save the world and who then had the appalling bad luck to run into a woman (*Anastasia's bust descends, likewise encircled by black crape, and*

remains suspended between Übelohe and Mississippi) who could
be neither changed nor saved, because she loved nothing but
the moment; though looking back on it I must say that this
is by far the pleasantest attitude to adopt to life. Anyhow, this
comedy might just as well have been called 'The Love of
Bodo von Übelohe-Zabernsee', or 'The Adventure of Mon-
sieur Saint-Claude' or, to keep it short and sweet, 'Anastasia
and her Lovers'. (*As he speaks he points in turn to the character
concerned.*) The fact that as the plot develops every project
finally comes to nothing, indeed that the whole thing de-
generates into violence and confusion, is regrettable, but that
is life, and in any case it is too late to change it now. (*The
busts disappear.*) And if at this moment you see one of the
few survivors staggering past outside the two windows –
look, there he goes – (COUNT ÜBELOHE *staggers past outside
with a blue banner*) running after some ridiculous detachment
of the Salvation Army, banner in hand, please overlook the
fact that this is completely impossible, since this room is on
the first floor, as may be gathered from the tops of the two
trees which you can see – an apple tree and a cypress, to be
precise. But let's make some sort of start with our story. We
might begin, for example, with myself in Rumania hatching
up the revolution that led to the fall of King Michael, or with
Count Übelohe in Tampang, a miserable dump in the interior of Borneo, trying to cut out a drunken Malay's appen-
dix while drunk himself (*two pictures showing what is being
described float down from above*), but let us remain in this room
that has now grown familiar to us. Let us go back (*the pictures
float upwards again*); we shall not find that difficult, since we
need not move from the spot – though it isn't even clear
where this house is situated; at one point the author decided
in favour of the south, hence the cypress, the temple and the
sea; at another, he settled for the north, hence the apple tree
and the cathedral. Anyhow, let us go back, if you please, just
five years before the disaster which you witnessed at the

beginning, back in other words to 1958 or 1959, always five
years before the present, so long as this remains possible at all.
Well, then, it is May, the windows are slightly open (*the
windows open slightly*), on the table stand red roses, above the
grandfather clock hangs the portrait of the first man who had
the good fortune to be married to Anastasia, the picture of a
beet-sugar manufacturer whose Christian name was François
(*the picture floats down*), and the maid brings in my old friend
Mississippi (*the* MAID *and* MISSISSIPPI *enter right*), who stands
there, correct as always and dressed as always in a black frock-
coat, and hands his stick, coat and hat to the girl, while I make
off in my usual way – I climbed through windows far too
often in my previous life; in fact this may not be the normal
manner for the dead to disappear, but how could I be
expected to have learnt their trick of fading into thin air all
on my own, when I was scarcely cold? In short, while I am
making for a place (*he looks somewhat suspiciously towards the
centre of the earth*) which I can't picture to myself at all (*he
climbs through the window left*), Mr Mississippi, five years ago
and at this particular spot, reaches an important decision.

(SAINT-CLAUDE *disappears*.)

THE MAID. Madam will be here in a moment, sir.

(*The* MAID *goes out right*, MISSISSIPPI *looks at the beet-sugar
manufacturer's picture*. ANASTASIA *enters left*. MISSISSIPPI *bows*.)

ANASTASIA. You wished to see me?

MISSISSIPPI. My name is Mississippi. Florestan Mississippi.

ANASTASIA. You told me in your letter that you had an urgent
matter to discuss with me?

MISSISSIPPI. Yes, very urgent. I'm afraid my work prevents me
from coming at any other time than in my lunch hour.

ANASTASIA. You were a friend of my husband's?

(*She glances briefly at the picture in the background*. MISSISSIPPI
also looks at it.)

MISSISSIPPI. I am deeply affected by his unexpected death.

(*He bows*.)

ANASTASIA (*somewhat embarrassed*). He died of a heart attack.

MISSISSIPPI (*bows again*). May I express my profound sympathy?

ANASTASIA. May I offer you a cup of coffee?

MISSISSIPPI. You are very kind.

(*They sit down.* ANASTASIA *on the left,* MISSISSIPPI *on the right.* ANASTASIA *pours out. The ensuing scene at the coffee table must be produced with great exactitude, the movements involved in drinking coffee being performed very precisely: e.g. both lift their cups to their mouths at the same time or stir the coffee simultaneously etc.*)

ANASTASIA. In your letter you urgently begged me to hear what you had to say. You did so in the name of my dead husband. (*She looks at the picture.*) Otherwise I should not have agreed to your visit so soon after François's death. I hope you understand me.

MISSISSIPPI. Perfectly. I too honour the dead. (*He too looks at the picture.*) Were my business not so urgent I should never have ventured to inflict my visit upon you, all the more so since there has also been a death in my family. My young wife died a few days ago. (*After a short pause, meaningfully.*) Her name was Madeleine.

(*He looks searchingly at* ANASTASIA, *who has almost imperceptibly started.*)

ANASTASIA. I'm sorry to hear that.

MISSISSIPPI. For years we had the same family doctor as you, old Dr Bonsels. It was from him that I heard the sad news of your husband's death. Dr Bonsels diagnosed heart failure as the cause of death in my wife's case too.

(*Again he looks watchfully at* ANASTASIA, *who once more starts.*)

ANASTASIA. May I too offer my heartfelt condolences?

MISSISSIPPI. In order to understand the request I am about to make it is most important that you should know all about me, Madam. I am the Public Prosecutor.

(ANASTASIA *drops her coffee cup in terror.*)

ANASTASIA. Forgive my clumsy interruption.

MISSISSIPPI (*bows*). Don't mention it. I am used to spreading fear and trembling.

(ANASTASIA *rings a small silver bell. The* MAID *enters right, mops the table, gives* ANASTASIA *a fresh cup and saucer and leaves again.*)

ANASTASIA. You haven't taken any sugar yet. Please help yourself.

MISSISSIPPI. Thank you.

ANASTASIA (*smiling*). What brings you to me now, Mr Public Prosecutor?

MISSISSIPPI. The reason for my visit concerns your husband.

ANASTASIA. Does François owe you money?

MISSISSIPPI. His debt is not of a financial character. We are totally unknown to one another, Madam, and I am sincerely sorry to have to speak ill of your husband, but he deceived you.

(ANASTASIA *starts and there is an awkward silence.*)

ANASTASIA (*coldly*). Who told you that?

MISSISSIPPI (*calmly*). My incorruptible powers of observation. I possess the ability to sniff out evil wherever it may be. It is a gift that causes me unimaginable suffering.

ANASTASIA. I really don't know how you can make such insane assertions about my husband's way of life so soon after his death and in this room, in which, so to speak, he still lives. Your accusation is monstrous.

MISSISSIPPI. The fact that your husband could deceive a woman such as you is a great deal more monstrous. Does it not occur to you that I have not come to you of my own free will, but only because we are bound together by an awful destiny? I beg you to steel your heart and listen to me calmly. Our mutual torment is already so dreadful that we must treat one another with the utmost consideration.

ANASTASIA (*after a brief pause, in a matter-of-fact tone*). Forgive my understandable agitation. François's unexpected death has exhausted my strength. Will you have another cup of coffee?

MISSISSIPPI. I should like one very much. My profession calls for iron nerves.

(*She pours out.*)

ANASTASIA. May I give you some sugar?

MISSISSIPPI. Thank you. Sugar has a calming effect. Unfortunately I am not in a position to set aside more than half an hour for our important discussion. I have to get a death sentence passed by a jury later this afternoon. Juries are very narrow-minded nowadays. (*He drinks coffee.*) So you still cling to the belief that your husband did not deceive you?

ANASTASIA. I swear that he is innocent.

MISSISSIPPI (*after a short pause*). Very well. You boast of his innocence. Will you continue to do so if I tell you the name of the woman with whom your husband deceived you?

ANASTASIA (*jumps up*). Who is this woman?

MISSISSIPPI (*after a short pause*). I have told you her name – Madeleine.

ANASTASIA (*horrified, because she has suddenly understood*). Your wife?

MISSISSIPPI. My wife.

ANASTASIA (*filled with horror*). But I thought she was dead?

MISSISSIPPI (*with the greatest possible calm*). Indeed she is. She died of heart failure. (*With dignity.*) We have been deceived by your husband François and my dead wife Madeleine, Madam.

ANASTASIA. It's terrible!

MISSISSIPPI. The facts of marriage are often terrible. (*He wipes the sweat from his brow with a handkerchief.*) Might I ask for another cup of coffee?

ANASTASIA (*crushed*). Please forgive me. I am upset and confused. (*She pours out.*)

MISSISSIPPI (*with relief*). The first stage of our terrible journey is behind us! You have confessed to knowing of your husband's infidelity. That is a tremendous step forward. Have you had proof for long?

ANASTASIA (*tonelessly*). For a few weeks. When I found a letter signed 'Madeleine' and filled with outpourings of the most ardent passion, the discovery stunned me like a blow from a club. I shall never understand my husband's action.

MISSISSIPPI. You didn't know my wife. She was the most lovable of women, young, radiantly beautiful and of medium height. The discovery of her infidelity cast me into the bottommost hell. I too found a letter imprudently headed with your husband's business address. Their love was already so wildly ablaze that they failed to take the most elementary precautions.

ANASTASIA. After my husband's death I wanted to forget his infidelity. I wanted to preserve the memory of him as the man who once loved me passionately and whom I shall never cease to love. That was why at first I evaded your question. I'm sorry. You have forced me to think once more about what has happened.

MISSISSIPPI. As the husband of the woman with whom your husband deceived you I'm afraid I couldn't possibly avoid it.

ANASTASIA. I too understand you. Being a man, you need clarity. (*She stands up.*) Thank you, Mr Public Prosecutor, for having given clarity to me too, weak woman that I am. Now I know all about François, and it is terrible to know all. (*Exhausted.*) Now you must excuse me, I am worn out. Your wife and my husband are dead. We can no longer call them to account. We can no longer beg them for love. They are now lost to us for ever.

(MISSISSIPPI *has now also risen.*)

MISSISSIPPI (*gravely*). At this unprecedented moment, when the first rays of truth are beginning to touch us, my twenty-five years as Public Prosecutor make it incumbent upon me to cry out to you that the time has come for us both to confess the whole truth, even if it destroys us.

(*He looks at her so resolutely that they sit down again.*)

ANASTASIA. I don't understand you.

MISSISSIPPI. I am referring to your husband's death.

ANASTASIA. I really don't know what you're getting at.

MISSISSIPPI. The fact that at the very beginning of our conversation, and for absolutely no apparent reason, you informed me of the cause of your husband's death, and your panic terror when I told you my profession, were all the evidence I needed.

ANASTASIA. Will you please be more explicit?

MISSISSIPPI. If you wish me to, I shall be utterly explicit. I doubt the cause of his death.

ANASTASIA (*quickly*). Many people die of a heart attack at the age of fifty.

MISSISSIPPI. His photograph alone disproves that. No man who enjoys such glowing health can die of a heart attack. Besides, people in whom I am interested never die of heart attacks.

ANASTASIA. What do you mean by that?

MISSISSIPPI. Could you really not have spared me the necessity of telling you to your face that you poisoned your husband?

ANASTASIA (*staring at him flabbergasted*). You believe that?

MISSISSIPPI (*distinctly*). I do.

ANASTASIA (*still as though stunned*). No, no!

> (*She is deathly pale.* MISSISSIPPI *wearily takes a rose from the Japanese vase and holds it to his nose.*)

MISSISSIPPI. Get a grip on yourself. It must be something of a relief to you to have been found out by Justice.

ANASTASIA (*in a wild outburst*). No!

> (MISSISSIPPI *replaces the rose in the vase.* ANASTASIA *rises to her feet with dignity.* MISSISSIPPI *does the same.*)

ANASTASIA. The physician, Dr Bonsels, had no hesitation in diagnosing the cause of my husband's death as heart failure. I presume that the Public Prosecutor will accept the verdict of medical science.

MISSISSIPPI. We belong to a social stratum, Madam, in which in cases of doubt medical science always diagnoses heart failure.

ANASTASIA. Now that I have told you everything that remained to be said regarding my husband's death, which came as a surprise to all of us, may I ask you to take your leave?

MISSISSIPPI (*worried*). In that terrible event it would be my duty to continue our discussion in a different room and under different circumstances.

ANASTASIA. I cannot prevent you from doing your so-called duty.

MISSISSIPPI. You can, if you take an unprejudiced view of your situation. You have the rare opportunity of confronting the Public Prosecutor between your own four walls. Do you wish to do so under the humiliating conditions of a Public Court? I hope not. I am altogether at a loss to understand why you refuse so disastrously to see the humanitarian nature of what I am doing. It is undoubtedly far easier to confess to a murder over coffee than before a jury.

(*They sit down again.*)

ANASTASIA (*in a low voice*). I am at your service.

MISSISSIPPI (*relieved*). That is unquestionably the best way.

ANASTASIA. But no power in the world will compel me to confess to the crime which you impute to me. You seem to be the victim of some terrible mistake.

MISSISSIPPI. Only the accused make mistakes, never the Public Prosecutor.

ANASTASIA. I shall defend my innocence like a wild beast.

MISSISSIPPI (*earnestly*). Pray to God, Madam, that you are spared such a fight. It is sheer madness to fight against me, and yet people are for ever trying to do so. For minutes, for hours, for days; then they break down. I shudder at the sight of my victims. Do you too wish to wriggle at my feet like a worm? Please realize that behind me stands the whole moral order of the universe, and that anyone who opposes me is lost. To confess may be difficult, but to be forced to confess is unimaginably frightful.

ANASTASIA. Are you a preacher or an executioner?

MISSISSIPPI. My terrible profession compels me to be both.

ANASTASIA. You can't come here and make the wildest accusations against me completely out of the blue like that.

MISSISSIPPI. Then I am afraid I must mention the name of Count Bodo von Übelohe-Zabernsee.

(ANASTASIA *is seized with fright, but recovers her poise.*)

ANASTASIA (*slowly*). I don't know that name.

MISSISSIPPI. You spent your youth with Count Übelohe in Lausanne, where your father was a teacher at a girls' boarding-school, and you grew up in a castle belonging to the Count's family. You parted, and a few years ago you met again in this town, you as the wife of your now dead husband and he as the head physician and founder of the St George's Hospital for the Poor.

ANASTASIA (*slowly*). I only see him very occasionally now.

MISSISSIPPI. On the sixteenth you asked him for two pieces of a white poison which looks exactly like sugar and about which he talked to you after you had been together to see *Götz von Berlichingen* and you came to speak of Weislingen's death. You are both great lovers of literature.

ANASTASIA (*stubbornly*). He didn't give me the poison.

MISSISSIPPI. Bodo von Übelohe-Zabernsee has confessed to everything.

ANASTASIA (*vehemently*). That's not true!

MISSISSIPPI. After I threatened to have his medical licence withdrawn he left our town as fast as he could and went to the tropics, no doubt to escape imprisonment.

ANASTASIA (*jumps up*). Bodo has gone?

MISSISSIPPI. The Count has fled.

(ANASTASIA *sinks back into the chair again.* MISSISSIPPI *wipes the sweat from his brow.*)

ANASTASIA (*after a long pause, dully*). Why did you threaten him with such a cruel step? The St George's Hospital for the Poor is his life's work.

MISSISSIPPI. I only acted according to the laws which govern the medical profession. (*After a short pause.*) According to the statement which he made when driven to utter despair, you told him that you wanted the poison in order to kill your dog, a statement which, of course, in no way excuses his giving it to you.

ANASTASIA (*quickly*). I did have to kill my dog. He was ill.

MISSISSIPPI (*politely*). You must permit me a brief incursion into your domestic rights.

> (*He stands up, bows and rings* ANASTASIA's *little silver bell. The* MAID *enters right.*)

MISSISSIPPI. What is your name?

MAID. Lucretia.

MISSISSIPPI. Has your mistress a dog, Lucretia?

MAID. He's dead.

MISSISSIPPI. When did the dog die, Lucretia?

MAID. A month ago.

MISSISSIPPI. You may go back to work, Lucretia.

> (*The* MAID *goes out right.* MISSISSIPPI *stands up.*)

MISSISSIPPI. You lost your dog a month ago and you fetched the poison from your childhood friend Count Übelohe-Zabernsee five days ago. Two pieces of a quick-acting poison that looked like lumps of sugar. Your husband died the same day. How much longer are we to keep up this comedy that is degrading for both of us, Madam? You force me to stoop to methods which a Public Prosecutor employs only reluctantly. Now I have even had to question your maid.

> (ANASTASIA *also rises. At this point a little dance round the coffee table may be executed in the heat of the duel.*)

ANASTASIA (*in a low voice*). I didn't poison my husband.

MISSISSIPPI. So you refuse to yield to lucid reason?

ANASTASIA. I am innocent.

MISSISSIPPI. Can no logic on earth persuade you to confess to murder?

ANASTASIA. I did not kill my husband.

MISSISSIPPI (*slowly*). Then Madeleine's belief that her lover's

141

death was due to an act of vengeance by his wronged wife, a belief which caused her such unutterable despair, was nothing but an insane fantasy?

ANASTASIA (*with shining eyes*). Your wife believed that?

MISSISSIPPI. The thought that you might have killed your husband brought Madeleine to the verge of madness.

ANASTASIA (*with barely restrained triumph*). She suffered before she died?

MISSISSIPPI. Terribly.

ANASTASIA (*jubilantly*). I achieved what I set out to do! I stabbed her to the heart! She groaned, raved, wept, cried out! She paid me back a thousandfold in despair for every second of her pleasure! I killed both of them! He perished at my hands and she through his death! They perished like beasts, they died like dogs!

(MISSISSIPPI *sits down again; so does* ANASTASIA.)

MISSISSIPPI. So you did poison your husband, Madam?

ANASTASIA. Yes, I poisoned him. We loved one another, he deceived me and then I killed him.

MISSISSIPPI. On the morning of the sixteenth of May you went to Bodo von Übelohe-Zabernsee. As a childhood friend of yours and as a friend of your husband's he gave you the poison, believing blindly that you would use it to destroy your dog, and you gave it to your husband with his after-lunch coffee instead of sugar.

ANASTASIA. He took one piece and died.

MISSISSIPPI. Did you do all that?

ANASTASIA (*with a terrible grandeur*). Yes, all of it.

MISSISSIPPI. And you do not regret your horrible deed?

ANASTASIA. I would do it again and again.

MISSISSIPPI (*white-faced*). I am gazing into an abyss of passion.

ANASTASIA (*indifferently*). Now you can take me away.

MISSISSIPPI (*rises slowly and solemnly*). I have not come to arrest you. I have come to ask you to be my wife.

(*He bows solemnly. A terrifying silence.*)

142

ANASTASIA (*her head spinning*). To ask me what?

MISSISSIPPI. To ask for your hand.

ANASTASIA. My hand?

MISSISSIPPI. I am well off, draw a very good salary, live a retiring life, am deeply religious, occupy my leisure chiefly with the collection of old engravings, for the most part idyllic landscapes which seem to me best to portray the original guiltless state of nature, and I can expect a pension fully adequate to our social standing.

ANASTASIA (*deathly pale*). That is monstrous!

MISSISSIPPI (*bows again*). Human life *is* monstrous, Madam.

(*He sits down. As if hypnotized,* ANASTASIA *sits down too.*)

MISSISSIPPI. Could I possibly ask for another cup of coffee? (*He looks at his watch.*) I have another twelve minutes.

ANASTASIA (*mechanically fills his cup*). I find it impossible to understand your behaviour. First you force me to confess to a deed that must inevitably fill any man with horror at what a woman is capable of, and then you ask me in cold blood to be your wife.

MISSISSIPPI (*helping himself to sugar, calmly*). Let me make to you the terrible confession that I too killed my wife with the same sugar-like poison with which you killed your husband.

ANASTASIA (*after a long pause, horrified*). You too?

MISSISSIPPI (*firmly*). I too.

(ANASTASIA *sits as though stunned.* MISSISSIPPI *stirs his coffee.*)

MISSISSIPPI. After I had confiscated the remainder of the poison from Count Übelohe – this time also there were two pieces – I went home and put one of them in Madeleine's black coffee after lunch. Half an hour later she gently fell asleep.

(*He drinks. He puts down the cup.*)

(*Dully*) It was the worst half-hour of my life.

ANASTASIA (*staggered*). So that is the destiny which binds us together.

MISSISSIPPI (*exhausted*). We have confessed our deed to one another.

ANASTASIA. You have killed and I have killed. We are both murderers.

MISSISSIPPI (*firmly*). No, Madam. I am not a murderer. Between your deed and mine there is an infinite difference. What *you* did in response to a dreadful impulse, I did in obedience to a moral judgment. You slaughtered your husband; I executed my wife.

ANASTASIA (*scared to death*). Executed?

MISSISSIPPI (*proudly*). Executed.

ANASTASIA. I don't know how to take your frightful words.

MISSISSIPPI. Literally. I poisoned my wife because she had earned the death sentence for her adultery.

ANASTASIA. There is not one code of laws in the world that prescribes the death sentence for adultery.

MISSISSIPPI. The Law of Moses.

ANASTASIA. That was a few thousand years ago.

MISSISSIPPI. I am firmly determined to bring it back.

ANASTASIA. You're mad.

MISSISSIPPI. I am merely a completely moral man, Madam. With the passage of time our laws have miserably degenerated. They are discounted paper money that still circulates for appearances' sake in a society whose only religion is pleasure, which has bestowed privileges upon robbery and does barter in women and oil. Only idealists out of touch with reality can still imagine that the cheque paid by Justice is covered. Compared with Old Testament law, which lays down the death penalty for *both* parties to adultery, our civil law is a wretched mockery. For this sacred reason, the murder of my wife was an absolute necessity. It was a question of reversing the course of world history, which has lost the Law and gained a freedom devoid of all moral responsibility.

ANASTASIA. Then I am completely at a loss to know why you are asking me to marry you.

MISSISSIPPI. You are beautiful. And yet you are guilty. You touch me deeply.

ANASTASIA (*uncertainly*). You love me?

MISSISSIPPI. I can no longer love.

ANASTASIA. What do you mean?

MISSISSIPPI. You are a murderess, Madam, and I am the Public Prosecutor. But it is better to be guilty than to see the guilt. Guilt can be repented; the sight of guilt is fatal. In my work I have stood for twenty-five years face to face with guilt; its look has destroyed me. I have spent whole nights begging for the power to love just *one* more person. In vain. I can no longer love what is lost, I can only kill. I have become a wild beast that springs at humanity's throat.

ANASTASIA (*shuddering*). And yet you expressed the wish to marry me.

MISSISSIPPI. It is absolute justice itself that compels me to take this step. I executed Madeleine in a private, not an official capacity. By this action I consciously offended against the existing law. For this misdemeanour I must be punished, even though my motives were as pure as spring water. But in this unworthy age, I am compelled to be my own judge. I have passed sentence. I have condemned myself to marry you.

ANASTASIA (*stands up*). Sir.

MISSISSIPPI (*likewise stands up*). Madam.

ANASTASIA. I have listened patiently to your monstrous talk. But what you have just said goes beyond the bounds of decency. You openly declare that marrying me is a punishment for the murder of your wife.

MISSISSIPPI. I wish you also to look upon marrying me as a punishment for the murder of your husband.

ANASTASIA (*coldly*). So you regard me as a common murderess?

MISSISSIPPI. You did not poison your husband out of respect for justice, but because you loved him.

ANASTASIA. Anyone else who killed her husband for love, as I did, you would have handed over to the Court?

MISSISSIPPI. I should have made it my life's ambition. In only very few cases have I failed to get a death sentence passed, and

every time that happened my health suffered so severely that
I was brought to the edge of the grave.

ANASTASIA (*after a long pause, resolutely*). Call the police!

MISSISSIPPI. That is impossible. By our deed we are indissolubly
bound together.

ANASTASIA. I desire no mitigation of the punishment.

MISSISSIPPI. There can be no question of that. With our marriage
I am not offering you mitigation, but an infinite intensifica-
tion of the punishment.

ANASTASIA (*close to fainting*). You are offering me marriage in
order to torture me unceasingly!

MISSISSIPPI. In order to torture *us* unceasingly. Our marriage
would mean hell for both parties!

ANASTASIA. There is no sense in it!

MISSISSIPPI. You are now a murderess; through our marriage I
shall change you into an angel.

ANASTASIA. You cannot compel me.

MISSISSIPPI. I demand your hand in marriage in the name of
absolute morality!

ANASTASIA (*staggering behind the folding screen*). Call the police!

MISSISSIPPI. In my twenty-five years as Public Prosecutor I have
obtained over two hundred death sentences, a figure that has
never been remotely approached anywhere else in the bourgeois world. Is this superhuman achievement to be destroyed
by a weak woman? We both belong to the highest stratum
of contemporary society, Madam. I am the Public Prosecutor
and your husband owned a beet-sugar factory. Let us now
act like beings of the highest degree of responsibility. Marry
me! Enter with me into the martyrdom of our marriage!

ANASTASIA (*yelling in a final despairing outburst*). Call the police!

MISSISSIPPI (*icy cold*). In an age when murder, adultery, robbery,
incest, lies, arson, exploitation and blasphemy are not inevitably punished with death, our marriage will be a triumph
of justice!

ANASTASIA (*deathly pale*). God above!

MISSISSIPPI (*monstrously*). Marry me!

ANASTASIA (*looking despairingly at the picture in the background*).
François!

MISSISSIPPI. So you accept my proposal of marriage?

ANASTASIA. I accept your proposal of marriage.

MISSISSIPPI (*slips his wedding ring off his finger*). Then will you
please give me the ring which you received from your dead
husband.

> (ANASTASIA *slips her wedding ring off her finger and places it on
> his finger.*)

MISSISSIPPI. Now take the ring which I received from Madeleine.

> (*He puts the ring on her finger. He bows.*)

You are now my wife.

ANASTASIA (*tonelessly*). I am your wife.

MISSISSIPPI. Before the legal formalities take place you will spend
six months in Switzerland. In Grindelwald or Wengen, or
possibly Adelboden. Your nerves are in a bad state. The
mountain air will do you good. I shall have prospectuses of the
afore-mentioned places sent to you by the travel agency.

> (*He rings the little silver bell. The* MAID *enters right.*)

My top hat, stick and coat!

> (*The* MAID *goes out.*)

We shall be married in the Calvinist church. The legal
formalities will be handled by the Minister of Justice, the
ecclesiastical ones by Bishop Jensen. They are both old friends;
we were undergraduates at Oxford together. We shall live here;
I shall be ten minutes closer to the Court. In case there is not
sufficient room for my collection of old engravings we shall
build an extension. Our life will be hard. As a loyal wife you
will have to stand by me in the sufferings and joys of my profession. We shall watch together the executions which I have
been able to bring about. They take place on Fridays. Moreover, I shall expect you to provide spiritual comfort for those
condemned to death, particularly those from the poorer
sections of the population. You will take them flowers,

chocolate and cigarettes, if they smoke. As far as my old engravings are concerned, attendance at a few lectures at the
university should suffice. (*He bows, then with a sudden shout*)
Now I shall get my death sentence passed this afternoon, that's
a dead certainty!

(*He stands motionless. Silence.*)

ANASTASIA (*seizes her forehead with both hands and suddenly cries out
in despair*). Bodo! Bodo!

(*She rushes out left.*)

MISSISSIPPI. This, ladies and gentlemen, took place five years ago
and was the dramatic beginning of a marriage which, although it was hell – and what hell – nevertheless, and this is
the important thing, had a basically ennobling effect upon
both my wife and myself. I threw myself wholeheartedly into
the work of the Court; Anastasia turned to stone; I exulted,
justice had triumphed, and my wife grew pale as death. Unfortunately I did not hear her despairing cry of 'Bodo, Bodo'
as she clutched her forehead – the incident you have just witnessed. I was already on the stairs, or possibly even in the
street. A circumstance which I profoundly regret, not because
I doubt my wife – I still consider her innocent and completely
incapable of the heinous sin of adultery even in thought; but I
should have attached more importance to the fact that she
was bound by ties of pure friendship to such an excessively
emotional and grossly over-imaginative Count (COUNT
ÜBELOHE *staggers by outside the window*) who constituted a
childhood memory to which she remained true. A great deal
might then have been avoided. A great deal – not the failure
of my truly monumental effort to rebuild the world from its
very foundations by the application of the Law of Moses
perhaps, but probably the bitter end to which we both came.
Yet despite the wealth of mental suffering they imposed, the
years of my second marriage were among the happiest of my
life; professionally too they were blessed, for, as is well
known, I succeeded in increasing the number of my death

sentences from two hundred to three hundred and fifty, of which only eleven – under scandalous circumstances, being prevented by acts of clemency on the part of the Prime Minister – could not be carried out. Our marriage moved with complete regularity within the proposed orbit. As I had foreseen, my wife's character grew substantially deeper and she even acquired a more positive attitude towards religious sentiments; she watched the executions at my side with perfect calm and composure, without ever losing her natural sympathy with the victims (*a picture floats down front stage showing Anastasia watching an execution*); her daily prison visits, which soon became an emotional need for her, continually increased her desire to help, so that she was universally known as the Angel of the Prisons; in short, it was a fruitful period which brilliantly confirmed my thesis that strict laws strictly obeyed are alone capable of making man a better, nay a higher being. (*The picture floats upwards again.*) Thus a few years passed. We have shown the beginning of my marriage; let us now show the end. The room has changed little. The maid is just hanging up two engravings by Rembrandt and Seghers (*the* MAID *enters right and hangs up the engravings*); this should be enough to convey to you the atmosphere of our home. Of the rest of the engravings some are in my study through the door at the back on the right – as you see it – some in Anastasia's boudoir and bedroom, through the door on the left, and some in the hall, through the door in front on the right. Beside the crape-encircled picture of the deceased beet-sugar manufacturer, who departed this life under such unfortunate circumstances, hangs the portrait of my first wife, Madeleine, who died in a similar manner, a fair-haired, rather sentimental-looking young woman, as you can see (*the picture descends backstage next to the portrait of the beet-sugar manufacturer, which has been there from the beginning*) likewise ringed with black crape. (*The Maid has meanwhile gone out right.*) Also in the room is my friend Diego, who did not, as just now, enter through the grandfather clock – a highly improbable action; on the contrary, I brought him in through the door on the right. (DIEGO *has entered the room through the grandfather clock and is now straightening his tie in front of the mirror through which the audience can see.*) Diego occupies the position of Minister of Justice in the undefined and undefinable country in which this room is situated; Diego – this too I should like to mention – takes a profound interest in my wife's philanthropic work. He is an honorary member of the Prisoners' Aid Society presided over by my wife. You are in the picture, ladies and gentlemen, we can begin. The Minister has lit a cigar, a sign that he wants to speak to me.

THE MINISTER. It must be ...

MISSISSIPPI. One moment –

(*He also lights a cigar.*)

THE MINISTER. It must be about five years ...

MISSISSIPPI (*again to the audience*). It is night, let us not forget that either, a gloomy November night. We are already changing the lighting, already a lighted chandelier is descending, bathing everything in a cloud of brownish gold.

THE MINISTER. It must be about five years now since you married the Angel of the Prisons.

MISSISSIPPI. The tremendous moral support I receive from my wife fills me with the keenest satisfaction.

THE MINISTER. It is indeed rare for a wife to console those whom her husband executes. Your zeal is astonishing. You have just obtained your three hundred and fiftieth death sentence.

MISSISSIPPI. One more professional triumph. Even though it was easy to bring the aunt-murderer to the gallows, no success ever did more to increase my self-confidence. You have come to congratulate me.

THE MINISTER. As a lawyer I do indeed admire you, but as Minister of Justice I am compelled to dissociate myself from you.

MISSISSIPPI. That's news to me.

THE MINISTER. Well, you see, the international situation has changed somewhat. I am a politician. I can't possibly afford to be as unpopular as you are.

MISSISSIPPI. I do not allow myself to be swayed by public opinion.

THE MINISTER. You are a genius, and judges are putty in your hands. The Government has repeatedly urged you to clemency.

MISSISSIPPI. The Government needs me.

THE MINISTER. Did need you. There is a slight difference. A high rate of death sentences was useful. It was a question of punishing political murders and restoring order. But now the best policy is to cut the ground from under the opposition's feet by modestly tempering justice with mercy again. At one moment we have to cut off heads in the name of God, at the next we must be merciful to please the devil; no state can avoid that. Once the way in which you exercised your office saved us, but now it is a danger to us. It has made us a laughing-stock throughout the Western world and has unnecessarily stirred up the extreme Left. We must take appropriate steps. A Public Prosecutor who has obtained three hundred and fifty death sentences and dares to declare in public that the Law of Moses ought to be brought back, is no longer to be tolerated. It is true that we are all rather reactionary nowadays, when you come to look at it, but in God's name there is no need to take such a radical line as you do.

MISSISSIPPI. What has the Government decided?

THE MINISTER. The Prime Minister wishes you to retire.

MISSISSIPPI. Did he depute you to convey this message to me?

THE MINISTER. That is the purpose of my visit.

MISSISSIPPI. According to law civil servants can be dismissed only when they are guilty of a felony, fraud, or associating with a foreign power or a political party that is planning the overthrow of the state.

THE MINISTER. You refuse to retire?

MISSISSIPPI. I refuse.

THE MINISTER. The Cabinet will have to compel you.

MISSISSIPPI. The Government must realize that it is fighting against the best lawyer in the world.

THE MINISTER. Your struggle is hopeless. You are the most hated man in the world.

MISSISSIPPI. Your struggle is equally hopeless. Thanks to me, you are the most hated government in the world.

THE MINISTER (*after a pause*). You know, we were undergraduates at Oxford together.

MISSISSIPPI. We were.

THE MINISTER. I can't understand how a man of your intelligence and your not insignificant origins can take such pleasure in beheading people. After all, we come of the best families in the country and that alone should make us exercise a certain restraint.

MISSISSIPPI. Exactly.

THE MINISTER. What do you mean?

MISSISSIPPI. My mother was an Italian princess and my father an American arms king, were they not? Your grandfather was a famous general who lost countless battles, and your father a colonial governor who suppressed various negro revolts. Our families caused heads to roll haphazard, I demand death for the guilty. They were called heroes, I am called a hangman. If my professional success throws an unfavourable light on the best families in the country, it only means that I am showing them up in their true light.

THE MINISTER. You are stabbing us in the back.

MISSISSIPPI. You are stabbing Justice in the back.

THE MINISTER. As Minister of Justice my job is to decide whether justice is politically feasible or not.

MISSISSIPPI. Justice cannot be changed!

THE MINISTER. Everything in the world can be changed, my dear Florestan, except man. You have to realize that before you can rule. To rule means to steer the ship of state, not to cut off heads. Ideals are all very well, but I have to stick to the possible and do without ideals except when I make a speech. The world is bad, but not hopeless; it only becomes hopeless when measured by absolute standards. Justice is not a mincing-machine but a compromise.

MISSISSIPPI. To you, Justice is primarily a slot-machine that provides you with an income.

THE MINISTER. I was best man at your wedding. But at tomorrow's Cabinet meeting I shall be forced to vote against you.

(*He puts his cigar down on the ashtray.*)

MISSISSIPPI. I have nothing more to say to the Government.

THE MINISTER. I have delivered the Prime Minister's message as deputed. Will you now please see me out?

(*They leave through the door on the right. The room is empty. Enter from the left* SAINT-CLAUDE, *now with a dark-brown goatee beard, whereas at the beginning he was clean-shaven. He is wearing rough clothes. A brown leather jacket. Is the audience mistaken in thinking that* SAINT-CLAUDE *has just come from* ANASTASIA, *whose hand he is kissing as he appears? The woman in the white nightdress may have been someone else, so fleetingly is she seen. We will leave this question open for the moment.* SAINT-CLAUDE *goes to the table, picks up the Minister's cigar, smells it, continues smoking it. Then he goes to the window backstage right and opens it. Admires the Venus. Then sits down on the left of the coffee table.* MISSISSIPPI *re-enters from the right.*)

SAINT-CLAUDE (*without looking up*). Good evening, Paul.

(MISSISSIPPI *stands motionless in the doorway.*)

MISSISSIPPI (*slowly getting a grip on himself*). You!

SAINT-CLAUDE. Yes, me. You've done it, Paul. You have become Prosecutor General, you bear the name Florestan Mississippi, you fill the newspapers with your deeds, you possess a home full of old furniture of various periods and no doubt also a beautiful wife.

(*He blows a smoke ring.*)

153

MISSISSIPPI. And what do you call yourself now?

SAINT-CLAUDE. Something even finer than you: Frédéric René Saint-Claude.

MISSISSIPPI. You don't seem to be doing badly either.

SAINT-CLAUDE. Yes, I've done it too. I have become a citizen of the Soviet Union, a colonel in the Red Army, an honorary citizen of Rumania, a member of the Polish parliament and a member of the Politburo of the Cominform.

MISSISSIPPI. How did you get in?

SAINT-CLAUDE. Through the window.

MISSISSIPPI. Then I'll shut it.

(*He goes backstage and shuts the window.*)

What do you want with me?

SAINT-CLAUDE. When you have been abroad for so long, the first thing you do when you get back is to visit your old friends.

MISSISSIPPI. I suppose you crossed the frontier illegally?

SAINT-CLAUDE. Naturally. After all, my job is to reorganize the Communist Party here.

MISSISSIPPI. Under what name?

SAINT-CLAUDE. The Party for People, Faith and Homeland.

MISSISSIPPI. What has that to do with me?

SAINT-CLAUDE. Well, you will have to start looking round for a new job, my dear Paul.

MISSISSIPPI (*walks slowly to the table*). What do you mean?

SAINT-CLAUDE. It seems to me you have no alternative but to comply with the Prime Minister's request.

MISSISSIPPI (*slowly sits down on the right of the table, facing SAINT-CLAUDE*). You eavesdropped on my conversation with the Minister of Justice?

SAINT-CLAUDE (*in amazement.*) Good heavens, no. I simply bribed the Minister for Internal Security.

MISSISSIPPI. Such interest in me on the part of a Soviet citizen makes me feel uneasy.

SAINT-CLAUDE. You have become such an internationally

notorious figure that even we are interested in you. I have come to make you an offer.

MISSISSIPPI. I can't imagine what business we could possibly have with one another now.

SAINT-CLAUDE. The Communist Party of this country has too long been without a head. We have chosen you to fill this vacancy.

MISSISSIPPI. That is a very curious proposition.

SAINT-CLAUDE. There can be no better recommendation for the position than to have obtained three hundred and fifty death sentences.

(MISSISSIPPI *stands up and goes to the window right, where he stands with his back to the audience.*)

MISSISSIPPI. And what if I refuse?

SAINT-CLAUDE. Then we shall have to attack your weak spot.

MISSISSIPPI. I have no weak spot. No one doubts the moral seriousness of my purpose.

SAINT-CLAUDE. Nonsense. Everyone has a vulnerable spot. Yours does not lie in your attack on society, it lies in yourself. You apply to the world the measure of absolute morality, and that is only possible because the world accepts you as moral. Your effectiveness would collapse the moment the halo of your virtue was destroyed.

MISSISSIPPI. It cannot be destroyed.

SAINT-CLAUDE. Do you really believe that?

MISSISSIPPI. I have trodden the path of righteousness.

(SAINT-CLAUDE *stands up.*)

SAINT-CLAUDE (*calmly*). You forget that *I* have come back.

(MISSISSIPPI *turns round. Silence.*)

MISSISSIPPI (*deathly pale*). You're right. I never expected to see you again.

SAINT-CLAUDE. Unfortunately our meeting was unavoidable. You have not only gained yourself a pre-eminent position in society by your death sentences – you also bear the name Florestan Mississippi, claim descent from an Italian princess

THE MARRIAGE OF MR MISSISSIPPI

and have an Oxford degree. You descended upon the world like a sun, and blinded by your fire the world has never looked into your origins.

MISSISSIPPI (*panting*). Louis!

SAINT-CLAUDE. That's right, Paul! Cry out to the darkness from which you came!

MISSISSIPPI. I want nothing more to do with it!

SAINT-CLAUDE. But it wants plenty to do with you.

MISSISSIPPI. Hyena!

SAINT-CLAUDE. I'm glad to see you returning to the language that comes naturally to us. Let us not forget our noble birth. No more than five lire was paid for our begetting; the gutter ran red as we came; rats showed us what life is, their fur wet with sewage; from the vermin that crawled over our bodies we learnt how time passes, never to return.

MISSISSIPPI. Be quiet.

SAINT-CLAUDE. Come, come. Let us sit down again in your Louis Quatorze chairs.

(*He sits down.* MISSISSIPPI *comes to the table.*)

MISSISSIPPI. When we parted thirty years ago we swore never to see each other again.

SAINT-CLAUDE (*smoking*). So we did.

MISSISSIPPI. Then go.

SAINT-CLAUDE. I'm staying.

MISSISSIPPI. You mean to break your word?

SAINT-CLAUDE. Of course. Keeping one's word is a luxury forbidden to us by our origins. What are we, Paul? First we stole the rags that covered our bodies, and filthy copper coins to buy mouldy bread for our bellies; then we were forced to sell ourselves, white victims in the hands of fat bourgeois whose cries of pleasure rose to heaven like the miauling of cats; and finally – with violated backsides, but with the pride of young capitalists – we used our hard-earned money to run a brothel, I as the proprietor and you as the doorkeeper.

(*A long pause.* MISSISSIPPI *sits down.*)

MISSISSIPPI (*panting*). We had to live!

SAINT-CLAUDE. Why? If we had hung ourselves from the nearest lamp-post, no one would have raised the slightest objection.

MISSISSIPPI. Why did I put up with all that unspeakable misery if not because I found in the corner of a damp cellar a half-mouldered Bible, from which I learnt to read, night after night, frozen stiff, by the light of the gas lamps? Should I have remained alive one day longer, if the vision of the Law had not flowed over me like a sea of fire bursting into our darkness, so that henceforth everything I did, the deepest humiliation I suffered and the meanest crime I committed, served the one goal of reading law at Oxford in order to become a public prosecutor and bring back the Law of Moses, driven by the knowledge that mankind must go back three thousand years in order to go forward again?

SAINT-CLAUDE (*wildly*). Did I too not have a vision of how this world that stinks of hunger, drink and crime could be improved? This hell that resounds with the singing of the rich and the howling of the exploited? Did I not find Karl Marx's *Kapital* in the pocket of a murdered ponce? And did I not go on with the terrible life we were forced to lead merely so that one day I could bring about the world revolution? We are the last two great moralists of our age. We have both adopted a disguise. You the mask of the hangman and I the mask of the Soviet spy.

MISSISSIPPI. Take your hands off my shoulders.

SAINT-CLAUDE. I'm sorry.

MISSISSIPPI. So you too have come to blackmail me?

SAINT-CLAUDE. If you won't see sense.

MISSISSIPPI. For ten years I did a menial job in your brothel, and in return you paid for my studies. We no longer owe one another anything.

SAINT-CLAUDE. There is something that cannot be paid for: life.

You chose it and I gave it to you. I showed you the terrible crooked path that leads from beast to man, and you followed it. Now it is my turn to make demands. Not for nothing did I pick you out of the gutter. The question is whether the Communist idea is to be or not to be. You are far too promising a genius for the Party not to try and make capital out of you.

MISSISSIPPI. I fight with the same ardour against the West as against the East.

SAINT-CLAUDE. I haven't the slightest objection to that, so long as you smash first one and then the other and don't attack both at the same time. That would be utterly foolish. What matters is not our sympathies, but reality. It is our historical misfortune that of all peoples it was the Russians who adopted Communism, although they are totally unsuited for it. Now we have to overcome this disaster.

MISSISSIPPI. Naturally you don't dare to advance this theory in public!

SAINT-CLAUDE. I have the freedom of Mikoyan's house. My task is not to commit suicide, it is to carry out a world revolution. Communism is the doctrine that teaches us how man can rule the earth without oppressing men. That is how I understood it in the holy nights of my youth. But I cannot put this doctrine into effect without power. Therefore we must reckon with the powers. They are the chessmen with which we make our moves. We must know what is; we must know what we want; and we must know what is to be done. These are three difficult things. The world as a whole has become immoral. Some fear for their business, others fear for their power. The Revolution must be directed against all. The West has gambled away liberty, the East justice; in the West Christianity has become a farce, in the East Communism. Both sides have betrayed themselves; the world situation is ideal for a true revolutionary. But reason compels us to give our backing to the East. Russia must conquer so that the

West goes under, and at the moment of the Russian victory there must be a universal uprising against the Soviet state in the name of Communism.

MISSISSIPPI. You're dreaming.

SAINT-CLAUDE. I am calculating.

MISSISSIPPI. Only the Law can change the world.

SAINT-CLAUDE. You see? Now we're back in our youth again, under the wet cellar vaults. The Law! When we argued about the Law, we fought all night long, till we were both battered and bleeding, and as the grey dawn broke to find us exhausted we rolled over one another down the slag heaps. We both wanted justice. But you wanted the justice of Heaven and I wanted the justice of the earth! You want to save an imaginary soul and I a real body!

MISSISSIPPI. There is no justice without God!

SAINT-CLAUDE. There is only justice without God. Nothing can help man but man. But you staked your money on another card – on God. That is why you must now give up the world; if you believe in God man is for ever evil, since goodness rests with God alone. Why do you still hesitate? Man cannot keep God's law, he has to create his own law. We have both shed blood; you have slain three hundred and fifty criminals, I have never counted my victims. What we are doing is murder, therefore we must do it to some purpose. You have acted in the name of God, I in the name of Communism. My deed is better than yours, for I am seeking something in time, while you are seeking something in eternity. What the world needs is not redemption from sin but redemption from hunger and oppression; it has no need to pin its hopes upon Heaven, it has everything to hope for from this earth. Communism is the Law in its modern form. Why do you still perform sacrifices when I am already carrying out surgical operations? Why are you still a theologian when I am already a scientist? Throw your God into the fire and you will have humanity, the drunken dream of our youth.

MISSISSIPPI. God cannot be thrown into the fire. He is Himself the fire.

(*Silence.*)

SAINT-CLAUDE. You won't come to us?

MISSISSIPPI. No.

SAINT-CLAUDE. We need your head, as I told you.

MISSISSIPPI. That is ambiguous.

SAINT-CLAUDE. That is unambiguous. I wanted your head as an instrument, now I want it as a prize. The papers that made you a relation of the Italian royal house were forged by me. The money for your studies came from my brothel.

MISSISSIPPI. What are you going to do?

SAINT-CLAUDE. Since I cannot have you as what you could be to us, I shall take you as what you are to us – as a hangman. The masses must be whipped up. It is true that without your co-operation I think it is the silliest thing we could do; but the order has been given. There is only *one* fight that will draw the masses, the fight against the man who has obtained three hundred and fifty death sentences, among them twenty-one Communists.

MISSISSIPPI. Who were common murderers!

SANIT-CLAUDE. The Trade Unions are demanding that you should be brought to justice; if the Government refuses, they will order a general strike.

MISSISSIPPI (*slowly*). I cannot prevent you.

SAINT-CLAUDE. You cannot prevent me and I cannot change you! (*He opens the window.*) Goodbye, I shall sink down before you once again. We were two brothers who looked for each other in a night that was too dark. We shouted for one another, but we did not find each other! The chance was unique, but the moment was wrong. We brought everything with us, you intelligence, I energy, you terror, I popularity, both of us an ideal origin. What a historic pair we should have been!

(*He climbs into the window frame. The 'Internationale' is heard from outside.*)

MISSISSIPPI. Louis!

SAINT-CLAUDE. Do you hear their singing, their drunken bawling, you friend of my youth, you trembling jackal with whom I walked through the underground passages of our first years, despairing at the indifference of all men, burning for their brotherhood, do you hear the song? This is the only place where they still sing those lines with enthusiasm, the only place where they still believe them, the only place where Communism can be made into a reality and not a ghastly pretence, this is the only place. And what prevents it? God, pulled out of a heap of refuse. What a farce! Go into a lunatic asylum, Paul.

(SAINT-CLAUDE *vanishes. Silence.* ANASTASIA *enters from the left in a white nightdress.*)

ANASTASIA. Are you still up?

MISSISSIPPI. It is midnight. You should be asleep, Madame. Remember the work you have to do tomorrow in the St John's Prison for Women.

ANASTASIA (*uncertainly*). Was there somebody here?

MISSISSIPPI. I was alone.

ANASTASIA. I heard voices.

(MISSISSIPPI *goes to the window and closes it. Then he steps back into the room.*)

MISSISSIPPI. I was talking to my memories.

(*A stone flies in through the window on the left. From outside shouts: 'Murderer, mass murderer!'*)

ANASTASIA. A cobblestone!

MISSISSIPPI. Pull yourself together. There'll be more than that smashed soon!

ANASTASIA. Florestan!

MISSISSIPPI. I have only you, Madame, the Angel of the Prisons, a shield which I hold up against the whole of mankind.

(*Curtain. Light in the auditorium.* ÜBELOHE *steps in front of the curtain.*)

ÜBELOHE. Ladies and gentlemen, if I ask you not to go for the interval yet, although the lights have been switched on, if I ask you to stay for my speech, it is only because in this very intricate plot the light which I shall cast upon Anastasia's former life is as important as that which Saint-Claude's appearance has cast upon the antecedents of the Public Prosecutor. You know me, you have twice seen me floating through the air past the cypress and the apple tree. I am Count Bodo von Übelohe-Zabernsee. I have come down in the world, unquestionably. I'm drunk, as you see. I wreck the whole play, I admit that too. But I can neither be left out nor toned down. My appearance on the scene is ridiculous, out of place, like me myself, like my whole grotesque life. My sudden return is highly embarrassing, and of course there is nothing more I can do to help, as you will see. But here, at this critical point in the action into which a crafty author has drawn you, ladies and gentlemen, as an audience, and us on the stage, we must ask ourselves *how* the author became involved in all this. Did he allow himself to be carried along from one free association to another without any preconceived idea, or was he guided by some secret plan? Oh, I can well believe that he did not create me light-heartedly, under the influence of some random hour of love, that he was concerned to investigate what happens when certain ideas collide with people who really take them seriously and strive with audacity and vigour, with insane fervour and an insatiable greed for perfection, to put them into effect. Yes, I can well believe that. And I can well believe that the curious author sought an answer to the question of whether the spirit – in any shape or form – is capable of changing a world that merely exists and is not informed by any idea, that he wished to ascertain whether or not the material universe is susceptible of improvement, to investigate the truth of a suspicion which perhaps arose in him during some sad and lonely night. This too I can well believe. But even so, ladies and gentlemen, I must bitterly deplore the fact that, having created us, he took no further hand in our fate. Thus he created me, Count Bodo von Übelohe-Zabernsee, the only one whom he loved with all his passion, because I alone in this play take upon myself the adventure of love, that sublime enterprise which, whether he survives or perishes in it, endows man with his greatest dignity. But probably for that very reason, he placed upon me the curse of a truly ludicrous life and gave me, not a Beatrice or a Proeza – or whatever lofty being a Catholic bestows upon his fine, upstanding heroes – but an Anastasia, not modelled upon heaven or hell, but only upon the world. Thus the lover of gruesome fables and futile comedies who created me, this stubborn Protestant with his morbid imagination, had me smashed in pieces so that he could taste my kernel – O horrible curiosity; thus he stripped me of my dignity in order to make me, not like a saint – saints are no use to him – but like himself, so that he could cast me into the crucible of his comedy not as victor but as vanquished – the only role in which man again and again appears. And all this merely in order to see whether in this finite Creation God's mercy is really infinite, our only hope. But let us raise the curtain again. (*The curtain rises. A large canvas covered with coloured drawings screens the centre of the stage. Underneath it can be seen the legs of* ANASTASIA *and the* MINISTER, *who are obviously embracing.* ÜBELOHE *continues in the tone of a market salesman.*) On this canvas which has been lowered to screen the centre of the stage we see what happened the following day and the following night, a space of time which we shall jump. As expected, the Public Prosecutor's position has become grave. Top left, as seen by you, newsvendor selling a special edition bearing the headlines: 'The Public Prosecutor as a brothel doorkeeper.' Top right, the Prime Minister turning pale. In the centre, Saint-Claude addressing the Trade

Unions. Bottom left, a furious mob carrying placards that read: 'Death to the three-hundred-and-fifty-fold mass murderer.' Bottom right, fellows from the police guarding the Public Prosecutor's house at night, while the sky is filled with stones being thrown at the villa; they look like flowers scattered over a red carpet. You are now in the picture. When the canvas rises you will see the room which we already know in the condition you would expect. The fin-de-siècle mirrors have been shattered. Venus has lost her head. The plaster has been knocked off the wall in places. The window-panes are in fragments. The shutters are closed; through the cracks fall the slanting rays of a sunny November morning. It is ten o'clock. I am going out into the hall on the right, where I shall press the maid to show me in. I shall wear dark glasses for the purpose. (ÜBELOHE *drops the glasses as he is about to put them on; as he bends down to pick them up he sees the legs of* ANASTASIA *and the* MINISTER. *He rises deathly pale.*) Anastasia, on the other hand, you find in a situation that embarrasses me and astonishes her. Here is the woman I love in the embrace of a man whom she must never love, at the same spot where we left her thirty-three hours ago.

(ÜBELOHE *goes out right; the canvas floats up; behind it* ANASTASIA *and the* MINISTER, *who is kissing her, become visible almost up to their heads.* MISSISSIPPI *enters from the left and pulls the canvas down again.*)

MISSISSIPPI. Before this messy canvas is finally drawn up to disclose a lying picture – the whole scene is an indecent exaggeration – my acute intelligence would long ago have divined all this, if there had been any truth in it – before this happens I should like to describe the following scene to you. (*Behind the canvas the* MINISTER *walks out backwards to the right; only his legs are seen stepping back; then the canvas rises.* ANASTASIA *is standing motionless by the table, a newspaper in her hand.*) It took place this morning. I had been working all night; this time I was trying to get a death sentence passed on a ponce – quite a tricky undertaking; outside was the raging mob, in the living-room my terrified wife. I entered the room and found the Angel of the Prisons. She was holding the special edition. The newspaper speaks the truth, I told my wife. You saw in me the natural son of an American arms king and an Italian princess. Madame, dismiss this idea from your mind, it is false, I am the son of a streetwalker whose name is as unknown to me as that of my father.

ANASTASIA. I thought for a moment, then I went up to Mississippi and solemnly knelt before him.

(*She kneels.*)

MISSISSIPPI. Deeply moved, I said: Madame, do you not despise me?

ANASTASIA. Thereupon I kissed his hand.

(*She kisses his hand.*)

MISSISSIPPI. And I said in a low voice: Madame, the purpose of our marriage has been achieved: we have done penance. Perhaps this very evening my attempts to bring back the Law of Moses will be finally shattered. You heard the tumult last night. The unworthy stones in this room, the broken mirrors, the damaged Venus speak volumes. Horrifying volumes describing a lost illusion. What is there to prevent us from publicly confessing that we are poisoners, you for love and I out of moral conviction? Then we can die a martyr's death. I am ready, Madame!

ANASTASIA. I solemnly rose and kissed his forehead.

(*She does so. The canvas descends again. Again we see the legs of the* MINISTER, *who once more approaches* ANASTASIA *from the right.*)

MISSISSIPPI. That was the scene. It staggered me and it will have staggered you. I have described it although a raging mob is now besieging me in the Court; in a few hours they will hound me through the building, up the stairs, along the galleries, down the stairs again, and finally beat me up in the entrance hall under the statue of Justice, where they will leave me streaming with blood. When this happens, I shall feel nothing but the lips of this outstanding woman – a laurel wreath flowering unwithered on my ravaged brow.

(MISSISSIPPI *leaves left.* ANASTASIA *and the* MINISTER *come into view, in a passionate embrace, as we have already seen. The room conforms to Übelohe's description. Outside, the 'Internationale'.*)

ANASTASIA. All night long they have been pelting the house with stones and singing their songs.

THE MINISTER. It was foolhardy to telephone me.

ANASTASIA. I was crazed with terror.

THE MINISTER. It is good to kiss when the world is falling apart.

ANASTASIA. You will set me free from this man. I want to go on kissing you for ever. For ever.

THE MINISTER. You shall go on kissing me for ever. One doesn't help a brothel doorkeeper.

ANASTASIA. The general strike will hit you too.

(*The* MINISTER *begins to undress. He puts his top hat on the statue of Venus, throws his coat over a chair, and so on.*)

THE MINISTER. My power is unassailable. It is not founded upon men's ardour, but upon their weariness. The longing for change is great, but the longing for order is always greater still. It will bring me to power. The mechanism is easy to see. The Prime Minister will have to go; the Foreign Minister will not be back from Washington for another hour. He will come too late. I have only to use the few minutes during which I shall be the only representative of the Government, and Parliament will proclaim me the new Prime Minister.

ANASTASIA. You will deliver my husband to the rabble?

THE MINISTER. You want him to die?

ANASTASIA. I desire his death.

THE MINISTER. You are an animal, but I love animals. You have no plan, you live only in the moment; as you have betrayed your husband, so you will betray me, and so on. For you what

166

is will always be stronger than what was, and what will be
will always triumph over the present. No one can grasp you;
whoever builds upon you will perish, and only he who loves
you as I love you will always possess you. No, my child! I
shall not deliver your husband to the mob. I shall strike him a
more radical blow than your hate could do; I shall have him
put away where fools are put away.

ANASTASIA (*who has not achieved her purpose*). Please leave now.
You have to go to Parliament.

THE MINISTER. It is unbearable only to meet in gaols, where
prisoners and warders watch us from all sides. At least we are
alone here for a change!

(ÜBELOHE *rushes in from the right.*)

ÜBELOHE (*with a voice of thunder*). Let me catch a glimpse of my
beloved, Madam!

(ANASTASIA *stands thunderstruck and the bewildered* MAID
appears in the doorway.)

THE MINISTER (*who has let go of* ANASTASIA *in dismay*). Under no
circumstances must I be seen here!

(*He hurries into the room on the left.*)

ÜBELOHE (*goes to* ANASTASIA *and kisses her hand*). I beg you to forgive my reckless and unseemly entry into your private room
and also my torn suit, but what is at stake is the last hope of a
now utterly ruined but once noble man, the final mercy
which you can show a poor soul. My name –

ANASTASIA (*cries out*). Bodo!

ÜBELOHE (*stands motionless for an instant, then he too gives vent to a
blood-curdling cry*). Anastasia!

(*He staggers and sinks white-faced into the chair on the right.*)

ÜBELOHE. Some black coffee, please.

ANASTASIA (*to the* MAID). Make coffee immediately.

THE MAID (*going out right*). Heavens above, the Count!

ÜBELOHE (*deathly pale*). Forgive me, Anastasia, for not recognizing you at once, but I became exceedingly short-sighted in
the tropics.

ANASTASIA. I'm sorry about that.

ÜBELOHE. It's of no importance. (*He stands up.*) You are free?

ANASTASIA. I am free.

ÜBELOHE. Pardoned?

ANASTASIA. I never went to prison.

ÜBELOHE. But five years ago I gave you poison disguised as sugar for your Pekinese, which was so fond of sweets, and you poisoned your husband with it.

ANASTASIA. I wasn't arrested.

ÜBELOHE (*staring dispiritedly into her face*). On your account I left the Continent and founded a hospital in the depths of the Borneo jungle!

ANASTASIA. Your flight was senseless.

ÜBELOHE. Was my medical licence not withdrawn?

ANASTASIA. No proceedings were taken against you.

ÜBELOHE (*tonelessly*). If the coffee doesn't come soon I shall lose my reason.

ANASTASIA (*suspiciously*). You wanted to see the Public Prosecutor?

ÜBELOHE. I came to this town from the feverish heat of the tropics on an old collier. I thought you had been condemned to life imprisonment. I intended to give myself up on condition that I could see you once more in my life. I came to this house for a permit to visit you in prison.

(*He stares at* ANASTASIA, *who, when he looks closer, turns out to be the damaged Venus. Fortunately* ANASTASIA *has already removed the Minister's top hat.*)

ANASTASIA (*anxiously*). Bodo!

ÜBELOHE. Mississippi's address struck me as uncannily familiar the moment I heard it; so did the garden, the house, the front door, the Picasso in the hall; but my extreme short-sightedness, the hallucinations from which I have suffered ever since I had yellow fever in Batavia, left open the possibility that I was under a delusion. I know that I can no longer entirely trust my senses. I suffered from all the tropical diseases.

168

Cholera has dulled my memory and malaria my sense of direction. Then the maid came. It was Lucretia. I could scarcely continue to doubt, but of course much can happen in five years. Naturally she had to look for a new job. In any case, she didn't recognize me; that was probably due to my dark glasses, which I have worn since my eye infection in South Borneo. Twice I was turned away. Then I acted. I entered this room, uttered a greeting, bowed, stepped closer, kissed a hand and stood before you.

ANASTASIA. Yes, you stood before me.

(*He looks at her helplessly.*)

ÜBELOHE. Anastasia, the tropics have affected me terribly. My health is no longer good. I know that I can make mistakes, frightful mistakes. Therefore I say to myself frankly and openly, without sparing myself: Is this all the ghastly delusion of my sick brain? Or have you become the wife of the Public Prosecutor, Florestan Mississippi?

ANASTASIA (*calmly*). Yes, I am his wife.

ÜBELOHE (*cries out*). So it's true!

(*He sways.*)

ANASTASIA (*in dismay*). Bodo!

(*She clasps him; he slips down her on to the floor, unconscious. ANASTASIA madly rings the little silver bell. The MAID rushes in from the right.*)

ANASTASIA. For heaven's sake bring that coffee, my guest keeps fainting!

THE MAID. Mother of God!

(*She rushes out again. The MINISTER enters from the left.*)

THE MINISTER. I haven't a minute to lose. I must get to the government building!

ANASTASIA. My guest may recover consciousness at any moment!

THE MINISTER. There's going to be a disaster! I know there's going to be a disaster. If the Foreign Minister makes his speech before me, he will be Prime Minister.

ÜBELOHE (*slowly opens his eyes*). Forgive me, Anastasia, in my physical condition I simply can't take this continual excitement any more.

(*The* MINISTER *rushes out left again;* ANASTASIA *throws his coat and scarf after him.*)

ÜBELOHE. If I could understand just a fraction of what is going on here, I should immediately feel better. I can't make head or tail of your marriage to Mississippi.

(*He slowly rises and sits down in the chair, wiping the sweat from his face. The* MAID *enters from the right.*)

THE MAID. The coffee!

(*She puts the coffee on the table and goes out again.* ÜBELOHE *laboriously stands up. On the left, the* MINISTER *pokes his head out of the door, but darts back again when he sees* ÜBELOHE. ANASTASIA *pours out the coffee.*)

ÜBELOHE (*takes the cup, stirs his coffee, remains standing.*) A Public Prosecutor can't possibly marry a woman knowing that she has poisoned her husband.

ANASTASIA. He married me because *he* poisoned his wife.

ÜBELOHE (*stands as though turned to stone, his coffee cup in his hand*). He did?

ANASTASIA. He did. With the poison which he confiscated from you.

ÜBELOHE. In black coffee like you?

ANASTASIA. In black coffee like me. In order to bring back the Law of Moses.

ÜBELOHE. To bring back the Law of Moses.

ANASTASIA. Our marriage is supposed to be the punishment for our crime.

ÜBELOHE. The punishment for your crime.

(*He sways.*)

ANASTASIA (*vehemently*). For heaven's sake don't faint again.

ÜBELOHE. No. I'm not going to faint. At one blow the truth has turned me to stone.

(*He slowly puts the cup down on the table.*)

ANASTASIA (*anxiously*). Bodo, don't you feel well?

ÜBELOHE. Please give me some brandy.

ANASTASIA. Coffee would do you far more good.

ÜBELOHE. You can't possibly expect me to drink any more coffee in this house.

(*He sits down again.* ANASTASIA *goes silently to the sideboard and comes back with a bottle of brandy and a glass. Fills the glass. Sits down on the chair on the left.*)

I gave you the poison fully believing that you wanted to destroy your dog with it; I fled to the tropics in the deepest despair and there did penance for your crime by charitable works among head-hunters and Malays; I renounced you, whom I have loved from the beginning, in order once more to sanctify our relationship by a sacrifice; and meanwhile you marry a man whose crime is infinitely greater than mine and go on living with him in the temperate zone in the best possible social conditions and unmolested by the Law!

(*The* MINISTER *rushes across the stage from the left and out right.*)

THE MINISTER. I *must* get to Parliament, otherwise I shan't be Prime Minister!

ÜBELOHE (*amazed*). Who was that?

ANASTASIA. Only the Minister of Justice.

ÜBELOHE (*utterly bewildered*). What is a Minister of Justice doing in your house?

ANASTASIA. My life too is a hell.

ÜBELOHE. Has your whole life's work been destroyed by a woman? Have you senselessly given up a great position to flee into the miserable interior of Borneo, and have you equally senselessly returned? Have you had cholera, sunstroke, malaria, typhus, dysentery, yellow fever, sleeping sickness and chronic liver complaints?

ANASTASIA. Were you forced to watch executions every Friday? Was it your duty to go every day to visit people in prison whom your husband had condemned and who poured out

171

the most horrible curses over you? Did you have to spend hour after hour with an unloved husband who condemned you to death without killing you? Did you have to keep the most complicated rules and the most absurd regulations, just because they were part of the Law of Moses? Do you not see that we have both suffered horribly, you physically and I mentally? You were able to flee and I had to stick it out here.

(*From the right three* CLERICS, *one Protestant, one Catholic, one Jewish, make a ceremonious entry. They bow.* ANASTASIA *rises with dignity.* ÜBELOHE, *much astonished, does the same.*)

THE FIRST. As the representative of the Synodal Council –

THE SECOND. Of the Diocese –

THE THIRD. Of the religious community of our city –

THE FIRST. We have come, honoured –

THE SECOND. beloved –

THE THIRD. gracious

THE FIRST. lady, to thank you in this grievous hour.

THE SECOND AND THE THIRD. To thank you!

THE FIRST. To thank you, for the

ALL THREE. exceptional.

THE FIRST. help, which you, honoured –

THE SECOND. beloved –

THE THIRD. gracious

THE FIRST. lady, ever bestowed upon the prisoners in our gaols. You performed this sisterly act time after time. At this critical moment may it be for you a –

THE SECOND AND THE THIRD. consolation

THE FIRST. and a source of fresh strength, a

ALL THREE. comfort in your tribulation

THE FIRST. that we not only give thanks, but also express hope.

THE SECOND AND THE THIRD. Hope!

THE FIRST. The hope that you, honoured –

THE SECOND. beloved –

THE THIRD. gracious

THE FIRST. lady, will continue to give your support to the
Prisoners' Aid Society of our city. We thank you, we hope
for you, we put our trust in you.

THE SECOND AND THE THIRD. We put our trust in you!

THE FIRST. To support you in your noble endeavours will now
be our unceasing task.

(*They bow.* ANASTASIA *bows her head slightly.* ÜBELOHE *bows
in helpless confusion.*)

THE THREE. True, we do oppose most strongly
Actions by your husband done.
Unpunished must not be who wrongly
Make the course of justice run.
But you yourself whose succour kind
Helped your brothers in their pain
Please now consolation find
In words of thanks we say again.

(*The three go out again right.* ANASTASIA *sits down.*)

ÜBELOHE (*takes his head in his hands*). That was Bishop Jensen!

ANASTASIA. They call me the Angel of the Prisons.

ÜBELOHE (*in despair, as he sinks into a chair*). And they expelled me
from the Church Council!

ANASTASIA (*passionately*). Don't you see that you are the only
person who can save me?

ÜBELOHE (*in surprise*). Are you in danger, then?

ANASTASIA. Now that my husband has ceased to be the Public
Prosecutor he wants to give himself up to the police with me
and confess our murders.

ÜBELOHE (*in dismay*). Anastasia!

ANASTASIA. This very night.

ÜBELOHE (*white-faced*). What are you going to do?

ANASTASIA (*resolutely*). I refuse to be thrust into the twilight
world of the prison cells, I absolutely refuse! There is only
one way to save our love, Bodo. Flee with me to Chile! It is
the only country that will not extradite a murderess. After all,
you're a millionaire! We'll take the plane. It leaves tonight at

ten o'clock. I've made inquiries. Five years I have waited for you and now you are here. We shall be happy in Chile.

ÜBELOHE (*slowly stands up again*). We cannot flee, Anastasia. I have lost my whole fortune.

ANASTASIA (*likewise stands up, deathly pale*). Bodo!

ÜBELOHE. The tropics have completely ruined me financially as well as physically.

ANASTASIA (*with a shudder*). Übelohe-Zabernsee Castle?

ÜBELOHE. Converted into a pharmaceutical factory.

ANASTASIA. Marienzorn ob Bunzendorf?

ÜBELOHE. Auctioned.

ANASTASIA. Mont Parnasse Castle on Lake Geneva?

ÜBELOHE. Distrained upon.

ANASTASIA. Your jungle hospital in Borneo?

ÜBELOHE. Mouldered away. The native medicine proved stronger. I wanted to help mankind with love and charitable works and have become a beggar myself in the process. The torn clothes I am wearing, this ghastly jacket, this sweater knitted for me by a woman missionary in Batavia, these ragged trousers and these worn-out shoes are my only possessions.

ANASTASIA. But the St George's Hospital for the Poor belongs to you! We don't need much, Bodo. You're a doctor and I shall give piano lessons.

ÜBELOHE. Before I left, I gave the hospital to Alcoholics Anonymous.

ANASTASIA (*crushed, sinks back on to the chair*). And my husband forced me to make over all my property to the Society for Fallen Girls.

ÜBELOHE (*shuddering*). We are both ruined for good and all!
(*He likewise sinks back on to the chair.*)

ANASTASIA. We are lost.

ÜBELOHE (*shyly*). We are not lost, Anastasia. We need only tell the truth.

ANASTASIA (*taken aback*). What do you mean?

174

ÜBELOHE. Have you confessed to your husband?

ANASTASIA (*mistrustfully*). Confessed?

ÜBELOHE. That you are my mistress?

ANASTASIA (*slowly*). You want to tell him that?

ÜBELOHE (*firmly*). I must tell him. I have always been extremely particular about the truth.

ANASTASIA (*resolutely*). That's impossible.

ÜBELOHE (*inexorably*). The night before François died, you gave yourself to me.

ANASTASIA. You mean that with your strict moral principles you are now going to go to my husband, five years later, and tell him that I seduced you?

ÜBELOHE. There is no other way.

ANASTASIA. That's ridiculous.

ÜBELOHE. Everything I set my hand to is ridiculous. In my youth I read books about the great Christians. I wanted to become like them. I fought against poverty, I went to the heathen, I became ten times sicker than the saints, but whatever I did and however terrible the things that happened to me, everything became ridiculous. Even my love for you – the only thing left to me – has become absurd. But it is our love. We must bear its absurdity.

ANASTASIA. It is always your decency that brings the most awful disasters upon us. It was the same in Lausanne. There you didn't marry me because you wanted to pass your exams first, so that a lieutenant-general was able to get me into his clutches. I seduced you; even then you refused to act. I killed François, so that at last I could become your wife; you fled to Tampang. And now you want to confess our love to the very man who poisoned his first wife as a punishment for adultery. For five years I have kept the truth from him in the clear knowledge that he would kill me if he found out. I changed myself into the Angel of the Prisons. I became a woman whom every clergyman spoke of with respect. And now you come along and want to open my husband's eyes, and at a moment that is critical enough already. It would be madness to tell him the truth.

ÜBELOHE. The truth is always madness. The truth has to be shouted, Anastasia. I shall shout it into this room, into this collapsing world of our sins. Do you want to lie, to go on and on lying? Our love can only be saved by a miracle. We must speak the truth, if we want to believe in this miracle.

ANASTASIA (*in astonishment*). You believe in a miracle?

ÜBELOHE. Our love demands a miracle.

ANASTASIA. That's nonsense!

ÜBELOHE. It is the only sense left to us. (*He lights a cigarette.*) I shall tell your husband the truth. It will burn our misery to ashes and our love will rise up, a plume of white smoke. (*He stamps out his cigarette.*) When is your husband coming back?

ANASTASIA. I don't know.

ÜBELOHE. I shall wait. Wait here among furniture and pictures. Wait till he comes.

(ANASTASIA *says nothing.*)

ÜBELOHE (*deathly pale*). Anastasia!

ANASTASIA. What is it?

ÜBELOHE. Do you love me?

ANASTASIA. I love you.

ÜBELOHE. Then come to me and kiss me.

(ANASTASIA *walks slowly towards him. She kisses him.*)

ÜBELOHE. Now I know that you will always love me. I believe in our love as I believe in the miracle that will save us.

ANASTASIA (*passionately*). Let us flee! Recklessly! Without thinking! And never return!

ÜBELOHE. No. I shall wait. I shall wait for the miracle!

PART TWO

The same room. By the coffee table, which is covered with brandy bottles, stands ÜBELOHE. *Backstage left by the window stands* ANASTASIA.

ANASTASIA. The mist is coming back.

ÜBELOHE. So is the mob.

ANASTASIA. The mist has risen from the river every evening this November.

ÜBELOHE. A Biedermeier table, two Louis Quatorze chairs, a Louis Quinze sideboard. A Louis Seize commode, an Empire sofa. I hate this furniture. I already hated it in Lausanne. I hate all furniture.

ANASTASIA (*although there has been no sound*). The cathedral is striking eight o'clock.

ÜBELOHE. Ten hours. I've been waiting ten hours.

ANASTASIA. Shots. Again and again shots.

ÜBELOHE. And this singing all the time. The kind of songs people will sing when the end of the world comes.

ANASTASIA. It will be high summer now in Chile, and at night you can see the Cross in the sky.

ÜBELOHE. Truth is the cross. I shall tell him the truth. (*He sits down at the table again.*) A Biedermeier table. Two Louis Quatorze chairs, a Louis Quinze sideboard. A Louis Seize commode. An Empire sofa. I hate this furniture. I already hated it in Lausanne. I hate all furniture.

ANASTASIA. Do you think the plane will take off in this weather?

ÜBELOHE. They fly in all weathers nowadays. Even if they smash themselves up. The truth. I shall tell him the truth.

ANASTASIA. You've drunk more than five bottles of brandy.

ÜBELOHE (*suddenly speaking wildly*). Can one put up with eleven hours of hell in any other way? Rembrandt Harmens van Rijn, 1606 to 1660, 'Landscape with Tower', etching. Hercules Seghers, 1589 to 1645, 'Old Mills', etching.

(*The two go rigid.* SAINT-CLAUDE *appears in the window on the left.*)

SAINT-CLAUDE. And while these two, man and woman, wait in their room, I, Saint-Claude, am hounding back into the gutter the friend of my youth whom I picked out of the gutter. A quiet word of command (*behind him appear men with small red flags*), and the crowd will drive the Public Prosecutor from the law courts over the bridge, round the Zwingli memorial, down towards the statue of Columbus by the docks, along the quay and into the gardens, beating and stoning him as they go – a slight movement of my hand (*he raises his hand in the air, the men disappear*), and the rabble will let him go.

(SAINT-CLAUDE *disappears. The* MINISTER *appears in the window on the right.*)

THE MINISTER. I, on the other hand, have just been elected Prime Minister. The situation appears catastrophic; foreign countries are holding their breath; U Thant is reading the newspapers with concern; Gromyko is rubbing his hands; the bottom is dropping out of the stock market; rumour is running wild; but in reality the situation is ideal for assuming power.

(*The clapping of an invisible multitude.*)

THE MINISTER. Lying on the sofa in my new office – the old Prime Minister is already in the sanatorium – I tear up the photograph of the agent smuggled in by the Cominform and throw the scraps in the fire. (*He tears up a photograph and throws the scraps in the fire.*) A fool, no more. As though a revolution directed against an individual were to be feared. You sacrifice the individual, and the bitch known as society remains untouched. That's a well tried rule – the beast called society is indestructible, if we put our money on the beast we shall stay on top for ever. (*Clapping.*) But it is important not to intervene too soon; we must profit from the apparently perilous situation created by a revolution. Think what credits America will give us if we put down a revolution that is thought to be dangerous. (*Clapping.*) The mob loves the first blood-lust, the wild hopes, the thrill of reckless destruction; but after a certain point in the revolt has been reached the masses' mood changes. If at first they were heated by the greed for more, they are now cooled by the fear of losing all. At this moment, which must be calculated exactly, one has a magnificent chance to appear as the saviour of order. (*Clapping.*) Let us profit by this. The Army is ready. Good. The police equipped with hoses. Still better. I swear by cold water. – John, a whisky. (*A servant brings a glass.*) For the time being I shall remain in the background. For the time being I shall let one fool hound another, shall let the mob rush with raised fists after our unfortunate Public Prosecutor, who at this moment is scrambling over his garden wall, filthy and spattered with blood, and now lies down under a tree – I think it's an apple tree. Too bad if they find you. Run, my dear rabbit, run. What a genius is going to perdition there.

(*He drains the glass, throws it over his shoulder and goes out. A shot rings out near by.*)

ÜBELOHE. Can you see anything?

ANASTASIA (*peers out*). There's someone lying under the apple tree.

ÜBELOHE (*rises laboriously to his feet*). Your husband?

ANASTASIA. He has got up and is limping across the terrace.

ÜBELOHE (*swaying*). I shall tell him the truth.

ANASTASIA (*steps back from the window*). Now they are shining searchlights into the garden.

(*Singing outside.*)

ÜBELOHE. And this singing all the time. The kind of songs people will sing when the end of the world comes.

ANASTASIA. He is opening the front door.

(ÜBELOHE *goes to the left of the coffee table, supports himself on it with his hands and stares spellbound at the door on the right.*)

ÜBELOHE. Do you love me?

ANASTASIA. He is about to come in.

ÜBELOHE. A miracle will take place. I shall tell him the truth and we shall be free.

(*The door on the right opens.*)

ANASTASIA (*calmly*). My husband.

(*In the doorway stands* MISSISSIPPI, *his clothes in tatters, his face smeared with blood.*)

MISSISSIPPI. Welcome to your homeland, Count.

ANASTASIA. Florestan!

(*She is about to rush to him;* MISSISSIPPI *signs to her to keep calm.*)

MISSISSIPPI. Let us not forget our guest, dear Anastasia. An attitude of unshakable calm is the only thing we can preserve in this perpetually changing world. (*He bows.*) It was five years ago last May, Count Übelohe, that I visited you in your rooms at the hospital. You will remember our conversation. It took place on a sofa under a poor copy of Raphael's 'St George'. I heard later that you had fled to the tropics. May I ask the reason for your return? You have appeared at a crucial moment for my wife and myself.

ÜBELOHE (*bowing*). Forgive me for being compelled to call upon you at such a late hour. My business is urgent.

MISSISSIPPI. You have come to give yourself up? Since my wife and I are about to take the same step, there is no longer any obstacle to your doing so.

(ÜBELOHE *pulls himself together.*)

ÜBELOHE. Mr Public Prosecutor! Five years ago you forced me, Count Bodo von Übelohe-Zabernsee, master of Marienzorn ob Bunzendorf, to leave this country. Those were difficult times for all concerned, we will not speak of them, since, Mr Public Prosecutor, I have not come to dispute with you. You married the woman to whom I gave the poison; well and good, a blow to me, a terrible blow, certainly; but you wanted to bring back the Law of Moses. I bow to such an immense passion for justice. It is a sublime thought. I bow in reverence. (*He bows.*) As an aristocrat whose forefathers fought at Pavia and Sempach, and even in the Crusades, I dissociate myself from those whose fiendish, God-forsaken singing echoes into this room. Having returned from the tropics, which bitterly disappointed me, I stand before you, Mr Public Prosecutor, ruined – I must confess – in every respect. I am not complaining. You too, Mr Public Prosecutor, as I can see, not without a shudder, by your bruised and scratched face, are ruined. It is the lot of both of us to be ruined, Sir, in this century. Ruined utterly. Decisions are no longer in our hands; history has repudiated us, you who with tireless and iron determination rose from the morass of the big city, and me, the Count, the scion of an aristocratic family. The mob is now singing your fate; mine too it will settle with mocking laughter. There is only one thing left for us to do in this foundering world – and who can still doubt that it is foundering? – one thing only and that absolute, fanatical, reckless. (*He is swaying more and more.*) We must get at the truth, Mr Public Prosecutor, to the terrible, perhaps ludicrous truth; we must stand by the truth with all our courage and all our strength.

(*He falls into the chair on the left and buries his head in his hands.* MISSISSIPPI *walks calmly to the table and rings the bell. The* MAID *enters from the left.*)

MISSISSIPPI. Bring a basin of cold water, Lucretia.

(*The* MAID *goes out.*)

ANASTASIA (*coldly*). He's drunk.

MISSISSIPPI. He will sober up and finish his speech.

ANASTASIA. Five bottles of brandy since this morning.

(*The* MAID *brings the basin.*)

MISSISSIPPI. Give the basin to the Count, Lucretia.

THE MAID. The basin, Count.

MISSISSIPPI. Dip your face in it, Count Übelohe.

(ÜBELOHE *obeys*.)

MISSISSIPPI (*to the* MAID). You can go, Lucretia.

(*The* MAID *goes out right*.)

ÜBELOHE (*slowly*). Forgive me, but it was waiting so long that reduced me to this state.

MISSISSIPPI. Go on, what is it you want to tell me?

ÜBELOHE (*stands up*). Mr Public Prosecutor! I want to tell you the truth. In my own name and in your wife's name. The truth is that your wife and I – the truth is that we – that I love your wife.

(*A tremendous burst of machine-gun fire crashes through the shutters into the room*.)

MISSISSIPPI. Back against the walls!

ÜBELOHE. The Communists.

(*A fresh burst of firing*.

All three press themselves against the walls. MISSISSIPPI *on the right*, ANASTASIA *and* ÜBELOHE *on the left. A fresh burst of firing. In the window left* SAINT-CLAUDE.)

SAINT-CLAUDE. They are already glued to the walls, pressing themselves against their sickening wallpaper. I shall smash this Louis Seize, Quinze, Quatorze furniture, the Empire chandeliers, the rococo mirrors, the engravings, vases, stuccoes, the remains of a plaster Venus, along with the sideboard it is standing on. I shall destroy all this bric-à-brac – a charcoal-burner who reduces this ridiculous world to charcoal in order to warm his coming kingdom.

(*He disappears. A fresh burst of firing*.)

MISSISSIPPI (*sharply*). Madame, go to your room. You will be safe there.

(ANASTASIA *goes out through the door on the left*.)

MISSISSIPPI (*shouting above the noise of firing*). Let us meet in the middle of the room. In view of the firing, however, I must unfortunately request you to crawl, Count.

ÜBELOHE. I'm already crawling, Mr Public Prosecutor.

(*They crawl towards the centre. A burst of firing. They duck.*)

MISSISSIPPI. Are you injured?

ÜBELOHE. Only a minor flesh wound.

(*They meet under the coffee table.*)

MISSISSIPPI. You have just made a confession, Count. As a husband, I feel obliged to put a few questions to you.

ÜBELOHE. I am at your disposal, Mr Public Prosecutor.

MISSISSIPPI. Count! Your fate is not devoid of a certain grandeur, albeit of a dubious character. Although a scion of one of our continent's oldest and most noble families. I nevertheless find you in rags. May I ask why you left Zabernsee Castle and entered what was to you an unknown world?

ÜBELOHE. I felt sorry for mankind.

(*A burst of firing. They duck.*)

MISSISSIPPI. You loved them all?

ÜBELOHE. All.

MISSISSIPPI. In their filth, in their greed?

ÜBELOHE. In all their sins.

(*A burst of firing. They duck.*)

MISSISSIPPI. Are you a Christian?

ÜBELOHE. I am a Christian.

(*A burst of firing.*)

MISSISSIPPI. What is left of your love for humanity, Count?

ÜBELOHE. Nothing but my love for your wife, Mr Public Prosecutor.

(*A burst of firing. They duck.*)

MISSISSIPPI. And what do you gain from this love for a woman who does not belong to you?

ÜBELOHE. Nothing but the hope that the soul of my beloved is not lost so long as I love her; nothing but this faith!

(*A burst of firing. They duck.*)

MISSISSIPPI. Abandon that groundless faith, Count. Love can accomplish nothing in this world. What would have become of my wife if she had only had your love? In addition to murdering her husband she would have committed adultery; I don't suppose I need say more.

ÜBELOHE. And what has Anastasia become through the Law of Moses, which you offered her?

MISSISSIPPI. An Angel of the Prisons, loved even by those whom I have condemned to death.

ÜBELOHE (*seizes hold of* MISSISSIPPI). You have no doubts about your marriage?

MISSISSIPPI. It is the most exemplary marriage of the twentieth century.

(*A burst of firing. They duck.*)

ÜBELOHE. You believe in your wife?

MISSISSIPPI. Unshakably.

ÜBELOHE. You believe that she has become better?

MISSISSIPPI. She has become better.

ÜBELOHE. You believe that there is truth between you and not fear, nameless fear?

MISSISSIPPI. I believe in her as I believe in the Law.

ÜBELOHE. You fool, whose bones I am now breaking in pieces, you clay giant into whose face I am now flinging the truth. How can you love a woman for her works? Do you not know that the works of man lie? How petty is your love, how blind your Law; *I* do not love your wife as a just woman, I love her as an unhappy one. Not as a woman who has been found, but as a woman who is lost.

MISSISSIPPI (*taken aback*). What do you mean by that?

ÜBELOHE. Sir –

MISSISSIPPI. May I ask for an explanation, Count Übelohe-Zabernsee?

ÜBELOHE. Mr Public Prosecutor, it is my duty to inform you that Anastasia was my mistress while she was still married to her first husband.

(*Deathly silence. Then orders are heard being given outside. The trampling of horses. Shrill whistles, the crowd moving back.*)

MISSISSIPPI. The revolt has been crushed. The Government has won. Rise, Count.

ÜBELOHE. Certainly.

(MISSISSIPPI *rises. So does* ÜBELOHE.)

MISSISSIPPI (*calmly*). Then my wife poisoned the beet-sugar manufacturer out of love for you?

ÜBELOHE. That was the reason for his death.

MISSISSIPPI. Open the door of my wife's boudoir, Count Übelohe-Zabernsee!

(ÜBELOHE *opens the door on the left.*)

ÜBELOHE (*uncertainly*). Are you going to ask Anastasia?

MISSISSIPPI. I consider that the most natural solution. You have accused my wife of adultery. I shall ruthlessly investigate your charge. But let us be clear about one thing: my wife's answer is going to crush one of us. Either I shall be shown up before you as a monstrous fool, or you before me as a totally degenerate alcoholic whose delirium makes his wildest wish-dreams appear true.

ÜBELOHE. I admire your objectivity.

MISSISSIPPI. Anastasia.

(ANASTASIA *appears in the door on the left and walks slowly towards the centre of the room, where she stops by the coffee table.*)

ANASTASIA. What do you want with me?

MISSISSIPPI. Count Übelohe has a question to put to you, Madame. Do you swear to speak the truth?

ANASTASIA. I swear.

MISSISSIPPI. By God?

ANASTASIA. I swear by God.

MISSISSIPPI. Now ask my wife, Count Bodo von Übelohe-Zabernsee.

ÜBELOHE. Anastasia, I have only one question to put to you.

ANASTASIA. Ask it!

ÜBELOHE. Do you love me?

ANASTASIA. No.

(ÜBELOHE *stiffens.*)

185

ÜBELOHE (*after a pause, reeling*). That cannot be your answer,
Anastasia!

ANASTASIA. I don't love you.

ÜBELOHE. That isn't true.

ANASTASIA. I have sworn by God to speak the truth.

ÜBELOHE. But you became my mistress!

ANASTASIA. I was never your mistress.

ÜBELOHE. You gave yourself to me the night before François died!

ANASTASIA. You never touched me!

ÜBELOHE (*as though crying out for help*). But you only killed
François because you wanted me to be your husband!

ANASTASIA. I killed him because I loved him.

ÜBELOHE (*slides on his knees to the table behind which* ANASTASIA *is
standing*). Have mercy! Tell the truth! Have mercy!

(*He embraces the table.*)

ANASTASIA. I have told the truth.

(ÜBELOHE *breaks down.*)

ÜBELOHE (*shattered*). Beasts! You are beasts!

(*From outside, the siren of an ambulance.*)

MISSISSIPPI (*cuttingly*). You have heard the truth. Anastasia does
not love you.

ÜBELOHE. Beasts! Beasts!

(*Loud knocking on the right-hand door.*)

MISSISSIPPI (*with dignity*). Count Bodo von Übelohe-Zabernsee,
the insane assertions which you sucked from the breasts of the
primeval forests, and which were unfortunately also inspired
by alcoholic excesses, have proved devoid of all truth.
Anastasia was never your mistress! By this act you have
regrettably increased the number of your misdemeanours; to
the unlawful supplying of a dangerous poison you have now
added a gross slander, a fact which leaves no doubt that you
are sinking into an ever more hopeless state not merely of
physical, but also of moral degeneracy.

(*The door on the right is suddenly opened and a doctor and two
male nurses enter, all in white coats.*)

THE DOCTOR. Professor Überhuber from the Municipal Hospital for Nervous Disorders.

MISSISSIPPI (*ignoring him*). Confess that you were lying.

ÜBELOHE. You are beasts!

(*Through all the doors to left and right and through the windows – from which Saint-Claude and the Minister have disappeared – and also from the grandfather clock, doctors in white coats and thick horn-rimmed spectacles throng on to the stage.*)

PROF. ÜBERHUBER. I am authorized by the Public Health Department to take you to the hospital for examination. Personal instructions from the new Prime Minister. The old one is already in our care.

MISSISSIPPI. Anastasia swore by God. Confess that you are lying, Count; I appeal to the last spark of an aristocratic sense of honour which must still be glimmering somewhere within you.

(*The male nurses seize* MISSISSIPPI.)

PROF. ÜBERHUBER. You are such an exceptionally interesting case, Mr Public Prosecutor, that I have invited the whole of the psychiatric congress here.

(*The doctors quietly clap in applause.*)

MISSISSIPPI. You were lying! Admit it! You were lying!

(*The male nurses lead* MISSISSIPPI *out.*)

MISSISSIPPI (*in despair*). Take me and my wife to the police! I poisoned my first wife and my second wife poisoned her first husband!

(*The male nurses lead* MISSISSIPPI *out.*)

PROF. ÜBERHUBER (*bows*). Don't let his words distress you, Madam. In his present remarkable state he is subject to the wildest delusions. We are quite familiar with such things. He will soon be better. Only yesterday the old Prime Minister considered himself totally incapable of governing, but today, after an electric shock and a few cold showers, he is thinking of serving his country either as an ambassador or as president of our national bank.

(*The doctors quietly clap in applause.* PROF. ÜBERHUBER *bows again to* ANASTASIA, *then goes out right. The doctors also leave through the doors and windows and the grandfather clock.* ANASTASIA *and* ÜBELOHE *are alone.* ÜBELOHE *slowly rises to his feet.*)

ANASTASIA. You told him the truth, and I betrayed you.

ÜBELOHE. Fear was greater than love.

ANASTASIA. Fear is always greater.

ÜBELOHE. And now they have come and taken your husband away.

ANASTASIA. The miracle has happened. We are free.

ÜBELOHE. And yet parted.

ANASTASIA. For ever.

ÜBELOHE. Faith is lost. A little water that trickled away into the sand.

ANASTASIA. Hope has vanished. A little cloud that turned to nothing in the light.

ÜBELOHE. Only love is left. The love of a fool, the love of a man who is ridiculous.

ANASTASIA. A love that has no further weight.

ÜBELOHE.

Henceforth I shall cry your name,
like the cry of a man with the plague
warning the wanderer, in the night into which I shall vanish.
You have cursed me, and I love you.
You have denied me, and I love you.
You have mocked the name of God, and I love you.
But from now on I shall turn away from you.
You shall never again see my face.
I am leaving you for ever.
But the love I bear you,
this love that will never grow weaker,
that has burnt me out, that has killed me,
and in whose name I am resurrected again and again,
I shall take with me.

I shall plant it in the countries through which I shall now roam,
unresting, a ruined Count, rotted by liquor,
I shall share it with every beggar.
Thus I have been flung upon a world that is now beyond
    salvation,
and nailed upon the cross of my absurdity,
I hang upon this beam
that mocks me,
exposed unprotected
to the gaze of God,
a last Christ.
    (ÜBELOHE *goes slowly out right.* ANASTASIA *stands motionless.*
    The sound of an aeroplane is heard.)

ANASTASIA. The plane for Chile has taken off.
    (*A canvas with a plane flying through clouds painted on it*
    screens the stage. SAINT-CLAUDE, *in evening dress as in Part*
    One, steps out in front of the curtain. He has a shaving towel
    round his neck.)

SAINT-CLAUDE. Let the plane fly to the highly commended
Republic of Chile. Let the Count leave too; he has given us
enough trouble. He will go under in the turmoil of the big
city, in the vast morass of liquor, perhaps through a knife in
the back, perhaps, if he is lucky, in a hospital for the poor
which he founded himself. We won't bother our heads about
him any more. Let us turn to the following morning. The
scene is sad enough. You will see for yourselves as soon as the
plane has finally vanished into the clouds. The room is in a
frightful state and ruined for good; the furniture is almost
indescribable, everything white with plaster and mortar.
You'll see. Only in the centre, unreal, obviously indestructible, stands the coffee table, still Biedermeier, laid for two
people as in the beginning; not for Anastasia and Mr Mississippi, however, but for Anastasia and me; we can't conceal
that. The fact that I now remove my beard will tell you enough.
That I am once more ruined and must start all over again,

you will have guessed. The end of the uprising was pathetic, the victory of the new Prime Minister total, the effect on my career painful. The Red Army has already reduced my rank and the Polish Parliament has withdrawn my mandate; in short, my rehabilitation is once more being cancelled and there is nothing left for me to do but to report how three people were checkmated in one game.

(*The canvas bearing the aeroplane goes up.*)

You are just hearing the first guns firing in salute from the classical temple. The city is preparing to celebrate the wedding of the new Prime Minister. (*Outside the window* DIEGO *and his* BRIDE *pass with two* CHILDREN *who are carrying the train, etc.*) You can see the exalted couple gliding past the window to the cathedral – him, whom we know well enough already, her, the new mother of the nation, the owner of the enormously popular *Evening Post*, blushing, in a wedding dress by Dior. Power has been preserved, order re-established, the old splendour and glory restored. With this festal event, with the ever renewed cheers of a happy people, the enthusiastic renderings of the combined girls' schools choir, municipal choral society and Philharmonic Association, who are bawling and blaring Beethoven's Ninth, and finally with the hollow majesty of the cathedral bells as they now start to ring, the following scene forms a painful contrast. Let us begin. (MISSISSIPPI *climbs into the room through the window on the right. He is wearing a mental-hospital uniform and disappears into his room on the right.*) That was the Public Prosecutor. He managed to escape from the lunatic asylum. Unfortunately I was not yet in the room when he climbed through the window, otherwise my friend Paul would have seen me as I shaved in front of the last fragment of this mirror, and would finally have caught on. As it was, he had no idea of my presence and I no idea of his, and by the time I had a chance to open his eyes there was no further point in it, so rapidly was he dealt with by the fate which he had prepared for himself. Anastasia – the equally ridiculous cause of my death – without her I should have been in safety long ago – came a little later. She had been in town, ostensibly in the St John's Prison for Women; in reality she had been trying in vain to speak to the new Prime Minister. He was not to be found – we know why. She had no alternative but to resign herself. Then she went to the bank, and now she is coming home, disguised as a charitable lady with her coat and crocodile handbag.

(ANASTASIA *enters breathless from the left*.)

ANASTASIA. Mississippi has broken out!

SAINT-CLAUDE (*indifferently*). So what?

ANASTASIA. Mental hospital nurses and police have surrounded him in the city park.

SAINT-CLAUDE. Like coursing a hare.

(*He turns round*.)

Where have you been?

ANASTASIA. In the St John's Prison for Women.

SAINT-CLAUDE. You're lying. You've been to the bank.

(*He seizes her handbag, opens it, takes out an envelope and puts it in his pocket*.)

How much?

ANASTASIA. Five hundred.

SAINT-CLAUDE. Good.

ANASTASIA. You've shaved?

SAINT-CLAUDE. Do I look different?

ANASTASIA. Yes.

SAINT-CLAUDE. Then put on your evening dress. The American ambassador is giving a party at his country house.

ANASTASIA. What do I care about the American embassy?

SAINT-CLAUDE. It's a chance to leave the city unrecognized. No one will expect me to go by that route. Why else do you think I'm wearing your husband's evening dress? (*He grips her arm and looks at her searchingly*.) I had a brilliant idea just now. We will flee together.

191

ANASTASIA (*anxiously*). Are the police after me?

SAINT-CLAUDE. No. They're after me. We'll go to Portugal.

ANASTASIA. Has the Party been banned?

SAINT-CLAUDE. The Party has expelled me.

ANASTASIA. What does that mean?

SAINT-CLAUDE. In response to the unerring instinct which tells it that it need fear only those who take Communism seriously, the Party will do all it can to kill me.

ANASTASIA. And what are we to do in Portugal?

SAINT-CLAUDE. Start all over again from the beginning. The world revolution that went astray in the Russian steppes must be carried out afresh from a different corner of the globe. No mean undertaking. It's a wretched state of affairs. Since the Soviet Union corrupted Communism the way it has, I have been like a man trying to blow up houses with wet dynamite. You can't send even the most miserable ruin sky-high with that.

(*He takes the little silver bell and rings it. The* MAID *enters from the right, still at her job though a bit the worse for wear.*)

SAINT-CLAUDE. Coffee!

(*The* MAID *goes out.*)

ANASTASIA (*goes up to him and gazes at him searchingly*). What are you planning to do with me?

SAINT-CLAUDE. We'll start in the sewers, rise to the doss-houses, move to the pubs and finally I shall build you a decent brothel.

ANASTASIA (*horrified*). I'm to sink to that?

SAINT-CLAUDE (*harshly*). You're to rise to that, you Public Prosecutor's wife.

(*He tears himself away and goes to the window on the left, turning his back to the audience. The* MAID *enters from the right.*)

THE MAID. The coffee.

SAINT-CLAUDE (*without turning round*). Pour out.

(*The* MAID *does so and goes out right.*)

ANASTASIA (*deathly pale, clutches at the locket hanging round her neck*). You are going to misuse me.

SAINT-CLAUDE. No. I am merely putting you to the use for which you are naturally fitted. What are you? A woman who consumes an immoderate quantity of men. In future you will live upon those against whom all revolutions have been directed – the rich. As the Angel of the Prisons you were an insult, in your new employment you will be one of the most natural means of obtaining money from the possessing class which will help to bring about its downfall. This is the only way of using you for the benefit of the world instead of its exploitation.

ANASTASIA (*opens the locket and takes out something that looks like a lump of sugar.*) You are ungrateful. I have kept you hidden in my room since the day you entered this country.

SAINT-CLAUDE. You became my mistress as an assurance against danger from our side, and I made you my mistress in order to make certain of your talents.

ANASTASIA. And if I don't come with you?

SAINT-CLAUDE (*looks at her*). Where else can you go?

ANASTASIA. The Prime Minister is my friend.

(*Cheers from outside.*)

SAINT-CLAUDE. It wouldn't do him any good to get mixed up with a poisoner just now. The only politician who can afford to have anything to do with you is I.

ANASTASIA. Are you threatening me?

SAINT-CLAUDE (*turns his back to her again*). Only for business reasons. You are the most gifted person there is for my requirements.

(*With a calm, elegant movement* ANASTASIA *stretches across the table and drops the thing like a lump of sugar into the cup on the right.*)

ANASTASIA. We shall see.

SAINT-CLAUDE. Is the coffee ready?

ANASTASIA. It's already poured out.

(SAINT-CLAUDE *comes to the table.*)

SAINT-CLAUDE. Is there any sugar in it?

ANASTASIA. No.

> (SAINT-CLAUDE *takes a lump of sugar from the basin, puts it in the cup on the right, stirs it with the spoon. Puts the cup to his lips, lowers it without drinking, looks fixedly at* ANASTASIA, *puts the cup down on the table again.*)

ANASTASIA. Aren't you going to drink it?

SAINT-CLAUDE. There was sugar in it.

> (*He wipes the sweat from his brow.*)

SAINT-CLAUDE. I think it would be better if I had my coffee in town, my dear. Lucky for you. It wouldn't have helped you, because the bank clerk you were going to run away with will be arrested this evening. Unfortunately he will be carrying a considerable sum of money that doesn't belong to him. As you see, I too have taken certain precautions. Go and put on your evening dress, it's time we were leaving. I'm going to fetch a car.

> (ANASTASIA *goes out left.*)

So she went into her room. I gazed after her, laughed, looked at my cup with a feeling of horror, reached across the table for hers and drank it. (*He does all this.*) Oh, I knew her, the poisoned coffee remained untouched, and if my overwhelming hope of bringing about the Revolution somewhere in spite of everything had not blinded me into believing myself unrecognized as I stole a newly-stolen, freshly painted car from a garage in the dock area – the garage hands had gone off to watch the public wedding ceremony and were listening to the girls' school choir – the bagpipers were playing at the time and the Ninth was about to begin – and if, on my return through the garden I had not failed to see the three men who were rather inadequately concealed behind the apple tree and the cypress – if I had not made all these mistakes I could have become master of the whole world with the help of that invaluable woman, that whore of Babylon!

> (*He leaves through the window on the right. But the room is only empty for a moment.* MISSISSIPPI *enters through the door on the*

right. He is in the ceremonial black robe of the Public Prosecutor. He goes to the coffee table, sees Anastasia's empty cup, fills it. Then he slips his hand under his robe and takes out a little golden box. Opens it. What happens now is easy to guess. He takes out a thing like a lump of sugar, reaches across the table and drops it into Anastasia's cup on the left. It is all done very simply and not without elegance. ANASTASIA *now enters from the left in a fiery red evening dress. She stops dead on seeing* MISSISSIPPI.)

MISSISSIPPI (*bows*). Madam.

ANASTASIA (*after a pause*). Florestan!

MISSISSIPPI. You might as well call me Paul. Everyone knows my name now.

ANASTASIA. It's madness to come here.

MISSISSIPPI. It isn't madness to want to see one's wife again before disappearing for ever, Madame. One doesn't escape from the madhouse twice. Won't you sit down?

(ANASTASIA *hesitates.*)

We drank coffee when we first met five years ago; now that the time has come to say goodbye let us do the same. The place is the same, but unfortunately sadly changed. The wallpaper ruined, the Venus almost unrecognizable, the Louis Quatorze, Quinze, Seize furniture smashed to pieces; only the Biedermeier coffee table has fortunately remained intact.

(ANASTASIA *sits down on the left,* MISSISSIPPI *on the right.*)

Would you pass me the sugar, please? (*She passes him the sugar.*) Thank you. I urgently need a pick-me-up. My escape called for tremendous exertions. I found the table laid for two, Madame. Were you expecting someone for breakfast?

ANASTASIA. I was expecting you.

MISSISSIPPI. You knew I should come?

ANASTASIA. I had a premonition.

MISSISSIPPI. Then you put on that magnificent and daring dress for me?

ANASTASIA. To receive you.

MISSISSIPPI. I don't remember seeing it on you.

ANASTASIA. I wore it the day François died.

(*She looks at the portrait.*)

MISSISSIPPI. As you see, I too have dressed in a manner worthy of our parting. I sit facing you in the robe of the Public Prosecutor. (*Watching her closely.*) Aren't you going to drink your coffee, Madame?

ANASTASIA. Yes. I'll drink it. It will do me good.

(*She drinks.*)

MISSISSIPPI (*breathes a sigh of relief*). We have now been married five years, Madam. (*He drinks.*) Good heavens, there's a lot of sugar in here.

ANASTASIA. I have done everything you demanded of me. I visited the prisoners, I comforted them and watched them die. I never forgot why I had to do it. Every day I thought of François.

(*She looks at the picture.*)

MISSISSIPPI. And I thought of Madeleine.

(*He also looks at the pictures. She watches closely as he drains his cup.*)

MISSISSIPPI. You have been faithful to me.

ANASTASIA. I have been faithful to you, as I was faithful to François.

(*She drinks up her coffee with a sigh of relief.*)

May I pour you another cup?

MISSISSIPPI. Yes, please.

(ANASTASIA *is about to pour out.*)

So you did not swear falsely, Madam?

(ANASTASIA *puts down the coffee pot.*)

ANASTASIA. Is that what you came home for? Is that why you are sitting there in front of me in that frightful cloak? Did you come to ask me *that*?

MISSISSIPPI. Yes, that is why I have come. The reasons for the death of the poor beet-sugar manufacturer are not yet clear. Madame, I shall now carry out the final interrogation.

ANASTASIA (*rises with dignity*). Sir, I am profoundly shocked that after five years of a self-sacrificing marriage you do not place more trust in me.

MISSISSIPPI (*likewise rises and bows*). Do not see in me the husband, but the Public Prosecutor who must do his terrible duty even when it involves someone he loves. Forget the hours you shared with me, your heart-warming work with the Prisoners' Aid Society. Cast out all thought of the marriage we had to lead together; physically it was hell, morally paradise. Go back in your mind to that grim afternoon on which I first visited you. Confide in me. Oh!

(*He groans, presses his hands to his right side and sinks back on to the chair.*)

ANASTASIA (*watching him closely*). Are you ill?

MISSISSIPPI. I felt a sudden violent stitch in my side, obviously of a rheumatic origin. I must have caught a chill yesterday as I lay under the apple tree. (*He stands up.*) But I feel better already. Let us continue the interrogation, Madam.

ANASTASIA. I do not understand your behaviour, Sir.

MISSISSIPPI. Do you stick to your story that you were never the Count's mistress?

ANASTASIA. I don't understand what compels you to harbour this absurd suspicion.

MISSISSIPPI. Human potentiality for evil, Madam. Count Bodo was drunk when he made his confession. In vino veritas.

ANASTASIA. I can only repeat that my childhood friend's assertion leaves me speechless and is utterly unfounded.

(*She sits down again. So does MISSISSIPPI.*)

MISSISSIPPI. You force me to take a step that I had to take once before.

(*He rings the little silver bell. The MAID enters from the right.*)

THE MAID. Yes, Sir?

MISSISSIPPI. Do you remember Count Bodo von Übelohe-Zabernsee, Lucretia?

THE MAID. He was a frequent visitor while the old gentleman was still alive.

MISSISSIPPI. Did Madam and the Count kiss in the manufacturer's absence, Lucretia?

THE MAID. Always.

MISSISSIPPI. You may go back to your work, Lucretia.

(*The* MAID *goes out right.*)

So you used to kiss Count Übelohe-Zabernsee in your husband's absence, Madam. Is this evidence not enough for you?

ANASTASIA. I am innocent. Call the police, if you don't believe me.

MISSISSIPPI. Since the police regard me as insane, they will not believe me. My confession that I poisoned my wife was dismissed with laughter. I have no alternative but to thrash this matter out with you on my own.

ANASTASIA. If you don't believe me, I can't help you.

MISSISSIPPI. It is impossible for one person to know another so well that he can dispense with belief, but in my case the issue is greater than that. I must be certain that you did not swear falsely. The very meaning of the Law is at stake. Our marriage was concluded in its name. The Law is meaningless if I have not succeeded in changing you, you, one single person; if throughout these five years you have been merely dissembling; if your sin, Madame, is greater than I know; if *nothing* has moved you to the depths of your soul. I *must* know what you are! An angel or a devil!

ANASTASIA (*stands up.*). That is something you cannot know; you can only believe.

(*From outside comes the beginning of the Ninth Symphony. Not as an accompaniment, but only, at infrequent intervals, a few bars for added emphasis.*)

MISSISSIPPI (*also stands up*). A sentence which in your mouth may be sacred or blasphemous, Madam.

ANASTASIA. I once more swear before God that I have spoken the truth.

MISSISSIPPI (*after a long pause, in a low voice*). Will you also swear to that if your last hour has come?

ANASTASIA (*suspiciously*). What do you mean by that?

MISSISSIPPI. If death awaits you.

(*Silence.*)

ANASTASIA (*alert*). You intend to kill me?

(*She suddenly presses her right hand to her right side and slowly sits down on a chair.*)

MISSISSIPPI. Do you not recognize the typical symptom? It generally stops almost at once, and after a while death supervenes painlessly.

ANASTASIA (*jumps up*). You have poisoned me?

MISSISSIPPI. The coffee which you drank contained the same poison with which you poisoned your husband François and I my wife Madeleine.

ANASTASIA. The coffee?

MISSISSIPPI. The coffee. Pull yourself together, Madame! We have reached the terrible conclusion of our marriage. You are facing death.

(ANASTASIA *prepares to rush out.*)

ANASTASIA. I'm going to Dr Bonsels!

MISSISSIPPI (*clasps her*). You know very well that no doctor in the world can help you.

ANASTASIA. I want to live! I want to live!

MISSISSIPPI (*embracing her with the force of a giant*). You must die!

ANASTASIA (*whimpering*). Why did you do it?

MISSISSIPPI. So that I should know the truth!

ANASTASIA. I have spoken the truth!

(MISSISSIPPI, *who has seized her by the shoulders, pushes her from right to left across the stage.*)

MISSISSIPPI. You loved only François!

ANASTASIA. Only him.

MISSISSIPPI. No other man ever possessed you? You were never an adulteress?

ANASTASIA. Never!

MISSISSIPPI. And this dress you are wearing? For whom did you dress, whom were you expecting?

ANASTASIA. You, only you.

MISSISSIPPI. You have been down to the prisoners, you have seen them lay their heads in the lap of the guillotine. Do not swear any more by God; swear by those dead to whom you now belong!

ANASTASIA. I swear!

(*In the distance is heard the final chorus from the Ninth Symphony.*)

MISSISSIPPI. Then also swear by the Law, in whose name I have been killing for thirty years, during which my hands became more and more red with blood and my soul more and more weighed down with despair and horror. Also swear by the Law!

ANASTASIA (*sobbing*). I also swear by the Law.

MISSISSIPPI. I can feel life leaving you, I can feel your body growing heavier and heavier in my arms, your face slowly turning to stone. You were beautiful and now your beauty is turning into carrion; but your soul shall not turn into carrion. Swear by your eternal bliss, swear by the immortality of your soul.

ANASTASIA. By my eternal bliss, by the immortality of my soul.

(*She sinks to the floor,* MISSISSIPPI *over her.*)

MISSISSIPPI. Then the Law is not senseless? Then it is not senseless that I have killed? Not senseless these everlasting wars and revolutions that add up to one single trumpet-blast of death? Then man does change when he is punished? Then there is sense in the Last Judgment?

ANASTASIA. I have spoken the truth.

MISSISSIPPI. How cold you are now as I embrace you; how wide your eyes are as they stare into the infinite. Is there any sense in lying now, in the sight of God? Can you be so depraved as not to speak the truth now, when you are passing over into another life?

ANASTASIA. I swear, I swear.

>(*She lies motionless.* SAINT-CLAUDE *climbs in through the window.*)

SAINT-CLAUDE. Well, Paul?

MISSISSIPPI (*slowly*). Louis!

SAINT-CLAUDE. Have you left the lunatic asylum?

MISSISSIPPI (*slowly*). I came back for a last visit.

>(SAINT-CLAUDE *goes to the coffee table and looks first at Mississippi's empty cup, then at Anastasia's empty cup.*)

SAINT-CLAUDE. Is that your wife?

MISSISSIPPI. I have killed her.

>(MISSISSIPPI *stands up.*)

SAINT-CLAUDE. Why?

MISSISSIPPI. To find out the truth.

SAINT-CLAUDE. And did you find it out?

MISSISSIPPI (*comes slowly to the table, his hand pressed to his right side again*). My wife didn't lie. She wasn't an adulteress.

>(*He sits down slowly on the left-hand chair.* SAINT-CLAUDE *looks at* ANASTASIA.)

SAINT-CLAUDE. Does one have to kill a woman to find that out?

MISSISSIPPI. To me she was the world. My marriage was a terrible experiment. I fought for the world and won. No one can lie when he is dying as she died.

SAINT-CLAUDE. One would have to take off one's hat to her if she could do that. It would make her a kind of saint.

MISSISSIPPI. She was the only person who stood by me, and now I also know, Louis, that I loved her.

SAINT-CLAUDE. That's no small thing.

MISSISSIPPI. But now I'm tired. I'm freezing. I feel once more the cold we felt in our youth, when I read the Bible and you Marx's *Kapital* under the gas lamps.

SAINT-CLAUDE. Those were the days, Paul!

MISSISSIPPI. Those were our best days, Louis! We were full of longing and full of wild dreams, feverish with the hope of a

better world. (*He stands up.*) I feel heavy. Lead me to my room.
(SAINT-CLAUDE *supports him.*)

MISSISSIPPI (*suddenly suspicious*). Why did you come here?

SAINT-CLAUDE. To say goodbye to you.

MISSISSIPPI. You knew I was here?

SAINT-CLAUDE. You weren't in the asylum.

MISSISSIPPI (*laughs*). Are you going away?

SAINT-CLAUDE. To Portugal. I must start all over again from the beginning.

MISSISSIPPI. We always have to start over again from the beginning. We are true revolutionaries. I shall flee with you, brother.

SAINT-CLAUDE. We belong together.

MISSISSIPPI. We'll found a brothel. I'll be the doorkeeper and you can do duty inside. Then if heaven and hell break apart, we shall plant the red flag of Justice in the midst of the tottering edifice of the world.

(*He suddenly collapses, and* SAINT-CLAUDE *lets him slide into the right-hand chair.*)

I am dizzy with fatigue. I can only see you as a shadow that is growing darker and darker. (*Collapsing over the table.*) I shan't give up. Never. All I want is to bring back the Law of Moses.

(*There is silence. Outside, the bells of the cathedral start to ring.* SAINT-CLAUDE *shakes* MISSISSIPPI, *takes away the cup, throws it on the floor, then the same with Anastasia's cup. He rings. The three* MEN *in raincoats enter from the right, their right hands in their pockets.*)

THE FIRST. You must allow us to come instead of the maid.

SAINT-CLAUDE. What do you want?

THE FIRST. You have been condemned to death, Saint-Claude. Put your hands behind your head.

(SAINT-CLAUDE *obeys.*)

Go and stand between the windows.

(SAINT-CLAUDE *obeys.*)

Turn your face to the wall. That's the simplest way to die.

(SAINT-CLAUDE *turns his face to the wall. The bells stop ringing. A shot.* SAINT-CLAUDE *stands where he is. The three* MEN *in raincoats go out right.* SAINT-CLAUDE *turns round.*)

SAINT-CLAUDE. So they fired their bullets into my body, you know the story.

(*He sits down on the right of the coffee table.*)

MISSISSIPPI (*sits upright again.*) So we perished through our own deeds, at once executioners and victims.

THE MINISTER (*appears in the right-hand window*). While I, who desire power and nothing else, embrace the world.

(ANASTASIA *has risen and goes to the* MINISTER, *who embraces her.*)

ANASTASIA. A whore, who passes unchanged through death.

SAINT-CLAUDE. But whether we too lie here in this ruin

MISSISSIPPI. Whether we die against a whitewashed wall, on a slowly sinking pyre, broken on the wheel, between heaven and earth

SAINT-CLAUDE. Again and again we return, as we have always returned

MISSISSIPPI. In ever new shapes, yearning for ever more distant paradises

SAINT-CLAUDE. Ever and again thrust out from among you

MISSISSIPPI. Nourished by your indifference

SAINT-CLAUDE. Thirsting for your brotherhood

MISSISSIPPI. We sweep by above your cities

SAINT-CLAUDE. Panting as we flap our mighty wings

MISSISSIPPI. That turn the mills which crush you.

(*In the window on the left appears* ÜBELOHE, *alone, a battered tin helmet on his head, a bent lance in his right hand, again and again submerged in the circling shadow of a windmill.*)

ÜBELOHE

Why do you raise your body from the morning mists
that lie outspread across the plain of Montiel

Why, circling your arms, do you thrust your head proudly
into the sun
which there before me
rolls up the slopes of the Catalan mountains, set free from the
   night

Look at me, windmill, giant licking your chops,
filling your belly with nations
hacked to pieces by your wing that is dripping with blood

Look at Don Quixote de la Mancha,
who knighted a drunken innkeeper,
who loves a pig-girl in Toboso

Many times battered and beaten, many times jeered at,
who yet defies you.

Forward then!

As you lift us up with your whirling hand,
horse and rider, both of them wretched,
as you hurl us into the swimming
silver of the glassy sky

I gallop on my sorry jade
away over your greatness
into the flaming abyss of the infinite

An eternal comedy

Let His glory blaze forth,
fed by our helpless futility

NOTE

Many productions, no doubt misled by the text, have made the mistake of using scenery that was too abstract. Since, among other things, this comedy is 'the story of a room', the room in which everything takes place must at the beginning be as real as possible. Only so will it be able to disintegrate. The unreal and fantastic may safely be left to the text, to the author.

DÜRRENMATT

AN ANGEL
COMES
TO BABYLON

*A Fragmentary Comedy
in three Acts*

Translated from the German by

WILLIAM MCELWEE

FIRST PUBLISHED IN GREAT BRITAIN 1964
TRANSLATED BY WILLIAM MCELWEE FROM THE GERMAN
Ein Engel kommt nach Babylon

© 1957 BY PETER SCHIFFERLI, VERLAGS AG 'DIE ARCHE', ZÜRICH
ENGLISH VERSION © 1964 BY WILLIAM MCELWEE

CHARACTERS

The Angel
The Maiden, Kurrubi
Akki
Nebuchadnezzar, King of Babylon
Nimrod, Ex-King of Babylon
The Crown Prince, Son of both of them
The Prime Minister
The Senior Theologian, Utnapishtim
The General
1st Soldier
2nd Soldier
3rd Soldier
A Policeman
The Banker, Enggibi
The Wine-Merchant, Ali
The Prostitute, Tabtum
1st Working Man
2nd Working Man, more class-conscious
1st Working Man's wife
2nd Working Man's wife
The Formal One
The Seller of Asses' Milk, Gimmil
A Large Number of Poets
Captain of the Guard
Cook
The People
Etc., Etc.

ACT ONE

To begin with the most important place – not, it is true, the setting, but only the background for this comedy – a vast sky is suspended over the whole scene. In its midst hovers the Andromeda Galaxy, seeming oppressively close, as it might look through the telescopes of Mount Wilson or Mount Palomar, and filling up half the background of the stage. Out of these heavens there have stepped down to us for this once, and this once only, an ANGEL *with a long red beard, dressed as a ragged beggar, and at his side a veiled* GIRL. *These wanderers have just reached the city of Babylon and found their way to the banks of the Euphrates. In the middle of the small square there burns an old-Babylonian gas-lamp, naturally very feeble in comparison with the sky overhead. Farther back, on the walls of houses and on hoardings, there are posters, some of them torn, which run roughly: 'Whoever begs harms his Country'; 'Begging is Anti-Social'; 'Beggars! Enter the service of the State'. Beyond these, stretching away into the background, one senses the maze of streets which make up the giant city with its millions of inhabitants, a mixture of magnificence and filth, a jumble of palaces, skyscrapers and hovels, dwindling away into the yellow sands of the desert.*

ANGEL. Since you, my child, were only created by our Lord, in the most remarkable way, a few moments ago, you should know that I – the I who walk beside you dressed as a beggar – am an Angel; that this harsh, unyielding stuff on which we are perambulating is – unless I have very much mistaken my way – the Earth; and those white blocks of buildings are the city of Babylon.

GIRL. Yes, Angel.

ANGEL (*pulling out a map and studying it*). The broad mass which is flowing by in front of us is the Euphrates. (*He goes down to the river bank, dips a finger in the water, and puts it to his mouth.*) It appears to consist of a vast agglomeration of dewdrops.

GIRL. Yes, Angel.

ANGEL. The curved, bright object above us – if you will be so good as to raise your eyes a little – is the moon; and the vast, limpid cloud behind us is the Andromeda Galaxy, which you know all about, since we have just come from there. (*He taps the map.*) That's quite right. It's all on the map.

GIRL. Yes, Angel.

ANGEL. You, however, who are walking beside me, are called Kurrubi and, as I have already indicated, were created by our Lord Himself a few minutes ago. For – and I can tell you this now – I saw Him with my own eyes reach out with His right hand into nothingness and rub His middle finger and thumb gently together, whereupon you were there, taking your first delicate steps across the palm of His hand.

GIRL. I remember, Angel.

ANGEL. Excellent. Remember it always, since from now on you are cut off from Him who created you out of nothing, and on whose hand you have danced.

GIRL. Where am I supposed to go now?

ANGEL. You are supposed to go just where you are, among human beings.

GIRL. What are human beings?

ANGEL (*embarrassed*). My dear Kurrubi, I must have you understand that I am not very well informed on this phase of the Creation. I only attended one lecture on this subject, and that was some thousands of years ago. According to that, human beings are beings of our present shape, which I must say I find unpractical. It seems to be equipped with a number of different organs whose immediate purpose escapes me. I shall be most relieved to be allowed soon to turn myself back into an angel.

KURRUBI. So now I am a human being?

ANGEL. You are a being in the form of a human. (*He clears his throat.*) According to that lecture, humans reproduce them-selves co-operatively, whereas you were made by God out of nothing. I might almost describe you as a non-human being. You are as eternal as nothingness, and as mortal as a human.

GIRL. Then what do I bring to mankind?

ANGEL. My dear Kurrubi, as you are only a quarter of an hour old, I will overlook all these questions. None the less you ought to know that really well-brought-up girls don't ask questions. You are to bring nothing. On the contrary, it is *you* who are being brought to mankind.

KURRUBI (*after a moment's reflection*). I don't understand.

ANGEL. What comes from the hand of Him who created us we never understand, my child.

KURRUBI. I beg your pardon.

ANGEL. I was ordered to hand you over to the lowliest of men.

KURRUBI. It is my duty to obey you.

ANGEL (*again consulting the map*). The lowliest of men are the beggars. You will, in consequence, belong to one Akki, who, if this map is accurate, is the last surviving beggar on earth, Probably a kind of living monument. (*With pride.*) Really, this map's marvellous. Everything's on it.

KURRUBI. If the beggar, Akki, is the lowliest of men, he will be unhappy.

ANGEL. What fine words we use when we are young. What is created is good, and what is good is happy. In all my exten-sive travels throughout creation I have never met with a particle of unhappiness.

KURRUBI. Yes, Angel.

ANGEL (*as they move across right he bends over the orchestra pit*). This is the place where there is a bend in the Euphrates. It is here that we must wait for Akki, the beggar. We'll sit down and sleep for a bit. The journey has tired me, and I feel as if, in skirting Jupiter, we had tripped over one of his moons.

(*They sit down, forward left.*)

Come close to me and put your arms round me. We will

cover ourselves with this wonderful map. I'm used to suns of a different temperature. I'm freezing, although, according to the map, this is one of the warmest spots on Earth. It seems we have to do with a cold star.

(*They tuck themselves under the map, snuggle up together, and go to sleep. Enter, right,* NEBUCHADNEZZAR, *a young man still, rather nice and somewhat simple-minded, with his suite, which includes the* PRIME MINISTER, *the* GENERAL, *the* SENIOR THEOLOGIAN, UTNAPISHTIM, *and a* HANGMAN *dressed in red.*)

NEBUCHADNEZZAR. Since in the north my armies have reached the Lebanon, in the south the sea, in the west a desert, and in the east a range of mountains which goes on rising for ever, I have conquered the world.

PRIME MINISTER. In the name of the Government ...

UTNAPISHTIM. Of the Church ...

GENERAL. Of the Army ...

EXECUTIONER. Of Justice ...

ALL. We congratulate His Majesty, King Nebuchadnezzar, on the New Order he has established in the world.

(*They all bow.*)

NEBUCHADNEZZAR. I spent nine hundred years as King Nimrod's footstool in an extremely cramped, unpleasant position. And that wasn't the only indignity. For nine hundred years, Prime Minister, you have been spitting in my face every time you had an audience.

PRIME MINISTER. Majesty, Nimrod compelled me. (*He abases himself.*)

(*There is a roll of negro drums in the distance.*)

NEBUCHADNEZZAR. Nimrod has been arrested. At daybreak he will arrive in Babylon, as the negro drummers given me by the Queen of Sheba have just signalled from Lamash. Now Nimrod will be my footstool. I shall compel you to spit in his face, Prime Minister.

PRIME MINISTER (*earnestly*). Majesty, when, in the distant past, you were King and Nimrod a footstool, I had to spit on him.

When, nine hundred years ago, Nimrod became King and Your Majesty a footstool, I had to spit on Your Majesty. Would it not be better to set me free from spitting altogether – a request which I make every time this reversal of fortune takes place –

NEBUCHADNEZZAR. What is just is just. You will do your duty and spit. (PRIME MINISTER *bows*.) This Empire is rotten to the core. I must lose no time in clearing up the mess. Life is short, and I have to carry out the plans I formulated while I was Nimrod's footstool.

PRIME MINISTER. I take it Your Majesty intends to inaugurate the Welfare State.

NEBUCHADNEZZAR. It astonishes me, Prime Minister, that you know what is in my mind.

PRIME MINISTER. Kings invariably think in socialist terms when they find themselves in a humiliating position, Your Majesty.

NEBUCHADNEZZAR. As always when Nimrod has been in power, private industry has done far too well, and the State has gone to the wall. There is a monstrous horde of dealers and middlemen, wholesalers and retailers, and the number of bankers and beggars is frightening. I can for the moment take no action against the bankers; I have to think of the budget. Begging, however, I have forbidden. Have my edicts been carried out?

PRIME MINISTER. All beggars have been enrolled as civil servants, Majesty. They now collect the taxes. Only one beggar named Akki insists on pursuing his wretched calling.

NEBUCHADNEZZAR. Has he been shown the error of his ways?

PRIME MINISTER. In vain.

NEBUCHADNEZZAR. Flogged?

PRIME MINISTER. Mercilessly.

NEBUCHADNEZZAR. Tortured?

PRIME MINISTER. There is no part of his body which has not been pinched with red-hot pincers, not one of his bones which has not been loaded with terrible weights.

NEBUCHADNEZZAR. And he still refuses?

PRIME MINISTER. Nothing will shake his determination.

NEBUCHADNEZZAR. It is because of this Akki that I find myself in the middle of the night on the banks of the Euphrates. It would be the easiest thing in the world to have him hanged. But it is not unbecoming in a great ruler to try to gain his ends humanely. I have therefore decided to share one hour of my life with the lowest of my subjects. Put on me the old beggar's cloak which I had fetched from the wardrobe of the Court theatre.

PRIME MINISTER. As Your Majesty wishes.

NEBUCHADNEZZAR. And now fix on my face the red beard which goes with this costume.

(NEBUCHADNEZZAR *stands dressed as a beggar.*)

See, all of you, what I am doing to create a faultless Empire, a grand design into which all will be fitted from the Minister down to the Executioner, with no one out of place, and getting the best out of each. Perfection, by definition, contains nothing superfluous. Yet a beggar is superfluous. I intend to persuade this Akki to enter the service of the State by appearing before him as a beggar myself, and so bring his own poverty home to him. If, however, he persists in remaining miserable, then he shall be strung up on this lamp-post.

(*The* HANGMAN *bows.*)

PRIME MINISTER. We are amazed by Your Majesty's wisdom.

NEBUCHADNEZZAR. Refrain from being amazed by what you do not understand.

PRIME MINISTER. Very good, O King.

NEBUCHADNEZZAR. Withdraw yourselves, but not too far, so that you may be at hand if I shout. Until I do, all of you keep out of sight.

(*They bow, withdraw to the back of the stage and hide.* NEBU-CHADNEZZAR *sits down forward, left on the Euphrates' bank. At the same moment the* ANGEL *and* KURRUBI *wake up.*)

ANGEL (*joyfully.*) Look. There's a man, now.

KURRUBI. He's dressed the same as you and has the same red beard.

ANGEL. We have met the man we were looking for, my child.

216

(*To* NEBUCHADNEZZAR.) I have much pleasure in making the acquaintance of Akki, the beggar.

NEBUCHADNEZZAR (*thrown into confusion by the sight of the* ANGEL *dressed up also as a beggar*). I am not Akki, the beggar. I am a beggar from Nineveh. (*Severely.*) I understood that Akki and I were the only beggars left alive.

ANGEL (*to* KURRUBI). I don't know what to think, my dear Kurrubi. My map is wrong. There is a beggar in Nineveh, too. There are two beggars left alive in the world.

NEBUCHADNEZZAR (*to himself*). I shall have the Minister of Information hanged. There are two beggars left in my Empire. (*To the* ANGEL.) Where do you come from?

ANGEL (*hesitatingly*). From beyond the Lebanon.

NEBUCHADNEZZAR. The great King, Nebuchadnezzar, has laid it down that the world ends at the Lebanon. All geographers and astronomers are of this opinion.

ANGEL (*consulting his map*). There are several villages beyond. Look. Athens, Sparta, Carthage, Moscow, Pekin. (*He shows the map.*)

NEBUCHADNEZZAR (*aside*). I shall also have the Geographer Royal hanged. (*To the* ANGEL.) The great King Nebuchadnezzar will conquer these villages too.

ANGEL (*to* KURRUBI). This second beggar alters our whole situation. I now have to discover who is the poorer, Akki, or this beggar from Nineveh, an investigation which will call for the greatest tact and delicacy.

(*From the left there comes a wild, ragged figure with a red beard, so that there are now three beggars with long red beards on the stage.*)

ANGEL. Here comes another human being.

KURRUBI. He has the same clothes as you, too, Angel, and the same red beard.

ANGEL. If this isn't Akki the beggar either, I shall begin to get confused.

NEBUCHADNEZZAR. If this isn't Akki the beggar either, then the Minister of the Interior hangs as well.

(*The figure sits down in the centre of the stage, on the Euphrates' bank, with his back against the lamp-post.*)

NEBUCHADNEZZAR (*clearing his throat*). You, I have no doubt, are Akki, the beggar, of Babylon.

ANGEL. The celebrated beggar Akki, whose fame has spread far and wide.

AKKI (*taking a pull from a gin bottle*). I never bother about names.

NEBUCHADNEZZAR. Everybody has a name.

AKKI. Who are you?

NEBUCHADNEZZAR. I'm a beggar, too.

AKKI. Then you're a very bad one. Your principles are all wrong from the begging point of view. A beggar has nothing; no money, and no name. He calls himself first one thing, then another, and takes a name as he would a piece of bread. That is why, every hundred years or so, I beg me a new name.

NEBUCHADNEZZAR (*reprovingly*). It is of the utmost importance to mankind that everybody should stick to his own name. Everybody should be who he is.

AKKI. I'm who I please. I've been everything, and now I'm Akki the beggar. But I might just as well be King Nebuchadnezzar.

NEBUCHADNEZZAR (*jumping up, shocked*). Impossible.

AKKI. To be a King? Nothing easier. It's one of the simplest tricks you learn when you start out to be a beggar. I've already been a king seven times in my lifetime.

NEBUCHADNEZZAR (*controlling himself*). There is no King greater than Nebuchadnezzar.

(*The whole suite stand up at the back of the stage, bow, and vanish again.*)

AKKI. Do you mean little Nebby?

NEBUCHADNEZZAR. Nebby?

AKKI. Mm. My chum, Nebuchadnezzar, King of Babylon.

NEBUCHADNEZZAR (*after a pause, with great dignity*). I find it hard to believe that you are acquainted with the great King of Kings.

AKKI. Great? A little twerp, body and mind.

NEBUCHADNEZZAR. All the statues show him as a fine, dignified figure of a man.

AKKI. Oh, well, statues. Who makes them? Our Babylonian sculptors. They make any king look like any other. They can't put it across on me. I know my Nebby. Unfortunately he doesn't take my advice.

NEBUCHADNEZZAR (*astounded*). Your advice?

AKKI. He has me fetched to the Palace whenever he's at his wits' end.

NEBUCHADNEZZAR. To his Palace?

AKKI. He's the stupidest king I've ever come across. He finds ruling very difficult.

NEBUCHADNEZZAR. It's an exalted and difficult task to rule the world.

AKKI. That's what Nebby always says, too. And every king I've ever known has said it. It's the excuse kings make. Everyone who isn't a beggar needs an excuse. There are bad times coming. (*He takes another pull at the bottle. To the* ANGEL.) And who are you?

ANGEL. I am a beggar, too.

AKKI. Your name?

ANGEL. I come from a village where we don't yet have any names.

AKKI. Whereabout is this attractive village?

ANGEL. Beyond the Lebanon.

AKKI. A pleasant district. What do you want with me?

ANGEL. Things are going very badly for beggars in my village. I find I can hardly make a living, and on top of that I have to feed my little daughter, whom you see standing here, veiled, beside me.

AKKI. A beggar who falls on hard times is an amateur.

ANGEL. Our Parish Council has paid my travelling expenses for a visit to the famous and successful beggar, Akki, so that I may learn more of the art of begging. I beg of you – make me into a properly trained, successful beggar.

AKKI. Your Parish Council did very well. There are still sensible Parish Councillors in the world.

KURRUBI (*distressed, to the* ANGEL). You are telling lies, Angel.

ANGEL. Heaven never lies, my child. It's just that from time to time it finds difficulty in making itself understood by mankind.

AKKI (*to* NEBUCHADNEZZAR). Why have you come to me?

NEBUCHADNEZZAR. I am Anashamashtaklakou, the great, the famous; outstanding and supreme among the beggars of Nineveh.

AKKI (*suspiciously*). You say you are the leading beggar in Nineveh?

NEBUCHADNEZZAR. Anashamashtaklakou, the leading beggar of Nineveh.

AKKI. What do you want?

NEBUCHADNEZZAR. Almost exactly the opposite to what this other beggar wants. I have come to convince you that we cannot go on being beggars. We are, of course, a tourist attraction, but, however much we prize the romantic glamour of the ancient East, now a new age has dawned. We have to accept the ban laid on us by the great King Nebuchadnezzar.

AKKI. Is that so?

NEBUCHADNEZZAR. There is no place for beggars in a socialist world. It is improper that it should continue to suffer the poverty which the begging profession brings with it.

AKKI. H'm.

NEBUCHADNEZZAR. All the other beggars in Nineveh and Babylon, in Ur and in Uruk, even in Aleppo and Susa, have thrown away their beggars' staves, since the King of Kings gives work and bread to all. They are, in comparison, much better off than before.

AKKI. You don't say!

NEBUCHADNEZZAR. Because of our outstanding artistry in begging, you and I have not felt the pinch so badly as our fellow beggars have, though even we are pretty wretched, as anybody can see from the clothes we wear. But even with consummate skill and with the present trade boom, we don't earn as much, for example – to take the lowest paid of all workers – as poets do.

AKKI. Rubbish!

NEBUCHADNEZZAR. For this reason, honoured Sir, I have decided to give up begging and to enter the service of His Majesty, King Nebuchadnezzar. I beg you to do the same and report to the Finance Ministry at eight o'clock. It's your last chance to obey the order. Nebuchadnezzar is a conscientious man, and he may otherwise have you hanged from that lamppost you're leaning against.

(*Backstage the* HANGMAN *rises and bows.*)

AKKI. You say you are the beggar, Anashamashtaklakou, from Nineveh?

NEBUCHADNEZZAR. The first and most renowned beggar in Nineveh.

AKKI. And you don't even earn more than a poet?

NEBUCHADNEZZAR. No more.

AKKI. There must be something wrong with your technique. I, alone, support fifty poets in Babylon.

NEBUCHADNEZZAR (*craftily*). It is, of course, possible that poets earn rather more in Nineveh than in Babylon.

AKKI. You are Nineveh's leading beggar and I am Babylon's. I've often wanted to try my skill against another champion. We'll have a match. If you win, we'll both enter the State service at eight in the morning. If I win, we'll both carry on begging, undisturbed by the dangers which beset our lofty calling. Day is breaking and people are getting up. It's a bad time of the day for begging. All the better test of our skill.

ANGEL. My dear Kurrubi, this is an historic moment. You are about to learn which is your husband, the poorest and lowest of beggars.

KURRUBI. How shall I be able to do that, Angel?

ANGEL. It is quite simple, my child. Whoever loses this begging match must be the lowliest of mankind. (*He taps his forehead proudly.*)

AKKI. Here come two workmen, trailing right across Babylon, up from the suburbs, with no food inside them and a three-hour walk to clock in for the early shift at Masherash's Brick-works. I'll give you first innings, beggar from Nineveh.

(*Two* WORKING MEN *enter from left.*)

NEBUCHADNEZZAR (*whining*). Alms, honourable workmen. Alms for a Comrade from the Nebo Mines who has fallen sick.

1ST WORKING MAN. Honourable workmen! Don't talk so bloody silly.

2ND WORKING MAN. The chaps up at Nebo have had a rise of tenpence a week. They should look after their own sick.

1ST WORKING MAN. At a time like this, when they're using granite instead of bricks for all the State buildings.

2ND WORKING MAN. Because it's more likely to last to eternity.

AKKI. A penny from each of you, you blacklegs. There you are, struggling to make ends meet at a shilling a week while I – I who uphold the honour of the working class and will not pander to this exploitation, but rather beg – I go hungry. Either tell the owners of the Brick-works to go to hell, or give me a penny each.

2ND WORKING MAN. How can I start a revolution all by myself?

1ST WORKING MAN. I've got a family to think of.

AKKI. Do you suppose I've no family? My families are running about in every street. What do you mean leaving me, the leader of Babylon's workers, to starve? A penny, or you'll find yourselves back in slavery, as you were before the Flood.

(*The two* WORKING MEN *reluctantly hand over their pennies and go out right.*)

(*Tossing the pennies in the air.*) I've won the first round.

NEBUCHADNEZZAR. Very strange. The workers in Nineveh react quite differently.

AKKI. Here comes Gimmil, the seller of asses' milk, limping along.

(GIMMIL *enters left, distributing milk bottles at the doors.*)

NEBUCHADNEZZAR. Tenpence from you, you greasy seller of

asses' milk, who sweat your milkmaids to death, or I'll set
Marduk, the Factory Inspector, on to you.

GIMMIL. Marduk, the Factory Inspector, who gets a rake-off
from City Dairies? Set him on to me? Just when it's all cows'
milk everywhere and me nearly ruined? D'you think I'd give
a halfpenny to a lousy beggar like you?

AKKI (*throwing down in front of him the two pennies he has just
acquired*). Here you are, Gimmil: my little all for a bottle of
the best asses' milk. I'm a beggar and you sell asses' milk. We
both stand for private enterprise. Long live asses' milk and
long live private enterprise. It was on asses' milk that Babylon
grew great, and asses' milk is the stuff for Babylonian patriots.

GIMMIL (*delighted*). Here you are – have two bottles and a shilling
over. With a Babylonian like you I'll go into battle against
all the State-subsidized cows' milk in the world. 'Asses' milk
is the stuff for Babylonian patriots.' Brilliant. That's a much
better slogan than 'Cows' milk for Progress.' (*Exit left.*)

NEBUCHADNEZZAR. Remarkable. I haven't struck form yet.

AKKI. Now here's a very rare occurrence – a real test case in the
art of begging. The prostitute, Tabtum, who's on her way
with her maid to Anu's Garden to buy fresh vegetables. An
easy and elegant little technical exercise.

(*The prostitute, TABTUM, comes from behind followed by her
MAID who carries a basket on her head.*)

NEBUCHADNEZZAR (*piteously*). Alms, most noble lady, Queen of
Virtue. Alms for a poor but honest beggar who has had
nothing to eat for three days.

TABTUM. Here's a shilling for you. In return say a prayer in the
Temple of the great goddess Ishtar, that she may send me
many rich lovers. (*She gives him a shilling.*)

AKKI. Ha, ha!

TABTUM. What are you laughing at, Thing?

AKKI. I am laughing, oh charming young lady, because you have
only given this poor devil from Nineveh a shilling. He's an
inexperienced beggar, most beautiful one, and he ought to be

given two shillings, if only to give his prayers a bit of strength.

TABTUM. Another shilling?

AKKI. One more.

(*The* PROSTITUTE *gives* NEBUCHADNEZZAR *another shilling.*)

TABTUM (*to* AKKI). Who are you, anyway?

AKKI. I am a proper, well trained, and accomplished beggar.

TABTUM. Will you, too, put up a prayer for me to the Goddess of Love?

AKKI. I very seldom pray, Most Beautiful, but I will make an exception for you.

TABTUM. Are your prayers ever answered?

AKKI. Always, my dear young lady, always. When I start praying to Ishtar, the four-poster bed on which the goddess lies is shaken by the tempestuous din of my invocations. You'll get more rich men than are found in Babylon and Nineveh put together.

TABTUM. I'll give you two shillings, too.

AKKI. I shall be content with just a smile from those ruby lips. That will be enough for me.

TABTUM (*astounded*). You don't want my money?

AKKI. Don't hold it against me, Most Wonderful One. I am a distinguished beggar. I beg from kings and financiers and ladies of the highest society, and I never accept less than a gold piece. A smile from your lips, Most Beautiful – just a smile – and I am content.

TABTUM (*interested*). And how much do the ladies of high society give you?

AKKI. Two gold pieces.

TABTUM. I can give you three gold pieces.

AKKI. In that case you will belong to the very highest society, Most Beautiful.

(*She gives him three gold pieces.*)

Even Madame Chamurapi, the Prime Minister's wife, gives no more.

(*In the background, the* PRIME MINISTER *can be seen listening, interested.*)

TABTUM. The Chamurapi? That West End snob? Next time you get four gold pieces.

(*She goes off right with her maid. The* PRIME MINISTER *fumes and vanishes.*)

AKKI. Well?

NEBUCHADNEZZAR (*scratching his head*). I admit you've won so far.

ANGEL (*to* KURRUBI). A highly gifted beggar, this Akki. The Earth seems to be a most entertaining star, at any rate for me, after rushing about among all those suns.

NEBUCHADNEZZAR. I'm only just getting into form.

AKKI. It's just as well, Beggar Anashamashtaklakou. Here comes Enggibi – Managing Director of the banking house of Enggibi & Sons, and ten times richer than the Great King Nebuchadnezzar.

NEBUCHADNEZZAR (*with a sigh*). These brazen capitalists!

(*Two slaves carry* ENGGIBI *in from right on a litter. In the rear of the cortège trots a fat eunuch.*)

NEBUCHADNEZZAR. Thirty pieces of gold, great Banker. Thirty pieces of gold.

ENGGIBI. Where do you come from, Beggar?

NEBUCHADNEZZAR. From Nineveh. I deal only with the upper classes. Never yet have I accepted anything less than thirty gold pieces.

ENGGIBI. Nineveh businessmen don't know what to do with their money. They're spendthrifts in small matters and miserly in important ones. I will, since you are a foreigner, give you one gold piece.

(*At a sign from him the* EUNUCH *gives* NEBUCHADNEZZAR *one gold piece.*)

ENGGIBI (*to* AKKI). Do you come from Nineveh, too?

AKKI. I am a native Babylonian beggar.

ENGGIBI. As a native you get a shilling.

AKKI. I never accept more than a penny. I became a beggar because I despise gold.

ENGGIBI. You despise gold, Beggar?

AKKI. There is nothing more despicable than that filthy metal.

ENGGIBI. I will give you a gold piece, the same as this beggar from Nineveh.

AKKI. A penny, Banker.

ENGGIBI. Ten gold pieces.

AKKI. No.

ENGGIBI. Twenty gold pieces.

AKKI. Run away and play, Genius of Finance.

ENGGIBI. Thirty gold pieces.

(AKKI *spits*.)

You refuse to accept thirty gold pieces from the Managing Director of the largest banking house in Babylon?

AKKI. The greatest beggar in Babylon only demands a penny from Enggibi & Sons.

ENGGIBI. Your name?

AKKI. Akki.

ENGGIBI. Such character must be rewarded. Eunuch, give him three hundred gold pieces.

(*The* EUNUCH *gives* AKKI *a sack full of gold. The cortège moves off, left.*)

AKKI. Well?

NEBUCHADNEZZAR. I don't know. I seem to be out of luck today. (*To himself.*) All the same, I'll make this chap my Finance Minister.

ANGEL. You are going to belong to this beggar from Nineveh, my dear Kurrubi.

KURRUBI. Oh, how glad I am. I love him. He's so helpless.

(*From left comes a younger man with appallingly long hair and beard, hands* AKKI *a clay tablet, and receives a gold piece, whereupon he goes off again, left.*)

NEBUCHADNEZZAR (*puzzled*). Who was that, then?

AKKI. A poet of Babylon. He received an honorarium.

(*He throws the clay tablet into the orchestra pit. From the right three soldiers drag in the captured* NIMROD. *He is dressed in*

226

royal robes exactly like NEBUCHADNEZZAR's *at the beginning of the scene.*)

NEBUCHADNEZZAR (*with sudden inspiration*). It may be that I'm a little rusty at this vulgar kind of begging. In Nineveh I confine myself to the higher forms of the art. Now, here are some soldiers dragging along a state prisoner whose evil deeds brought the world to the brink of destruction, as the historians unanimously agree. Whoever can beg him shall be the winner of our contest.

AKKI (*rubbing his hands*). Done. A trifling, but attractive little problem in the art of begging.

1ST SOLDIER. This man whom we are dragging along, bound and helpless, is Nimrod, who was once King of the World.

NIMROD. Look, Beggars, how my own soldiers have put fetters on me, and how the blood pours down my back from the stripes they have given me. I left the throne vacant to go and put down the rebellion of the Duke of Lamash, and who sits on it now? My footstool!

NEBUCHADNEZZAR. Who seized his chance.

NIMROD. I am down now, but I shall get on top again. Nebuchadnezzar is on top now, but one day he'll be down again.

NEBUCHADNEZZAR. That will never happen.

NIMROD. It has been happening continuously for thousands of years. I'm thirsty.

(KURRUBI *scoops up water from the Euphrates in her hands and gives it to him to drink.*)

NIMROD. The filthy water of the river Euphrates tastes better from your hands than the wine of the Kings of Babylon.

KURRUBI (*shyly*). Would you like more to drink?

NIMROD. I have wetted my mouth. That's enough. Have this for your thanks, child of a beggar. If soldiers try to take you, kick them between the legs.

KURRUBI (*shocked*). Why do you say that?

NIMROD. No king could give you anything more valuable, my

girl. In this world there is nothing better worth knowing than how to handle curs.

1ST SOLDIER. Shut the ex-King's mouth.

KURRUBI (*weeping*). Did you hear what he said, Angel?

ANGEL. Do not be frightened by what he says, child. When you see how the first beams from an unknown star touch the Euphrates, you must realize that the world has been made perfect.

(*A moment before the sun has broken through the slowly thinning morning mist.*)

1ST SOLDIER. Come on. Drag the ex-King along.

NEBUCHADNEZZAR. Hi!

1ST SOLDIER. What's that fellow want?

NEBUCHADNEZZAR. Come here, all of you.

SOLDIERS. Eh?

NEBUCHADNEZZAR. Bend down to me. I've something to say to you.

SOLDIERS (*bending their heads to him*). Well?

NEBUCHADNEZZAR (*quietly*). Do you know who I am?

SOLDIERS. Nope.

NEBUCHADNEZZAR. I am your Supreme Commander, Nebuchadnezzar.

SOLDIERS. Ha, ha, ha!

NEBUCHADNEZZAR. Do as I tell you and you shall all be promoted to lieutenant.

1ST SOLDIER (*with cunning*). What are Your Highness's orders?

NEBUCHADNEZZAR. You will hand the ex-King over to me.

1ST SOLDIER. Very good, Your Highness.

(*They strike* NEBUCHADNEZZAR *to the ground with the pommels of their swords. The* GENERAL *springs forward from behind with drawn sword, but is dragged back by the* PRIME MINISTER.)

1ST SOLDIER. Fool!

KURRUBI. Oh.

ANGEL. Peace, child. A simple accident which in no way disturbs the harmony of the spheres.

AKKI. Why have you knocked down this good beggar from Nineveh, soldiers?

1ST SOLDIER. The blighter alleged he was King Nebuchadnezzar.

AKKI. Is your mother still alive?

1ST SOLDIER (*puzzled*). Yes. In Uruk.

AKKI. Your father?

1ST SOLDIER. Dead.

AKKI. Are you married?

1ST SOLDIER. No.

AKKI. Engaged to be married?

1ST SOLDIER. Broken off.

AKKI. Then there will only be your mother to mourn you.

1ST SOLDIER (*bewildered*). Eh?

AKKI. Your name?

1ST SOLDIER. Mumabitu, soldier in King Nebuchadnezzar's army.

AKKI. Very soon your head will roll in the sand, Mumabitu. Very soon vultures will make a meal of your flesh, soldiers of the King, and the dogs will be fighting over your bones.

SOLDIERS. What do you mean?

AKKI. Bend your heads down to mine. You won't be able to much longer.

SOLDIERS (*bending down to* AKKI). What, then?

AKKI. Do you know who it is you have knocked down?

1ST SOLDIER. A lying beggar who tried to have us on that he was King Nebuchadnezzar.

AKKI. He spoke the truth. You have struck Nebuchadnezzar, the King, to the ground.

1ST SOLDIER. What do you take us for?

AKKI. You've probably never heard of the habit kings have of dressing up as beggars and sitting by the banks of the Euphrates to study how the people live.

SOLDIERS. Never.

AKKI. All Babylon knows that.

1ST SOLDIER. I come from Uruk.

2ND SOLDIER. From Ur.

3RD SOLDIER. From Lamash.

AKKI. And now you're all going to die in Babylon.

1ST SOLDIER (*looking anxiously across at* NEBUCHADNEZZAR). What a bit of bad luck.

2ND SOLDIER. Bloody awful luck.

3RD SOLDIER. There's a rattle in his throat.

AKKI. Nebby is renowned for his inhuman and carefully thought-out death sentences. He had Lugalzagesi, the Governor of Akkad, thrown to the great sacred snake.

1ST SOLDIER. Nebby?

AKKI. Nebuchadnezzar is my best friend. I am the Prime Minister, Chamurapi, likewise dressed as a beggar and studying the life of the common people.

(*This time it is the* PRIME MINISTER *who would have rushed forward and the* GENERAL *who pulls him back.*)

SOLDIERS (*coming to attention*). Excellency!

AKKI (*in the grand manner*). Is there anything further?

1ST SOLDIER (*with relief*). He gave a sigh.

2ND SOLDIER. He groaned.

3RD SOLDIER. He is moving.

AKKI. His Highness is coming to.

SOLDIERS (*falling on their knees in despair*). Help us, Prime Minister, help us.

AKKI. What is it the Most High wished you to do?

1ST SOLDIER. He ordered us to hand over the ex-King.

AKKI. Then hand him over. I will give orders that you are only to have your ears cut off.

SOLDIERS (*in terror*). Our ears?

AKKI. When all's said and done, you did knock His Majesty down.

1ST SOLDIER (*humbly*). Here is the ex-King for you, Excellency. He is fettered and gagged, so that he may not defile you with his chatter.

(*He throws* NIMROD *down in front of* AKKI.)

AKKI. Now, run for your lives. His Majesty is getting up.

(*The* SOLDIERS *rush off and* NEBUCHADNEZZAR *gets painfully to his feet.*)

(*Grandly.*) Look at this brave ex-King I've begged for myself.

ANGEL (*delighted.*) You have won the begging duel, Akki of Babylon.

KURRUBI. The earth is a lovely place, Angel. Now I can belong to the beggar I love.

NEBUCHADNEZZAR (*depressed*). Those soldiers were louts. How did you do it?

AKKI. Very simple. I told them you were the King of Babylon.

NEBUCHADNEZZAR. But I did that, too.

AKKI. That was just your mistake. Nobody will believe you if you say that you are the King yourself, because that sounds unbelievable; but they will if you tell them somebody else is.

NEBUCHADNEZZAR (*gloomily*). You've beaten me.

AKKI. You're a bad beggar, man from Nineveh. You work yourself to death without achieving anything.

NEBUCHADNEZZAR (*exhausted*). This miserable profession is nothing but the most exhausting drudgery.

AKKI. How little you know of beggars. Secret teachers, we are, educators of the people. We go in rags as a tribute to man's wretchedness, and we obey no law, that freedom may be held in honour. We eat as greedily as wolves and drink like drunkards to expose the appalling hunger and torturing thirst which poverty brings with it; and we fill the arches of the bridges under which we sleep with the treasures of long-forgotten empires, to show that everything ends up with the beggar, in the course of time. So now go back to Nineveh and beg better and more wisely than before. And you, beggar from the far lands – follow the example you have been set and the village beyond the Lebanon is yours.

(*The* PROSTITUTE *and her* MAID *come back from the market, right.*)

TABTUM (*to* AKKI). Here are four gold pieces for you.

(*She gives them to him.*)

AKKI. Your benevolence, young lady, is developing on the grandest scale. I shall tell Madame Chamurapi of it.

TABTUM (*jealous*). You are going to the Chamurapi?

AKKI. I've been invited to lunch.

(*The* PRIME MINISTER *rises wrathfully up in the background.*)

TABTUM. What are you having?

AKKI. Oh, the sort of food one gets with Prime Ministers. Salted Red Sea fish, an Elam cheese, and onions.

TABTUM. I'm having Tigris pike.

AKKI (*jumping up*). Tigris pike?

TABTUM. With butter sauce and fresh radishes.

AKKI. With butter sauce!

TABTUM. Spring chickens à la Sumérienne.

AKKI. Spring chickens!

TABTUM. With some rice, and a bottle of Lebanon to drink with it.

AKKI. That's a meal fit for a beggar.

TABTUM. You can come if you like.

AKKI. I'm coming with you. Give me your arm, Most Beautiful. The Chamurapi can keep her middle-class meal.

(*He goes off left with* TABTUM *and the* MAID, *dragging* NIMROD *along with him. The* PRIME MINISTER, *shaking his fists, disappears again.*)

ANGEL (*standing up*). Now that this very remarkable man has left us, the time has come for me to reveal myself. (*He throws off his beggar's garment and beard, and stands revealed as a bright and glorious* ANGEL. NEBUCHADNEZZAR *falls on his knees and covers his face.*)

NEBUCHADNEZZAR. Your countenance dazzles me. The fire of your robe burns me up. The power of your wings brings me trembling to my knees.

ANGEL. I am an Angel of God.

NEBUCHADNEZZAR. What is your will, Most Glorious?

ANGEL. I have come to you from Heaven.

NEBUCHADNEZZAR. Why do you come to me, O Angel? What have you to do with a beggar from Nineveh? Go, Messenger of God, to Nebuchadnezzar the King. He alone is worthy to receive you.

ANGEL. Kings, O Beggar Anashamashtaklakou, do not interest

Heaven. On the contrary, the poorer a man is, the more pleasing he is in the sight of Heaven.

NEBUCHADNEZZAR (*astounded*). How can that be?

ANGEL (*after a moment's thought*). I've no idea. (*He thinks again.*) Actually it is rather extraordinary. (*Apologetically.*) But, I'm not an anthropologist. I'm a physicist. I specialize in suns. Especially giant red ones. I have been allotted the task of finding the lowliest of men, but have no means of knowing Heaven's reason. (*With sudden enlightenment.*) Perhaps it's like this: that the poorer a man is, the more fully does he reflect the perfection of Nature.

(*Backstage,* UTNAPISHTIM *rises with his hand up, like a schoolboy who knows the answer.*)

NEBUCHADNEZZAR. You believe that I am the lowliest of men?

ANGEL. Absolutely.

NEBUCHADNEZZAR. The poorest?

ANGEL. The poorest of the poor.

NEBUCHADNEZZAR. And what have you to bring to me?

ANGEL. Something unbelievable and unique; the grace of God.

NEBUCHADNEZZAR. Show me this grace.

ANGEL. Kurrubi.

KURRUBI. Yes, Angel?

ANGEL. Come here, Kurrubi. Come to me, thou who wast created out of the hand of God. Stand before the poorest of mankind, the beggar, Anashamashtaklakou, from Nineveh.

(*She stands before* NEBUCHADNEZZAR *and the* ANGEL *unveils her. With a cry,* NEBUCHADNEZZAR *covers his face.* UTNAPISHTIM, *terrified, disappears.*)

ANGEL (*joyfully*). There! Is not that a noble gift from Heaven, a magnificent gift, my beggar from Nineveh?

NEBUCHADNEZZAR. Her beauty, Messenger of God, surpasses even your majesty. You are a shadow in the glory of it, and I am but darkness in the brightness of her eyes.

ANGEL. A lovely girl. A good girl. Created this very night, out of nothing.

NEBUCHADNEZZAR (*desperately*). She is not for me, the poor beggar from Nineveh; she is not for this unworthy carcase. Go,
she is not for me, Angel. Go to King Nebuchadnezzar – go!

ANGEL. Out of the question.

NEBUCHADNEZZAR (*imploringly*). The King alone is worthy of
this purity – this glory. He will clothe her in silks; he will lay
costly carpets before her feet and place a golden crown on her
head.

ANGEL. He's not getting her.

NEBUCHADNEZZAR (*bitterly*). So you're going to hand over this
Holy One to the lowest of beggars?

ANGEL. Heaven knows what it is doing. Take her. A good girl.
A well-brought-up girl.

NEBUCHADNEZZAR (*in desperation*). What is a beggar supposed to
do with her?

ANGEL. I'm not a human being. How should I know your
customs? (*He has an idea.*) Kurrubi!

KURRUBI. Yes, Angel?

ANGEL. Did you observe the astounding success of that beggar,
Akki?

KURRUBI. Everything, Angel.

ANGEL. Then do as he did. You belong to this beggar from
Nineveh and you are to help him to become as successful a
beggar as Akki. (*To* NEBUCHADNEZZAR.) She will help you to
beg, Anashamashtaklakou.

NEBUCHADNEZZAR (*shocked*). This jewel of a Grace is to beg?

ANGEL. I can't think what else Heaven can have had in view when
it gave her to a beggar.

NEBUCHADNEZZAR. At Nebuchadnezzar's side she would rule
the world. At mine she will beg.

ANGEL. Learn, once and for all, that ruling the world is Heaven's
business and begging is mankind's. So carry on and beg dili-
gently. In decent moderation, of course. Not too much, and
not too little. If you can manage to beg yourselves to a solid,
middle-class status, that will be enough. Fare you well.

KURRUBI (*horrified*). You're not going to leave me, Angel?

ANGEL. I am going, my child. I have brought you to mankind, and now I must fly away.

KURRUBI. But I don't know them yet.

ANGEL. Do I know them, my child? It is my job to leave mankind and yours to stay with them. We must both obey. Farewell, Kurribi, my child, farewell.

KURRUBI. Stay, Angel.

ANGEL (*spreading his wings*). Impossible. After all, I have a job to do too. I have to investigate the Earth. I must hurry away to measure, to dig and collect, to discover new wonders in the grandeur of the Universe. For so far, my child, I have only been acquainted with the material world in gaseous form.

KURRUBI. Stay, Angel, stay!

ANGEL. I must fly away. I must fly away into the silver of the morning. Climbing gently, in ever wider circles round Babylon, I must disappear; a small, white cloud, dissolving in the light of Heaven.

(*The* ANGEL *flies off, the beggar's coat and beard carefully laid over his arm.*)

KURRUBI. Stay, Angel!

ANGEL (*from afar*). Farewell, Kurribi, my child, farewell. (*As he disappears altogether.*) Farewell.

KURRUBI (*softly*). Stay! Stay!

(KURRUBI *and* NEBUCHADNEZZAR *are left alone facing each other in the silver of the morning.*)

KURRUBI (*softly*). He has disappeared.

NEBUCHADNEZZAR. He has departed in all his glory.

KURRUBI. Now I am with you.

NEBUCHADNEZZAR. Now you are with me.

KURRUBI. I am freezing in this morning mist.

NEBUCHADNEZZAR. Dry your tears.

KURRUBI. Don't human beings cry when an Angel from Heaven leaves them?

NEBUCHADNEZZAR. Of course they do.

235

KURRUBI (*after closely examining his face*). I don't see any tears in your eyes.

NEBUCHADNEZZAR. We have forgotten how to cry and learnt to swear instead.

(KURRUBI *shrinks away from him.*)

Why are you afraid?

KURRUBI. My whole body is trembling.

NEBUCHADNEZZAR. Do not be frightened of men. Be frightened of God. He created us in His image. All is His doing.

KURRUBI. What He does is good. I was safe in His hand. I have stood close to His countenance.

EBUCHADNEZZAR. And now He has flung His toy into my lap – the lap of the lowliest and most tattered article in all His creation, the beggar, Anashamashtaklakou from Nineveh. Descended from the stars, you stand in front of me. Your eyes, your face, your body, declare the beauty of Heaven, but what is the use of heavenly perfection to the poorest of mankind on this imperfect Earth? When will Heaven ever learn to give each man what he needs? The poor and the powerless are packed together like sheep and starve. The mighty are full-fed, but alone. The beggar hungers for bread, and Heaven ought to give him bread. Nebuchadnezzar hungers for a human being, so Heaven ought to give him you. Why doesn't Heaven understand the loneliness of Nebuchadnezzar? Why should you be sent to mock both me, the beggar, and Nebuchadnezzar the King?

KURRUBI (*thoughtfully*). I have taken on a difficult job.

NEBUCHADNEZZAR. What is your job?

KURRUBI. To look after you and beg for you.

NEBUCHADNEZZAR. Do you love me?

KURRUBI. A woman bore you that you might love me to all eternity, and I was created out of nothing to love you to all eternity.

NEBUCHADNEZZAR. Leprosy has made my body under my cloak as white as snow.

KURRUBI. I still love you.

NEBUCHADNEZZAR. Because of your love men will tear at you with wolfish fangs.

KURRUBI. I still love you.

NEBUCHADNEZZAR. You will be driven into the wilderness. You will end in the red sand beneath a burning sun.

KURRUBI. I still love you.

NEBUCHADNEZZAR. Then kiss me, if you love me.

KURRUBI. I will kiss you.

NEBUCHADNEZZAR (*striking* KURRUBI *to the ground as the kiss comes to an end and placing his foot on her*). So I throw you to the ground, you whom I love more than ever man loved, and trample you underfoot, Gift of God, on whom my whole happiness depends. There and there! Those are the kisses I give – that's how I return your love. Heaven shall see how a beggar treats its gift; how the lowliest of men spurns one whom King Nebuchadnezzar would have loaded with love and all the gold of Babylon.

(AKKI *comes in, left, dragging the captive* NIMROD *with him.*)

AKKI (*in surprise*). What are you doing, kicking that girl, beggar from Nineveh?

NEBUCHADNEZZAR (*with bitter scorn*). I am trampling underfoot the gift of God. A new, lovely gift, as you can see for yourself, created only last night, intended for the most pitiable of men and handed over personally to me by an Angel. Do you want her?

AKKI. Created only last night!

NEBUCHADNEZZAR. Out of nothing.

AKKI. Then it will be a very useless gift.

NEBUCHADNEZZAR. For that reason going cheap. I'll swap her for your prisoner.

AKKI. Well, after all, he is an ex-king.

NEBUCHADNEZZAR. I'll throw in the gold piece that I succeeded in begging.

AKKI. And what about his historic value?

NEBUCHADNEZZAR. The two shillings.

AKKI. It's not a very good business proposition.

NEBUCHADNEZZAR. Well, will you close on the deal?

AKKI. Only because you're a singularly inept beggar. There! (*He throws the* EX-KING *to his feet.*) And you, my girl, belong to me. Get up. (KURRUBI *gets up slowly, with bowed head.*) An Angel is supposed to have brought you here. I like fairy stories, and I will believe the unbelievable. I will lean on you, who have been created out of nothing. That man from Lebanon upset me rather. You won't know the Earth, but I know it, so console yourself. You have been knocked down once – I, a thousand times. Come. We'll go to Anu's Garden Market. It's a market day, a good moment and I smell profit. We shall now see what we can get by begging, you with your beauty and I with my red beard; you, covered with bruises from kicking, and myself persecuted by a king.

KURRUBI (*softly*). I love you all the same, my beggar from Nineveh.

(AKKI *goes out right, leaning on* KURRUBI. NEBUCHADNEZZAR *is left standing alone with* NIMROD, *fettered and gagged at his feet. He throws off the beggar's costume and red beard, stamps on them, and then stands sunk in deep thought, gloomy and motionless.*

The SUITE *come creeping cautiously forward.*)

PRIME MINISTER (*disturbed*). Your Majesty!

NEBUCHADNEZZAR. A reprieve of ten days will be granted to the beggar, Akki. If he wishes to become a civil servant, the highest offices of state are open to him. If not, I send my hangman to him. And you, General, will lead my army out beyond the Lebanon. Conquer these ridiculous villages – Spartens, Mosking, Pekow, and Athage – or whatever they're called. We, on the other hand, will withdraw with the captive King into our palace to continue our work of improving mankind, tired and saddened, insulted by Heaven itself.

ACT TWO

The Second Act is to be played beneath one of the Euphrates bridges, in the very heart of Babylon. The sky is shut out by towering skyscrapers and palaces. The orchestra pit again represents the river, and the bridge makes a great vault forwards from the back of the stage, so that it appears in cross-section and from below. High overhead the traffic of the giant city makes itself heard. There can be heard the steady rattle of the ancient Babylonian trams and the tuneful cries of the litter-bearers. Left and right of the bridge narrow steps lead down to the river bank. Akki's dwelling is a wild hotch-potch of various objects of every period: sarcophagi, heathen idols, an ancient royal throne, Babylonian bicycles and car tyres and so forth, all covered with the dirt of ages, mouldy, heaped with dust. Above all this mess, halfway up the vault of the bridge, there is a relief of the head of Gilgamish. Beside it, torn copies of the notices about begging with strips pasted across them saying 'Today is your last chance.' Outside on the right, clear of the bridge, a kitchen range and a kettle. The ground is red sand, littered with jam tins and poetic manuscripts. Everywhere hang parchments and clay tablets closely written with poetry; in short the characters seem to be moving about on an enormous rubbish dump. Forward, right, several croaking, muffled figures are bathing in the Euphrates; on the left, two filthy members of Babylon's criminal class, Omar the pickpocket and Yussuf the burglar, are lying asleep on the top of a sarcophagus. Akki and Kurrubi, both in tatters, come in from left. Akki has a sack on his back.

AKKI. Clear yourselves off, scum. I won't have you sleeping off your pilferings and burglaries on my sarcophagus.

(Omar *and* Yussuf *slip out.*)

Wash your bodies farther down the filthy stream, you pied crows. It's no good your croaking. This bridge was built in

239

honour of our national hero, Gilgamish, and is not to be used
as a health resort. National heroes are the outstanding killers
of mankind; doctors aren't in the same class.

(*The muffled figures vanish.*)

KURRUBI. What are those muffled-up creatures, creeping away
over there?

AKKI. Lepers. Folk without hope, who still seek it in the Euphrates. This would be a snug enough billet if every kind of
riffraff didn't nest in it the moment one's back was turned.

KURRUBI. The Earth is awfully different from the Angel's idea of
it, my Akki. With every step I take I see more injustice, more
sickness, more despair around me. Human beings are not happy.

AKKI. The important thing is that they should be good customers.
There. Once again we have begged a splendid haul between
us. A short midday rest, and then we will resume our voca-
tion in the Hanging Gardens.

(*He puts down his sack.*)

KURRUBI. Yes, my Akki.

AKKI. You've made progress. I'm pleased with you. There's only
one thing wrong. You smile when people throw you money.
Fundamentally wrong. A sad face has far more effect – it's
more moving.

KURRUBI. I will bear it in mind.

AKKI. Practise it for tomorrow. Despair is what pays off best. (*He
takes the proceeds of their begging out of the sack.*) Pearls, precious
stones, pieces of gold, shillings, pennies – away with them.
(*He throws the lot into the Euphrates.*)

KURRUBI. Now you are throwing the money back into the
Euphrates.

AKKI. Well?

KURRUBI. It is senseless to beg if you always throw everything
away.

AKKI. It is the only way of maintaining a really high standard in
beggary. Prodigality is the essential. I've begged millions, and
I've thrown millions into the mud. It's the only way to

relieve the world of riches. (*He goes through his pockets.*)
Olives. They're more useful objects. Bananas, a tin of finest
sardines, gin, and a Sumerian goddess of love carved in ivory.
(*He examines it.*) But that you mustn't see. It was not made for
little girls to look at.

(*He pitches the goddess of love into the back of the vault.*)

KURRUBI. Yes, dear Akki.

AKKI. 'Yes, my Akki' and 'Yes, dear Akki', endlessly the whole
day. You are sad about something.

KURRUBI. I'm in love with the beggar from Nineveh.

AKKI. Whose name you've forgotten.

KURRUBI. It is such a difficult name. But I shall never stop looking
for my beggar. One day, somewhere, I shall find him. By day,
in the squares of Babylon and on the steps of the palaces, I
think of him all the time; and when I gaze at the stars at night,
high and distant above the cobbled streets, I seek his face in
every pool of their light. Then he is close; then he is by my
side. Then he lies on the earth of the countryside, my beloved,
and gazes into my face, white and large against the starry
mist from which the Angel brought me down.

AKKI. Love is without hope.

KURRUBI. It is the only hope. How could I live on this Earth
without the love I have for my beloved?

AKKI. Since one cannot live on this Earth, I have decided to live
off it and have become a beggar. Here we are under the best
bridge I could find in Babylon. I won't have my apartment
polluted by thoughts about a man who in one hour could beg
no more than a single gold piece and two shillings. (*He starts
up.*) What are these hanging all over the place? Oh, of course,
poems. The poets have been here.

KURRUBI (*delighted*). Oh, can I read the poems?

AKKI. In the present decadence of the poetic art in Babylon, reading is not to be recommended. (*He takes one sheet and, after a
glance at it, throws it into the Euphrates.*) Love poems. Nothing
but love poems ever since I swapped you for the ex-king.

Make some soup – that'll be much better. Here – some fresh-
begged beef to go with it.

KURRUBI. Yes, my Akki.

AKKI. I, on the other hand, shall withdraw into my favourite
sarcophagus.

(*He opens the sarcophagus in the middle of the stage, but springs
back from it as a* POET *heaves himself out of it.*)

(*Angry.*) What are you doing in that sarcophagus?

POET. Writing poetry.

AKKI. That's no place for writing poetry. That's the sarcophagus
of the enchanting Lilith who was once my mistress. What's
more, it saw me through the Flood. Light as a bird it carried
me over the raging seas. Off with you – find somewhere else
to write poetry. Here – a few more onions.

(*He throws some onions to* KURRUBI *and lies down in his
sarcophagus. The* POET *slinks away.* KURRUBI *busy at the range.
The Policeman,* NEBO, *comes down the steps, left, mopping his
forehead.*)

POLICEMAN. A hot day, Beggar Akki. An exhausting day.

AKKI. Greetings, Policeman Nebo. I would gladly rise in your
honour, for I have an enormous respect for the police; but I
still have to take care of my back. Last time I visited the
police station you pinched me with red-hot pincers and
loaded considerable weights on to all my limbs.

POLICEMAN. I was only doing it for your own good. I was
strictly obeying the orders for the rehabilitation of recalci-
trant beggars as regular civil servants.

AKKI. Decent of you. Can I offer you a sarcophagus for an over-
zealous policeman?

POLICEMAN. I'd rather sit on this stone. (*As he sits.*) Sarcophagi
make me feel sad.

AKKI. That's the throne of the last chief of the cave men. I got it
from his widow. Have a drop of red Chaldea.

(*He takes a bottle from his cloak and passes it across.*)

POLICEMAN (*drinking.*) Many thanks. I'm all in. My job gets more exhausting every day. I've just had to collect up all the school textbooks and arrest all the geographers and astronomers.

AKKI. What have they done?

POLICEMAN. The world turned out to be larger than they thought. Apparently they overlooked a few villages on the other side of the Lebanon. Science, like everything else in our State, has got to be infallible.

AKKI. The beginning of the end.

POLICEMAN. And now the army is off to conquer them.

AKKI. They were rolling over the Gilgamish Bridge northwards the whole night. I smell total disaster in the offing.

POLICEMAN. As an official I have only to obey, not to think.

AKKI. The more perfect a State, the more stupid the officials it needs.

POLICEMAN. So you say now. If you ever become an official you will learn to marvel at our State. You will perceive its excellence like a blinding light.

AKKI. I see. That's why you've come. You want to continue my education as a civil servant.

POLICEMAN. I never let go.

AKKI. I noticed that at the police station.

POLICEMAN. I am here in an official capacity.

AKKI. I thought as much.

(*The* POLICEMAN *takes out a notebook.*)

POLICEMAN. Today is the last day.

AKKI. You don't say so?

POLICEMAN. You were begging in Anu Square.

AKKI. It was an oversight.

POLICEMAN. I've a piece of news for you.

AKKI. A new instrument of torture?

POLICEMAN. A new decision. In recognition of your abilities you have been appointed President of the Board of Management and Bankruptcy. The Treasury has its eye on you, too, and there are rumours in official circles that a career worth watching lies before you.

AKKI. Careers, Policeman Nebo, do not interest me.

POLICEMAN. You refuse to accept this important post?

AKKI. I intend to remain an independent artist.

POLICEMAN. You are going on begging?

AKKI. It's my profession.

(*The* POLICEMAN *puts his notebook away.*)

POLICEMAN. Bad. That's bad.

(AKKI *starts to get up.*)

AKKI. All right, Policeman Nebo, you can take me back to the police station.

POLICEMAN. Unnecessary. The hangman will come to you.

(*A silence.* AKKI's *hands go involuntarily to his neck. Then he starts cross-examining the* POLICEMAN.)

AKKI. The little fat one?

POLICEMAN. Lord, no. The hangman for this district is a tall, lean chap – a master of his art. It's a real pleasure to watch him. Outstanding technically.

AKKI. You mean that well-known vegetarian?

POLICEMAN (*shaking his head*). Forgive my saying so – you're a bit of a novice on executions. You're muddling him up with the Nineveh hangman. Ours is a great reader of old books.

AKKI (*relieved*). Ah! That makes all the difference.

POLICEMAN. The man is on his way here.

AKKI. I shall be delighted to make his acquaintance.

POLICEMAN. He means business, Beggar Akki, I warn you. He will hang you if he does not find you in the office in the morning enrolled in the civil service.

AKKI. I am at his disposal.

KURRUBI (*terrified*). Do they mean to kill you?

AKKI. No need to get excited, my girl. I've been threatened so often in the course of a stormy life that I don't notice it any more.

(*All the sarcophagi open as* POETS *leap up in them and creep out from under every conceivable object.*)

POET. A new subject.

244

ANOTHER. A powerful subject.

A THIRD. What material!

A FOURTH. What possibility!

ALL. Tell us, Beggar, tell us.

AKKI. All right, I'll give you the saga of my life. When I was young, several thousand years ago, and was still inexperienced, I was the son of a merchant. My father went in cloth of gold, my mother was loaded with silver jewels, the house was full of carpets and silks and satins. The silver tarnished, the gold rolled and rolled away. In Babylon the firm of Enggibi & Sons gobbled everything. My father perished at the stake, and then my mother, and nothing was saved from the wreck.

POETS. Nothing was saved from the wreck.

AKKI. There came a prophet from the mountains of Elam who took me with him and treated me as his own son. I lay night and day before the altar and made sacrifices there to the gods, dressed in rags, and with ashes in my hair. Religion tarnished. Grace rolled and rolled away. In Babylon there was a change of high priests. The prophet perished at the stake, and then the gods, and nothing was saved from the wreck.

POETS. Nothing was saved from the wreck.

AKKI. My education was taken over by a general, armed in steel from head to foot and a faithful soldier of the King; no mother's son was ever held in greater honour. Knocked his enemies from the saddle, owned a castle, and his baggage train stretched for miles. The honour tarnished. The offices rolled and rolled away from him. In Babylon there was a change of dynasty. The general perished at the stake, and then all his officers, and nothing was saved from the wreck.

POETS. Nothing was saved from the wreck.

AKKI. As the rich man was ruined and the pious man died, and even the strong man perished, my mother's son said to himself: Man should be as sand, for sand alone does not show the footprints of the evil-doer or of the hangman on the ground. Of all Babylon there only remains one beggar, poppy-

245

crowned, and his beard may perish and his coat may perish, but he will be saved from the wreck.

A POET. The tale of your night of love with the Princess Thetis.

ANOTHER. Of how you begged the whole State Treasury.

A THIRD. The giants Gog and Magog.

AKKI. There's nothing in those. I have visitors. Kurrubi, go on cooking.

POLICEMAN (*in wonder, as the* POETS *disappear*). In the name of Heaven, your dwelling seems to be full of poets.

AKKI. So it is. It has taken me by surprise too. Perhaps I ought to give my bridge vault another spring-clean.

(POLICEMAN *rises and puts on a solemn manner.*)

POLICEMAN. Oh much-sung one, are you quite determined to let yourself be hanged?

AKKI. Entirely and absolutely.

POLICEMAN. A bitter decision, but I have to respect it.

AKKI (*puzzled*). What's the matter with you, Policeman Nebo? You've gone all formal and you keep on bowing.

POLICEMAN. Most Noble, you must be very worried about what is to happen to Kurrubi when you are no more. I am very anxious about it myself. Every Babylonian envies you. They are deeply shocked that Kurrubi lives in poverty. They are seeking every means of taking the girl away from you. You have knocked down five people already.

AKKI. Six. You're forgetting the general I threw over the parapet of Ishtar Bridge. He soared through the night into the deeps like a comet.

POLICEMAN (*bowing yet again*). Most Noble, the girl needs a protector. I never saw a prettier child. All Babylon talks of her. People come here from Ur, from Uruk, from Chaldea and Uz, from all over the empire, to admire her. The whole city is lost in a transport of love. Every man thinks of Kurrubi, dreams of her, loves her. Every house, every square, the Hanging Gardens, the Gondolas on the Euphrates, all are full of sighs, full of songs. Three sons of the highest nobility have

246

drowned themselves because of her. Bankers are beginning to write poetry and civil servants to make music.

(*Above on the steps, right, appears the Banker,* ENGGIBI, *with an old-Babylonian guitar.*)

ENGGIBI.   I was once very fond of an exchequer bond
            And studied the closing prices,
            Now damn the gilt-edged; to Kurrubi I'm pledged
            And I'm facing a capital crisis.

POLICEMAN. What did I tell you?

ENGGIBI.   I no longer care for a bull or a bear
            And Kurrubi my heart entrances,
            A banker's pride, I lay aside
            And make unlimited advances.

AKKI (*amazed*). The banker.

(*Above on the steps, left, appears* ALI, *also with a guitar.*)

ALI   I used to deal in red, red wine,
            And now I'm a poet, a poet.
            Oh, lovely beggar's child, be mine,
            Your heart on me please bestow it.

POLICEMAN. Another one.

AKKI. Ali, the wine merchant.

ENGGIBI. I am astonished, Wine-merchant Ali, that you make use of my metre.

ALI (*with dignity*). My metre, Banker Enggibi, if you will pardon me; my metre.

ALL POETS (*appearing suddenly*). My metre! My metre!

(POETS *disappear again.*)

AKKI. It's always the same. Let a man once start writing poetry, someone will at once accuse him of plagiarism.

(*With sudden decision the* POLICEMAN *pulls a poem from his tunic.*)

POLICEMAN.   I was a decent traffic cop,
            Loyal, honest, severe;
            And now all the time my heart goes pop
            With love for the girl I revere.

AKKI. Policeman Nebo!

POLICEMAN.   Now I send the traffic all over the shop;
           It goes I know not whither.
           For a lovely girl has me on the hop
           And I dream of a nice come-hither.

AKKI (*severely*). What's come over you? You're supposed to clear all the poets out, not to swell their numbers.

    (*The* POLICEMAN *folds his poem away in embarrassment. He is, moreover, confused throughout the following speech by the continued strumming of the banker and wine-merchant.*)

POLICEMAN. Forgive me. It suddenly came over me. As a general rule I'm inarticulate, but last night, as the moon rose above the Euphrates, huge and yellow, and as I thought of Kurrubi, with everyone writing poetry all round me, I suddenly had to break out into a poem. (*He bows again.*) My beggar. I am a Nebo. I own a nice little house in Lebanon Street. I shall be promoted Station Sergeant at the new year.

    (*The two* WORKING MEN *come in left.*)

1ST WORKING MAN. There he is, the beggar, Akki, who upholds the honour of the working classes.

2ND WORKING MAN. Of course. In a sarcophagus.

1ST WORKING MAN. In broad daylight he idles about everywhere – Babylon's chief worker.

2ND WORKING MAN. And the girl, dirty and in rags.

1ST WORKING MAN. It's a disgrace.

2ND WORKING MAN. What's more, he shovels gold and silver into the Euphrates.

1ST WORKING MAN. Poets are the only ones who get anything out of him. As though we couldn't write poetry too, if we tried.

    (*Both unfold poems with the intention of reading them aloud. Akki heaves himself up in his sarcophagus in a fury.*)

AKKI. For God's sake, no.

1ST WORKING MAN. It's a marvel to me where he can have got such a lovely girl.

AKKI. I had her off that incompetent beggar on the quay who couldn't even screw a penny out of you two.

2ND WORKING MAN. That bloody fool?

1ST WORKING MAN. And where did he get her, then?

AKKI. It sounded like a fairy tale. An angel brought the girl to him, flying down with her from the Andromeda Galaxy.

(*The* POETS *appear.*)

POETS. An angel?

ALI. Precisely.

POETS. What a splendid new subject for poetry.

AKKI. I most emphatically forbid anything of the kind.

(*The* POETS *vanish.*)

1ST WORKING MAN. Are we supposed to believe this?

ENGGIBI. From the Andromeda Galaxy. That is scientifically quite impossible.

(*Laughter.*)

2ND WORKING MAN. It's all a swindle. There aren't such things as angels. They were invented by the priests.

ENGGIBI. I suspect an abduction.

ALI. The police ought to investigate it.

POLICEMAN. The police have no official reason to throw doubt on the Angel. On the contrary. It is in fact the atheists who come under suspicion.

(*The prostitute* TABTUM *comes down the steps, right.*)

TABTUM. It's a scandal – an outrage.

AKKI. Greetings, young lady.

(*The* PROSTITUTE *runs a hand over* KURRUBI, *as though she were a horse.*)

TABTUM. That's the creature. Has she got better teeth than anyone else? Better developed thighs? A lovelier figure? There are girls like her by the thousand, and going cheap.

KURRUBI. Keep your hands off me. I've done you no harm.

TABTUM. Not done me any harm? Now, listen to the little innocent! And I must keep my hands off the little lamb! I'll get my hands on you – you may be sure of that. All Babylon has forsaken me because of you, and you dare to play the prude.

KURRUBI. Nobody has forsaken you because of me. I love my beggar from Nineveh, and nobody else.

TABTUM. You love a beggar from Nineveh? You've got your eye on all the bankers in Babylon, and on them alone.

(*She tries to get* KURRUBI *by the hair, but she flies to* AKKI.)

1ST WORKING MAN. Leave the girl alone, whore!

ALI. What terrible words for the child to learn!

ENGGIBI. The girl belongs in a quite different milieu.

TABTUM. A different milieu? Indeed? My milieu has always been good enough for bankers and wine-merchants.

AKKI. What's biting you, Most Beautiful?

TABTUM. Is there a more discreetly conducted house than mine? Have I not the most beautiful breasts in Babylon?

AKKI. I don't understand what those structures have to do with Kurrubi.

TABTUM. I take endless trouble to stay young and beautiful. I diet, I take baths and have myself massaged. And what's the result? The moment this creature appears all my clients go off to write poetry.

ENGGIBI (*from above, right*). Kurrubi inspires us to better things.

ALI (*from above, left*). She enchants us.

1ST WORKING MAN. Now we know what we are toiling for.

2ND WORKING MAN. At a shilling a week.

POLICEMAN. She has uplifted us.

(ENGGIBI, ALI, *the* WORKING MEN *and the* POLICEMAN *chant slowly and solemnly in unison.*)

ALL. It is true. There burns a fire
Deep within and hard to master.

AKKI. I will not tolerate any more poems in my apartment.

(*The* POETS *reappear and join in.*)

ALL. Never does mankind stand higher
Than when love makes hearts beat faster,
When all that's wicked's laid aside
And only the good and true abide.

TABTUM. So you're all uplifted, are you? Am I supposed to

250

believe that? If so, the little thing isn't coming to me. In my profession we do an honest job of work.

(*From the right arrive the* WIVES *of the two* WORKING MEN. *The* POETS *take fright and vanish.*)

1ST WIFE. So my old man is carrying on under the Gilgamish Bridge, in this most unsavoury neighbourhood, is he?

1ST WORKING MAN. But dear, I only happened to be passing here by chance, dear.

2ND WIFE. Mine's there, too.

2ND WORKING MAN. What's it got to do with you? Shall I tell them all about your goings on with the Union Secretary?

(*The* POLICEMAN, *his mind made up, goes over to* KURRUBI *who has taken refuge with* AKKI *and is crouching by the sarcophagus in which he is sitting.*)

POLICEMAN. Miss. I am a Nebo. I own a little house in Lebanon Street. At the new year I am going to be promoted Station Sergeant. The Nebos have always made good husbands. If I may say so, they have, in our particular circle, quite a reputation for this. You would be happy. It is my deep desire to make you entirely and …

1ST WORKING MAN (*plunging forward*). Miss. I'm a Hassan. It is my deep desire to make you entirely and completely happy. I live almost in the country, and I have an allotment. The missus here will fit up the best room for you. You will have a healthy life, a simple life, a contented life.

1ST WIFE. He's gone off his head.

2ND WORKING MAN (*also plunging forward*). Miss. I'm a Sindbad. You belong in a sound proletarian background. My old woman will also fit up the best room for you. I will enlighten you. I will open your eyes to the intrigues of the capitalists. Day and night I will work ceaselessly to prepare you for the great Workers' Crusade.

2ND WIFE. And now my old man has gone round the bend, too.

(*The* SELLER *of asses' milk bursts on to the stage from right, and throws himself on his knees before* KURRUBI.)

251

GIMMIL. Miss. I'm a Gimmil. I own an apartment in the Euphrates district. Live on the sixth floor, with lift and view over
the Hanging Gardens if required. You would breathe good,
middle-class air, and breathe it happily.

WOMEN. Hound her out of the city. Hound her out of the city.

(*Both* ALI *and* ENGGIBI *have now drawn near.*)

ALI. Miss. I am Ali, owner of the firm of Ali, Wine-Merchants
Ltd. I have a town house and a villa on the banks of the Tigris.
What you need, Miss, above all things is a rock: a rock to cling
to. I am that rock. You can cling to me. I am convinced that ...

THE POETS (*reappearing*). Kurrubi belongs to us. Kurrubi
belongs to us.

ENGGIBI. Miss. I am an Enggibi, Managing Director of the world-
wide banking house of Enggibi & Sons, but that is not what
is most important. My palaces, my shares, my country properties, may all pass away. What matters is that you need a heart,
the living, loving, sympathetic heart of a man; and it is in my
breast that this heart beats.

WOMEN. Hound her out of the city. Hound her out of the city.

POETS (*simultaneously*). Kurrubi belongs to us. Kurrubi belongs
to us.

(*As the growing tumult reaches a climax, the* ANGEL *is suddenly
there again, sitting on the head of Gilgamish. Fir cones and
poppies are tangled in his hair and his arms are full of things like
sunflowers and twigs of trees.*)

ANGEL. Kurrubi. Kurrubi, my child.

ALL (*in terror*). An angel!

(ALL *except* KURRUBI *fall to the ground and seek to hide themselves.*)

KURRUBI. Angel! My Angel.

ANGEL. Quite by chance, my dear girl, as I was flying by, I
caught a glimpse of you in the midst of this merry tumult.

KURRUBI. Help me. Angel.

ANGEL. The Earth, my child – what a wonderful discovery! I am
transported with happiness. I tremble with awe in every limb.

Wonder upon wonder glows within me and I am shaken
through and through by the knowledge of God. I cannot
leave off studying and experimenting and I flutter excitedly
hither and thither, admiring, collecting, taking notes. Day and
night, unceasingly, untiringly, I pursue my researches. And
even so I haven't yet once dived into the sea, into all this
water which surrounds us. I only really know the middle
regions and the North Pole. Look what I found there:
frozen dew. (*He holds up an icicle.*) As a sun-researcher I have
never found anything nearly so precious before.

KURRUBI. The beggar from Nineveh has deserted me, Angel. I
love him and he has deserted me.

ANGEL. It's a muddle, my child, just a muddle. Only be patient,
and he will come back. The Earth is so out of all reason
beautiful that one does get a bit muddled by it. That is to be
expected. Who could experience the delicate blue of the sky,
the red of the sand or the silver of the streams without some
disturbance? To behold it moves one to prayer. And then the
plants and the animals. The white lilies, the yellow lions and
the brown gazelle. Even the men are different colours. Just
look at this for a miracle. (*He holds up a sunflower.*) Things like
that are not to be found on Aldebaran, on Canopus, or on
Arcturus.

KURRUBI. Men are plotting against me, Angel. I have brought
unhappiness on the city of Babylon. The Euphrates is carrying
tears down to the sea. Whether I meet love or hatred, it is
killing me.

ANGEL. It will all turn out for the best, dear girl. It will all turn
out for the best.

(*He spreads his wings.*)

KURRUBI. Don't leave me, Angel. Stay with me. Help me with
your heavenly strength. Carry me to my beloved.

ANGEL. I must use every moment of my time down here. I must
confine myself to what is strictly necessary. All too soon I have
to return to the Andromeda Galaxy to creep about among the

giant red suns. I must study, dear girl. I must study. I am
wholly absorbed in new discoveries.

> Over the continents, over blue seas,
> Dazzled, my silver way I thread;
> Over the hills and the fields and the trees
> Soaring through clouds or gliding under,
> Moving softly on wings outspread,
> Absorbed in Earth's unceasing wonder.

AKKI (*wearily*). Now even *he* is going in for poetry.

ANGEL.
> Embodied in beasts and flowers I find
> What in the stars is formless and blind.
> Intoxicated by every sight,
> I plunge and soar in a blinding light.

KURRUBI. Stay, Angel, stay!

ANGEL. Farewell, Kurrubi, my child, farewell (*as he vanishes*),
farewell.

> (KURRUBI *has fallen to her knees and covered her face. Very
> slowly they all get up, pale and tottering.*)

POETS (*as their heads emerge cautiously from the sarcophagi*). Then it
really was an angel.

GIMMIL (*stammering*). In broad daylight.

POLICEMAN (*wiping sweat from his forehead*). And sitting down
calmly on the head of our national hero.

1ST WORKING MAN (*still in a dream*). A glorious messenger of God.

1ST WIFE (*likewise*). Full grown, and with coloured feathers.

2ND WORKING MAN. It fluttered round my head like a huge bat.

ENGGIBI. I shall endow a bell. The Enggibi Bell.

ALI. Free meals for theologians. The Ali Endowment.

WOMEN. We'll go to confession.

GIMMIL AND WORKING MEN. We will at once become converts to the Established Church.

POLICEMAN. Thank goodness I've always been a churchgoer.

ENGGIBI. Men of Babylon! An angel has flown down to us. It is a
moment for careful reflection. As a banker, as a man of cool
judgment, I must tell you that we are living in critical times.

1ST WORKING MAN. Wages will go down.

GIMMIL. Cows' milk sales will go up.

ALI. The wine trade will suffer.

ENGGIBI. On top of that, bad harvests.

1ST WIFE. Earthquakes.

2ND WORKING MAN. Swarms of locusts.

ENGGIBI. The stock exchanges are unstable. Last year an epidemic of smallpox. The year before that, the plague. What does all this mean? It is because we did not believe in Heaven. All of us, more or less, were atheists. Now God has revealed Himself through an angel. All depends now on what we do with this girl whom the angel brought down to Earth, diving down from the Andromeda Galaxy.

GIMMIL. She must not live in poverty any longer.

1ST WORKING MAN. She must be taken away from this beggar.

2ND WORKING MAN. And from these poets.

ENGGIBI. Let us invest her with the greatest honour that we have in our power and Heaven will be propitiated. Let us enthrone her as our Queen. Otherwise we may fear the worst. We cannot allow the wrath of Heaven to continue against us. Already we have had to struggle, with much pain and loss, through the Great Flood. An economic crisis now might bring upon us an even greater catastrophe.

1ST WIFE. To the King with the maid from Heaven!

ALL. To Nebuchadnezzar.

1ST WORKING MAN. She shall be our Queen.

ALL. Our Queen.

POETS. Stay with us, Kurrubi. Stay with us.

KURRUBI. I will stay with you, Beggar Akki; beside you under this bridge, close by the waters of the Euphrates – close to your heart.

(*The crowd begins to look threatening.*)

SEVERAL VOICES. Throw the beggar in the river.

(*They would fall on* AKKI, *but the* POLICEMAN *stops them, waving his arms furiously.*)

POLICEMAN. You know my feelings, Beggar. You know that I own a little house in Lebanon Street and how well placed I am, as a Nebo, to make Kurrubi happy. In modest circumstances, of course. Nevertheless, it is now my duty to bring the maiden before the King, and yours to let her go.

(*He wipes the sweat from his face.*)

CROWD. Long live the Police.

KURRUBI. Help me, Akki.

AKKI. I cannot help you, dear girl. We must bid each other good-bye. For ten days we have wandered, both in our torn clothes, through the streets of the city of Babylon and about her squares, and at night you have slept, breathing gently, in my warmest sarcophagus, with my poets moaning all around you. Never have I begged with greater genius. Yet now we must part. I have no right to you. You came to me, a fragment of Heaven, in a chance bargain, and clung to me, like a thread of God's Grace, uncomplaining and cheerful, until another puff of wind has come to carry you away again.

KURRUBI. I have to obey you, my Akki. You took me in. You gave me food when I hungered and drink when I was thirsty. When I was afraid, you sang me your splendid songs, and when I despaired, you clapped your hands and stamped your feet in a rhythm which set me dancing around you. You wrapped me in your cloak when I was cold and when I was tired you carried me under the burning evening sun in your strong arms. I love you as I would love a father, and I shall think of you as I would think of a father. So I shall not resist any longer, if they take me away.

(*She bows her head.*)

AKKI. Go to Nebuchadnezzar, the King, my child.

POETS. Stay with us, Kurrubi. Stay with your poets.

CROWD. To Nebuchadnezzar. To Nebuchadnezzar.

(*They take* KURRUBI *with them out to the right.*)

POETS.   So the hope which tantalizes
           Snatches back the Grace we sought,

        Leaving the accursed ones nought,

        But ruined houses, corpses, bats.

KURRUBI. Farewell, Akki. Farewell, my poets.

POETS.   Eating gutter filth like rats,

        Hoping God would hear our anguished

        Prayer to let the maiden stay,

        We watched the Angel fly away.

        Gone the Grace for which we languished,

        We, the poets, man despises.

CROWD (*in the distance*). Kurrubi! Our Queen, Kurrubi!

    (AKKI *sits down gloomily by the range and stirs the soup.*)

AKKI. I've nothing against your tuneful complaints, O poets, except that they go a bit too far. 'Eating gutter filth like rats,' you sing, and then sit down cheerfully to a plate of my soup. Your despair is not entirely convincing. The art of cookery, rightly cultivated, is the only capacity of man for which nothing but good can be said, and it must not be mishandled by poets.

    (*An elderly man comes down the steps left, tall and thin and dressed formally in depressing black. He carries a small suitcase.*)

FORMAL ONE. Greetings, Beggar Akki. Greetings.

AKKI. What do you want?

FORMAL ONE. Breath-taking how that girl's improved. Makes one giddy. I watched from the bridge. Saw them leading her away.

AKKI (*angrily*). I would have made that child into the best female beggar in the world, and now she's just going to be a queen.

FORMAL ONE. Be a wild, strange marriage.

AKKI (*fuming*). Nebuchadnezzar will handle her with kid gloves.

FORMAL ONE. Be stormy. Wouldn't care to be there. When one thinks the King trampled her underfoot, horrifying to think what the next few nights'll be like.

AKKI. Trampled on her?

FORMAL ONE. Down by the Euphrates.

AKKI. By the Euphrates?

FORMAL ONE. That morning.

AKKI (*jumping up*). The beggar from Nineveh was the King?

FORMAL ONE. Was present. Saw it myself. Majesty disguised himself.

AKKI. Why?

FORMAL ONE. Talk you into joining the civil service. Then the Angel handed the girl over. Great moment. Solemn moment.

AKKI (*mopping his face, frightened*). A moment which might have ended unfortunately. I was lucky again that time. (*Mistrustfully.*) And who are you?

FORMAL ONE. Hangman.

(*The* POETS *disappear.*)

AKKI. Pleased to meet you. (*He shakes him by the hand.*)

FORMAL ONE. How do you do?

AKKI. You are in mufti.

FORMAL ONE. Not allowed to hang beggars in uniform. Very strict instructions.

AKKI. You'll have some soup with beef?

FORMAL ONE. Is that a trap? I don't think I ought.

AKKI (*innocently*). A trap?

FORMAL ONE. You've already escaped from the hangman of Lamash, from the hangman of Akkad, and from the hangman of Kish.

AKKI. They were only ducal hangmen, not royal ones. I only permit myself to be hanged by a King's hangman. Only the best is good enough. After all, I have my pride. Merely to do you honour I offer you a plate of soup with beef.

FORMAL ONE. Feel it an honour, assure you. With my salary am restricted to a very meagre diet. Only know soup with beef by hearsay.

AKKI. Sit on this throne of a long-since mouldered ruler of the world.

FORMAL ONE (*sitting down carefully*). Sure it's not a trap?

AKKI. Of course not.

FORMAL ONE. Incorruptible. Bribes, gold, carnal lusts, roll like

water off a duck's back. Once, as a young man, had to hang
a whole tribe in Mysia. Was offered herds of asses and
sheep. Useless. The Mysians were hanged in their thousands –
neat rows under the evening sun.

AKKI. Well believe it.

FORMAL ONE. Care to try me?

AKKI. No point in it.

FORMAL ONE. Do. Beg you will. Like nothing more than tests of
integrity.

AKKI. Right. Suppose I offered you a wife – a fresh, plump one?

FORMAL ONE. Out of the question.

AKKI. A nice, slippery, rosy little boy?

FORMAL ONE (*beaming*). Firm as a rock.

AKKI. Whisper a word in your ear, where all my treasure lies in
the Euphrates.

FORMAL ONE. Not interested. You'll hang. (*Triumphantly.*) They
call me Sidi the Unbribable.

AKKI. On the strength of that you can have the best bit of beef.
Soup! (*He hammers with his ladle on the pot, which gives out a
gong-like note. The* POETS *appear.*)

POETS. That note. That heavenly note!

(*Each of them brings a small bowl to the pot.*)

AKKI. The Poets, Distinguished One.

FORMAL ONE. A pleasure. Pure, unalloyed pleasure.

(*The* POETS *and the* FORMAL ONE *bow to each other. From
right,* OMAR *and* YUSSUF *come timidly in, also with small
bowls.*)

AKKI. Omar, the pickpocket, and Yussuf the burglar.

FORMAL ONE. Know them both. Got to hang them next week.

(*The muffled lepers come in from the right.*)

FIGURES (*croaking*). Hungry. We're hungry.

AKKI. Right, crows. There's your share.

(*He throws a large piece of meat to them and they vanish. The
soup has been served out and all begin to eat. The* FORMAL ONE
has tucked a red handkerchief into his collar.)

FORMAL ONE. Delicious, this soup. What a luxury feast for my poor old bones.

AKKI. You sound contented.

FORMAL ONE. I am. I am. Beef's delicious. An orgy. An unrestrained orgy, this meal. But you'll hang all the same.

(AKKI *refills his plate for him.*)

AKKI. Have another helping.

FORMAL ONE. Making pig of myself. Absolute pig.

AKKI. Try a bottle of the best Egyptian.

(*He pours wine out all round.*)

FORMAL ONE. Tongue's hanging out for it. Very thirsty. It's Bacchanalian, a thundering great Bacchanalian feast, this meal. Let us celebrate the hundredth time that your profession has been forbidden, and the tenth time they've tried to hang you. Been looking it up. Painstakingly accurate on dates of secret history. Keep a diary. World empires go, world empires come. Note it all down. And men? They change. They alter. Changes in employment, fashion, class relations, customs. Get confused without a diary to fix them. You alone don't change. Whatever happens, whoever persecutes you, you remain a beggar. A toast – a royal toast to you. (*They all drink.*) You hang on, just as the Prime Minister hangs on, with his thousand government departments. A toast – a royal toast to him, too. (*They all drink.*) He holds his own, as you hold your own. Rules kings, quietly rules the world with his Civil Service lists. And I am the third. A toast – a royal toast, finally, to me. (*They all drink.*) I, too, never alter, never change, don't migrate – remain a hangman. I shout it with pride to the heavens. Bureaucracy, beggary, and hanging – these three are the hidden framework of the world, within which all else rises and falls. (*All clink glasses.*)

AKKI. Drink up what's left.

FORMAL ONE. What's left. Tragic thought. Shocking thing that I should be here in an official capacity. The world will be a poorer place when I have done my business with you. Still, we come fresh to the dismal work. Soup's eaten, beef's gone, bottle's empty. One of those lamp-posts over there do you, or do you insist on hanging in the city park?

AKKI. What I'd like best would be a lamp-post in front of the King's palace.

FORMAL ONE. Noble thought, but difficult. Lamp-posts in front of the palace are reserved for members of the government. Simplest to hang you from the railing of the bridge. My assistant is up there already. Halef!

VOICE ABOVE. Yes, Master. Just coming.

(*A rope with a noose is lowered from above.* POETS, OMAR *and* YUSSUF *shriek and vanish.*)

FORMAL ONE. If you'll be so good.

(AKKI *mounts the king's throne in the middle of the stage.*)
Any last wishes?

(*He puts the noose round* AKKI's *neck, after softening it with soap.*)

AKKI. Whatever's left I bequeath to the Poets. The only puzzle is what to do with my second-hand bookshop in Flood Street.

FORMAL ONE. You have a second-hand bookshop?

(*The* POETS *reappear.*)

POETS. A second-hand bookshop?

AKKI. Begged last week. I was inspired with the very highest form of beggar's intuition and at the very top of my form that day.

FORMAL ONE. To own a second-hand bookshop is the dream of my life.

AKKI. I had no idea that you were interested in such things.

FORMAL ONE. To sit as an antiquary, surrounded by manuscripts and reading the classics seems to me the highest form of bliss.

AKKI (*shaking his head*). Remarkable. The hangmen of Lamash, Kish and Akkad were wild about culture, too.

FORMAL ONE. Lead a bitter, joyless life. Must be admitted, with bitter regret. Hanging all the time, and never getting any-where. At the most, an occasional perk from one of the ministers. When I think of your calling – what a contrast: daily intercourse with poets; roaring celebration dinners, of soup with beef.

AKKI. Great hangmen are fed fat, and only the lesser ones are left to starve. I will do a bargain with you. Swap your profession for my second-hand bookshop.

FORMAL ONE (*hesitating*). Do you want to become a hangman?

AKKI. It's the only profession I haven't yet begged off someone.

FORMAL ONE (*sinking down on the throne*). Good heavens!

AKKI (*anxious*). What's the matter, then, Sidi the Unbribable, prop of the hidden framework of society?

FORMAL ONE. Water, I beg you. One of my heart attacks coming on.

AKKI. Have some gin. It's better for you.

(*He steps carefully down from the throne, the noose still round his neck, and offers him a bottle.*)

FORMAL ONE. My head is going round. Oh, my head. Where then is honour? The characteristic Babylonian pride?

AKKI. What the devil have they to do with life under the arch of this bridge?

FORMAL ONE. Perfectly entitled to hand over my job to anyone I've got to hang. It's in the contract I signed in my youthful over-confidence, thinking I should get an opportunity to study the fine arts. Thought I'd make money. And yet – the lowliest worker, the most disreputable of ministers, the seediest of tramps I've had to hang over the dreary thousands of years never let himself be talked into becoming hangman in my place and saving his life. Proverbial Babylonian sense of honour – stronger than the desire to live.

AKKI. You know, I've always thought Babylon was going to ruin by letting its sense of honour run riot.

FORMAL ONE. Very fact that your proposal would release me from a painful way of life makes me all the more unsure of myself. You really want to exchange the most contemptible, meanest of professions for a second-hand bookshop?

AKKI. Your whole attitude to your job is wrong, Hangman. It is precisely the mean, the despised, the distasteful professions which must be raised up, so that they may be redeemed from their lowliness and stand for something. Otherwise they are lost. I, for example, was once a millionaire.

FORMAL ONE (*astounded*). A millionaire?

POETS. Tell the story, Beggar. Tell the story.

AKKI. Very well. Listen to the saga of my career as a beggar.

(*He takes his head out of the noose and holds on to it with his right hand.*)

When flowers were at their height, and the May moon was bright, in the middle of the night, I begged from a millionaire's daughter with art and skill, the entire contents of her papa's till. For I had quite determined that before I died I would put in its place the stinking rich man's pride. Hear then what the wise man did. I set myself with the greatest haste to let forests and properties run to waste. Drank up my money early and late; squandered herds and flocks – the whole estate. Got rid as fast as I was able of pictures and marbles, the farms and the stable. The carpets and tapestries went for a bet, the mirrors and the works of art, and yet, in spite of all I ran into debt. So by galloping spending, out of rhyme, out of reason, I made myself bankrupt by the end of the season. In the larder no bone, in the cellar no booze; no cash in my pocket and no more to lose. And in all this profusion, with the skill of a master, I involved in confusion and total disaster five other financiers, all multi-rich, whose shares fell to nothing, who lost every stitch. So you see, hangman, in my crusade against oppression, how I redeemed from discredit an evil profession.

POETS. And what became of the millionaire's daughter?

AKKI. She married the Official Receiver.

(*He tosses the noose in the air and the rope is drawn up.*)

When after that in my sarcophagus I lay, pondering human destiny night and day; why mankind was lost in sin; why the mean always win; in my inspired, masterly fashion I satisfied

my ruling passion to have before I grew much older another
adventure, this time as a soldier. By being courtly and charming and cunningly disarming, by working the lobbies and
flattering the snobbies, by under-dogs kicking, back-
scratching, boot-licking, and needling and wheedling – by
every device I could use, to be brief, I begged the appointment
as Commander-in-Chief. With the conviction I was filled
that soldiers never should be killed. So I devoted all my great
military talent to relieving my troops of the need to be gallant.
Against Akkad I marched with three hundred thousand men;
and when we saw the enemy we marched them back again,
thereby achieving what generals never can – losing a battle
without losing a man.

FORMAL ONE. What an achievement! But how did you do it?
Generally defeats are the most costly of battles.

AKKI. I omitted to send out orders for the attack.

FORMAL ONE. Remarkable. Astonishing.

AKKI. So you see how mean professions should be exploited.
Some good can be got out of every one.

FORMAL ONE (*cautiously*). And you think that, as a bookseller,
I should be able to have soup with beef? With a feast like that
once a month I should be content – even delighted.

AKKI. You'll eat soup with beef three times a week and a goose
on Sundays.

FORMAL ONE. What a change! Orgiastic reversal of fortune!

AKKI. Your robe, hangman.

FORMAL ONE. In this suitcase. After you, I was to have hanged the
geographers and astronomers.

AKKI. Hanging means letting go.

FORMAL ONE. You'll miss the poets dreadfully.

AKKI. On the contrary. I rejoice in the thought of the silence of
the royal dungeons.

(*He puts on the* HANGMAN's *cloak.*)

POET (*shocked*). Don't put that garment on.

ANOTHER. Don't dishonour yourself.

264

A THIRD. Don't become a hangman.

ANOTHER. Remain an object for poetry.

AKKI. Is it to be your everlasting ill-fortune, poets of Babylon,
that you never perceive the hour of danger? You do not fore-
see the horror that is coming upon us. Kurrubi seeks a beggar
and she will find a king. Every day and night there are fresh
arrests, the army has marched off to the north, and the State
is claiming infallibility; it has set itself to catch the lot of us.
Have I got to relate to you my last and most bitter saga? The
saga of the weapons of the weak?

A VOICE. Your last and bitterest saga.

POETS. Before you escape – before you vanish.

AKKI. To withstand the world the weak must know with certainty which way they go. The strong are strong and without
truth. Essential we should face this truth. Whoso a hero's death
would seek betrays the real strength of the weak. We have to
learn one simple rule: to meet strength with strength is the
act of a fool. Hear then the Beggar, ragged, tattered, harried
by the police, tortured and battered ... In this world the
powerful man seizes your house, your wife, whatever he
pleases. Only what he despises escapes, and the clever can
learn from this; that even the clever cannot fight a strong man
unarmed; that only he who is nothing and has nothing remains unharmed. So draw this conclusion: if you wish to
grow old pretend to be stupid. Attack from within. Be
already in the cells before the trials begin. Slip by, eyes downcast, as boon-companion, as slave, as poet or debt-collector.
Be lowly and all the walls will go down before you. Put up
with insults, walk delicately, and bury for the time being all
the wildness of hope and the warmth of love, all the sorrows
and all the graces, all long-suffering and all kindliness – bury
all beneath the hangman's cloak.

(*He pulls the black mask over his face and stands there, a red-
cloaked hangman.*)

265

ACT THREE

It is not necessary to say very much about the Throne Room, which is the scene of the Third Act. Its luxury, its sophistication, its secluded remoteness may be taken for granted, and also an element of cruel and bestial barbarity. Set in a background of the highest culture, this element of negro barbarism is apparent, for example, in the bloodstained standards of the Empire's conquering armies. A giant screen, which stretches out of sight on either side, divides the stage into a fore- and background, and here and there giant stone statues gaze down on the scene. The throne, left, in front of the screen, is raised on steps. On it sits NEBU-CHADNEZZAR, with his feet resting on NIMROD's shoulders, the head appearing between them. There is a door, left, in the screen leading to the back of the stage, and doors in the side walls, left and right. Forward right, at the edge of the orchestra, two stools.

NIMROD. Now, now, King Nebuchadnezzar, why do you sit in your palace staring at nothing day and night and why stamp ceaselessly with your feet on my shoulders?

NEBUCHADNEZZAR. I love Kurrubi.

NIMROD. In that case you are in love with a girl you swapped for your footstool.

NEBUCHADNEZZAR. I'll have you whipped.

NIMROD. Carry on. Can you torment me as much as I'm tormenting you?

NEBUCHADNEZZAR. Silence, head between my feet.

NIMROD. Very well.

(*Silence.*)

NEBUCHADNEZZAR. Say something.

NIMROD. You see? You can't even stand my silence.

266

NEBUCHADNEZZAR. Talk of Kurrubi. You have seen her. She gave you a drink out of the filthy waters of the Euphrates.

NIMROD. You're jealous of me.

NEBUCHADNEZZAR. I'm jealous.

NIMROD. She was veiled. But through her veils I saw her beauty before you perceived it.

NEBUCHADNEZZAR. Her beauty fills the whole city of Babylon with a heavenly glory and the songs of her lovers can be heard even within my palace.

(*A page can be heard singing outside.*)

PAGE.   She was not for the King,
                    The heavenly maid,

NIMROD. Do you hear? Even your page is turned poet.

PAGE.   Dressed in golden light,
                    In the gutter she stayed.

NEBUCHADNEZZAR (*quietly*). Hangman!!

(*From the left* AKKI *walks in in his hangman's uniform.*)

AKKI. Majesty.

NEBUCHADNEZZAR. Kill that poetic page.

PAGE.   We burn for her sake
                    Who comforts a beggar –

AKKI. With pleasure, Majesty. Energetic measures are clearly called for.

(*He goes out right.*)

PAGE.   The dazzling snow flake,
                    From the snow of the ...

(*The voice breaks off suddenly.*)

NEBUCHADNEZZAR (*quietly*). All who love Kurrubi shall die.

NIMROD. In that case you'll have to exterminate the whole human race.

NEBUCHADNEZZAR. I'll have your eyes put out.

NIMROD. Put out my eyes with red-hot irons, stuff my ears with molten lead, stop my mouth; you still cannot tear the memory out of my body.

NEBUCHADNEZZAR. Prime Minister!

PRIME MINISTER. Majesty?

NEBUCHADNEZZAR. Clap the ex-King into our deepest dungeon.

PRIME MINISTER. I am the lawgiver. In this capacity I have already laid down that by definition the King's feet must rest on the shoulders of his predecessor. If this definition goes, the King goes with it.

NEBUCHADNEZZAR. Then alter the definition.

PRIME MINISTER. Impossible. All five hundred thousand paragraphs of the Babylonian legal code would become worthless, since all develop logically from the definition of Kingship. It would be complete chaos.

(PRIME MINISTER *withdraws*. NIMROD *laughs*.)

NIMROD. That's what he always used to say to me, too.

NEBUCHADNEZZAR. And each time the number of the paragraphs has grown. They have become innumerable.

NIMROD. So has the number of government departments.

NEBUCHADNEZZAR. Nothing is left to me except a footstool.

NIMROD. And your son, the Crown Prince.

(*From the left at the back a dandified figure of an idiot dances, grinning and cartwheeling, across the stage and out again right.* NEBUCHADNEZZAR *covers his face with his hands.*)

NEBUCHADNEZZAR. Your son.

NIMROD. Our son, the heir to all our power. Nobody knows who begat him. If you remember, we both slipped into his mother's bed when we were drunk.

NEBUCHADNEZZAR. We are chained together, you and I.

NIMROD. For ever and ever.

NEBUCHADNEZZAR. It has been so for thousands of years.

BOTH. I beneath and you on top. I on top and you beneath. For ever and ever.

(*Silence.*)

NEBUCHADNEZZAR. Hangman!

(AKKI *comes in*.)

AKKI. Majesty?

268

NEBUCHADNEZZAR. Have the geographers and astronomers been dealt with?

AKKI. The dungeons are cleansed of their presence.

NEBUCHADNEZZAR. Has begging now been stamped out?

AKKI. Entirely.

NEBUCHADNEZZAR. The Beggar Akki?

AKKI. Transformed. Were he to appear before Your Majesty, you would find him unrecognizable.

NEBUCHADNEZZAR. Strung up?

AKKI. He has gone up in the world. He moves now in the highest circles.

NEBUCHADNEZZAR. That great patron of the poets will hardly have got to Heaven.

AKKI. A little lower than that.

NEBUCHADNEZZAR. The beggars have been rooted out. For the first time since the Flood there is perceptible progress. Mankind begins to take on clearer forms – to achieve a greater humanity. On the social plane the worst abuses have been eliminated. The next step towards a rational society is to move against either the poets or the theologians.

(AKKI *shudders*.)

AKKI. Above all, no poets. It has been so peaceful down there in the dungeons, and now even pages are spouting poetry.

NEBUCHADNEZZAR. You did not kill that page?

AKKI. Court ceremonial only permits pages to be hanged during the hours of darkness. I beg that Your Majesty will proceed against the theologians. They are much pleasanter.

NEBUCHADNEZZAR. A talk with the Senior Theologian should settle that question. Do your duty and have the State gallows set up.

(AKKI *goes*.)

Utnapishtim!

(*The Senior Theologian*, UTNAPISHTIM, *comes in right. He is a venerable old man*.)

UTNAPISHTIM. What is your will, King Nebuchadnezzar?

NEBUCHADNEZZAR. Spit in the face of the man between my feet.

UTNAPISHTIM. According to the law which you laid down, I am excused this ceremony.

NEBUCHADNEZZAR. In that case, curse my footstool to all eternity.

UTNAPISHTIM. My duty is to pray for the salvation of men.

(NIMROD *laughs.* NEBUCHADNEZZAR *pulls himself together.*)

NEBUCHADNEZZAR. You may sit.

UTNAPISHTIM. I thank you.

NEBUCHADNEZZAR. I need advice.

UTNAPISHTIM. I am listening.

NEBUCHADNEZZAR (*after some hesitation*). You were present on that painful occasion the other morning when the Angel appeared on the bank of the Euphrates.

UTNAPISHTIM. For a theologian a bewildering experience. I have set myself against belief in angels, and have written various theses condemning it. Two professors of theology have even been burnt for holding it. It seemed to me that God needed no agents, since He is all-powerful. Now I find myself almost compelled to revise my dogma in respect of angels: a difficult undertaking, as even a layman may understand, since the omnipotence of God must naturally not be called in question.

NEBUCHADNEZZAR. I don't understand you.

UTNAPISHTIM. It does not matter, Your Majesty. Even professional theologians scarcely ever understand each other.

NEBUCHADNEZZAR (*embarrassed*). You saw how I kicked that girl.

UTNAPISHTIM. It upset me very much.

NEBUCHADNEZZAR. I love that girl, Utnapishtim.

UTNAPISHTIM. We all love the child.

NEBUCHADNEZZAR. The whole city is singing songs to her.

UTNAPISHTIM. I know. Even I have attempted some verses in praise of her.

NEBUCHADNEZZAR. You, too? The oldest living man.

(*Silence.*)

Heaven has insulted me.

UTNAPISHTIM. You are only jealous of yourself, King Nebuchadnezzar.

(*The* IDIOT *passes across the back of the stage in huge cartwheels, right to left.* UTNAPISHTIM *bows.*)

NEBUCHADNEZZAR (*embarrassed*). Speak on.

UTNAPISHTIM. If we wish to understand, O King, the behaviour of the universe, which is, I admit, often puzzling, we must start out with the assumption that Heaven is always right.

NEBUCHADNEZZAR (*gloomily*). In this conflict between Heaven and myself you are taking Heaven's side. I am sorry, but I shall have to have you executed. Hangman!

(AKKI *comes in left.*)

AKKI (*joyfully*). So it's to be the theologians, Majesty. Allow me.

UTNAPISHTIM (*rising with great dignity*). As you will.

NEBUCHADNEZZAR (*shocked*). Sit down again, my dear Utnapishtim. I'm not in such a hurry as all that. The hangman can wait a bit longer. Meanwhile, talk further.

AKKI. I implore you not to weaken, Majesty. With theologians one must be firm.

UTNAPISHTIM (*undisturbed*). You seem to think that Heaven has allowed itself to be deceived by you and mistook you that night for a beggar. That is ridiculous. You confused the Angel, but God, who sent him, knew to whom He was giving the girl. To you, King Nebuchadnezzar. Nothing else is possible, since God is not only all-powerful, but all-knowing, as I have proved.

NEBUCHADNEZZAR (*gloomily*). Heaven intended Kurrubi for the poorest of mankind.

UTNAPISHTIM. Heaven's words should never be taken literally, but must be understood against a general background. All men are pretty well equally lowly if we remember the enormous differences in outlook with which Heaven regards events here below. By your own folly you have frustrated God's intention to present you with His grace.

271

NEBUCHADNEZZAR (*amicably, after a short silence*). All that about hanging you is, of course, nonsense.

UTNAPISHTIM. I thank you.

NEBUCHADNEZZAR. The study of theology must be insisted on throughout my empire. I shall have all other branches of learning forbidden.

UTNAPISHTIM. Praiseworthy as your zeal is, it should not be carried too far.

NEBUCHADNEZZAR. In that case, it is the poets who will now be hanged.

UTNAPISHTIM. I am sorry for that.

NEBUCHADNEZZAR. The perfect State cannot allow the spreading of untruths. Poets advertise feelings which do not exist, stories they make up themselves, and sentences which don't make sense. I should have thought that theology, too, was interested in preventing this.

UTNAPISHTIM. Not unreservedly.

NEBUCHADNEZZAR. Hangman.
    (AKKI *comes in left.*)

AKKI. I come – I run. The State gallows is all ready for the Senior Theologian.

NEBUCHADNEZZAR. Have the poets arrested.

AKKI (*shocked*). The poets?

NEBUCHADNEZZAR. They are to be liquidated.

AKKI. Then let it be only the epic poets. They are relatively the quietest.

NEBUCHADNEZZAR. Lyric poets and playwrights too.
    (*Resigned,* AKKI *departs.*)
That should put an end to the conflict between Church and State.

UTNAPISHTIM. Once again.

NEBUCHADNEZZAR. And you think I ought to marry the girl.

UTNAPISHTIM. I can't think why you didn't do so long ago.
    (*The* PRIME MINISTER *comes in right.*)

PRIME MINISTER. Majesty! The Angel has touched down in the

272

city park and is collecting coconuts and humming birds as he hops from palm to palm.

(*One of the Senior Theoligan's* SECRETARIES *comes in, also right, and whispers something in his ear.*)

UTNAPISHTIM (*rejoicing*). My secretary informs me that conversions to the Established Church are suddenly surpassing the wildest expectations.

(*The* SECRETARY *unrolls an enormous list signed by all the converts.*)

PRIME MINISTER. From the political point of view this unearthly appearance is not so easy to assess. The people are intoxicated. They are storming into the palace courtyard, and demanding that Your Majesty should marry Kurrubi. The girl is being brought here in the Banker Enggibi's litter, crowned with flowers.

UTNAPISHTIM. A revolt?

PRIME MINISTER. A spontaneous uprising which shows some indication of a sound Babylonian conservative character, but which nevertheless gives some cause for anxiety.

NEBUCHADNEZZAR AND NIMROD (*together*). Mow the people down.

PRIME MINISTER. An uprising need not necessarily be suppressed if it can be diverted in a direction advantageous to oneself.

(NEBUCHADNEZZAR *and* NIMROD *both adopt attitudes of profound thought.*)

NEBUCHADNEZZAR AND NIMROD (*together*). I am listening.

NEBUCHADNEZZAR. What's all this taking up my words, Footstool?

NIMROD. Not only yours – our throne is threatened.

(*Both resume their thinking postures.*)

NEBUCHADNEZZAR AND NIMROD. Our throne is threatened. We are waiting for your proposals, Prime Minister.

PRIME MINISTER. Your Majesties. The throne of Babylon, this noble institution which has come down to us from time immemorial, founded by Gilgamish, our national hero, this true centre of the whole earth, round which the peoples have gathered themselves ...

NEBUCHADNEZZAR AND NIMROD. What a striking and brilliant exposition.

PRIME MINISTER. ... has in the course of thousands of years fallen into such discredit that it is generally spoken of as the shabbiest institution of all time.

NEBUCHADNEZZAR AND NIMROD. You dare to say so! Hang- ...

(AKKI *appears left, but is waved away by the* PRIME MINISTER.)

PRIME MINISTER. There is no need for Your Majesties to get upset. This is a statement of political fact, not a personal opinion.

NEBUCHADNEZZAR AND NIMROD. You may continue.

PRIME MINISTER. In the best circles in Babylon it is fashionable to be Republican. This great throng packed in the Inner Court is only a symptom. It must be dealt with firmly, or our world empire will vanish away.

NEBUCHADNEZZAR AND NIMROD. Like snow in the north at the coming of spring.

UTNAPISHTIM. What do you propose, Prime Minister?

PRIME MINISTER. This girl, Kurrubi, whose beauty stirs even my old bones, should immediately be crowned queen.

UTNAPISHTIM. Religion and political expediency see most happily eye to eye.

PRIME MINISTER. Never before have events played so positively into our hands. As a politician I am delighted. We have the chance to use religion to stabilize a structure which stands on very weak political foundations. Today everybody believes both in Kurrubi and in God. If we make this girl Queen, the Republican idea will be obliterated for some thousands of years. We have only to give way to the people's will and all will be in splendid order. Furthermore, we may hope before very long to have a new heir to the throne. For, although the efficiency of my Civil Service is such that no great inconvenience would be caused by a ruler of somewhat limited

274

capacity, this is naturally from the political standpoint not to be desired.

NEBUCHADNEZZAR AND NIMROD. Bring the maiden in.

(*The* PRIME MINISTERS *and the* SENIOR THEOLOGIAN *make to go through the door in the screen.*)

NEBUCHADNEZZAR. But first I must have some speech with my hangman.

(UTNAPISHTIM *and the* PRIME MINISTER *stand, puzzled.*)

UTNAPISHTIM. Your Majesty, what can the hangman have to do with such a joyous occasion?

NEBUCHADNEZZAR. There is no occasion in my empire with which the hangman has not something to do, Senior Theologian. You may go.

(*The* MINISTERS *go.* AKKI *comes in left. There is a noise of cheerful singing.*)

AKKI. Majesty?

NEBUCHADNEZZAR. What's all that singing, Hangman?

AKKI. It's the poets. They are striking up an ode.

NEBUCHADNEZZAR. They are singing remarkably cheerfully.

AKKI. The poets of Babylon have lived so tragic a life that they rejoice at the thought of the next.

NEBUCHADNEZZAR. Come closer.

AKKI. Certainly, Majesty.

NEBUCHADNEZZAR. Close to me. You may take off your mask.

AKKI. I prefer not.

NEBUCHADNEZZAR. I don't feel safe unless I have you somewhere near me.

AKKI. But my duties, Majesty. I'm busy with a sort of gigantic spring-cleaning of the dungeons.

NEBUCHADNEZZAR. You are hanging the poets?

(*A* POET *staggers on to the stage, left, drinking out of an enormous tankard.* AKKI *waves him vigorously away and he staggers off.*)

AKKI. I'm altering their circumstances for them.

NEBUCHADNEZZAR. I want to talk to you as man to man, as to

a brother. You are the poorest paid of all the officials of my court and you have the most to do. I am going to give you a cheque for a thousand gold pieces.

(*He takes out a cheque book.* AKKI *hands him a pen and he writes a cheque.*)

AKKI. As long as it doesn't bounce.

NEBUCHADNEZZAR. You are the only person in the whole of my empire who does not misrepresent himself – who is what he seems to be.

AKKI. I think Your Majesty goes a bit far.

NEBUCHADNEZZAR. You are the only one I can trust. I am about to receive the girl I love. I want to test her. It is possible that she does not love me any more. She's been knocking about with some poets, and above all, with the beggar, Akki.

AKKI. What do you want me to do?

NEBUCHADNEZZAR. Kill the girl if she doesn't love me any more.

(*The* PRIME MINISTER *and* UTNAPISHTIM *lead* KURRUBI *in through the door in the screen. She is barefooted and her clothes are torn.*)

PRIME MINISTER (*entranced*). The maiden.

(AKKI *disappears.* NEBUCHADNEZZAR *and* NIMROD *cover their faces with gold masks.*)

UTNAPISHTIM. Come, dear daughter.

PRIME MINISTER. Come in, my dear child.

(*The* PRIME MINISTER *and* UTNAPISHTIM *draw back, right.*)

NEBUCHADNEZZAR AND NIMROD. We bid you welcome.

(KURRUBI *stands still, terrified.*)

KURRUBI. Twins!

NEBUCHADNEZZAR AND NIMROD. You stand before the King of Babylon.

(*The* IDIOT *bounds across the back of the stage.*)

KURRUBI (*frightened*). Who is that?

NEBUCHADNEZZAR AND NIMROD. A harmless creature who hops about the palace from time to time.

(KURRUBI *creeps tentatively a little nearer.*)

276

KURRUBI. Are you the mightiest of mankind?

NEBUCHADNEZZAR AND NIMROD. The mightiest.

KURRUBI. What will you do with me?

NEBUCHADNEZZAR AND NIMROD. The Babylonians wish you to become my wife.

KURRUBI. I cannot become your wife.

NEBUCHADNEZZAR. You love another?

(NEBUCHADNEZZAR *waves and* AKKI *appears behind* KURRUBI.)

KURRUBI. I love another.

NEBUCHADNEZZAR. One of the poets? They seem to be the people who are most preoccupied with you.

KURRUBI. I love the poets. They're so nice.

NEBUCHADNEZZAR. There are two possible opinions about that.

KURRUBI. But I love them only as one does love poets.

NEBUCHADNEZZAR. You've been seen about with an old swindler and teller of fairy stories in the streets and under the bridges.

(AKKI *stamps his foot in a rage.*)

KURRUBI. I love the beggar Akki as one would love a father.

NEBUCHADNEZZAR (*relieved*). And whom do you love as a girl loves a young man – a beloved?

KURRUBI. I love a beggar with a complicated name, great King.

(*At a sign from* NEBUCHADNEZZAR, AKKI *withdraws.*)

NEBUCHADNEZZAR. The beggar from Nineveh?

KURRUBI (*delighted*). You know him?

NEBUCHADNEZZAR. Forget that luckless young man. He was tragic, he was in despair, and he was lonely.

KURRUBI. I cannot forget him.

NEBUCHADNEZZAR. He has disappeared. His name is not to be found on any of the official lists.

KURRUBI. I shall go on seeking him for ever.

NEBUCHADNEZZAR. It was a ghost that appeared in the Euphrates mist. Apart from the few on the quay, nobody saw him again.

KURRUBI. I saw him.

277

NEBUCHADNEZZAR. One sometimes sees what one imagines.

KURRUBI. I put my arms round him. I kissed him.

NEBUCHADNEZZAR. You are seeking somebody who does not exist.

KURRUBI. He does exist, because I love him.

NEBUCHADNEZZAR. You love one whom you will never find.

KURRUBI. I shall find the one I love some time, somewhere.

NEBUCHADNEZZAR. Then go.

KURRUBI (*bowing*). I thank you, great King.

(NEBUCHADNEZZAR *and* NIMROD *unmask.* KURRUBI, *as she looks up, recognizes* NIMROD *first.*)

KURRUBI. The prisoner I gave drink to!

NIMROD. I am he.

(*She recognizes* NEBUCHADNEZZAR *and gives a cry.*)

KURRUBI. My beggar!

NEBUCHADNEZZAR. I am he.

KURRUBI. The King!

NEBUCHADNEZZAR. Who never doubted your love.

KURRUBI. My beloved.

(*Pale and uncomprehending, she stares at him as he comes down to her from the throne.*)

NEBUCHADNEZZAR. The beggar whom you seek does not exist because he never did exist. He was the figment of one night who disappeared into the void. You have lost him and found me. You loved a beggar. Now love a King. For the kicks I gave you I now give you the whole earth, since my army is marching against those villages beyond the Lebanon. You shall sit on my right hand with your foot on Nimrod. The great ones of my empire shall bow down before you, and I will make sacrifices to Heaven such as cannot be counted.

(*He makes to lead her to the throne.*)

KURRUBI (*as though waking up*). You are the King. But the Angel gave me to you because you were a beggar.

NEBUCHADNEZZAR. I was never a beggar. I was always a King. Then I was merely disguised.

278

KURRUBI. It is now that you are disguised.

NEBUCHADNEZZAR. You are confused, dear girl.

KURRUBI. By the Euphrates you were the man I loved. Now you are a ghost who frightens me.

NEBUCHADNEZZAR. You are confusing appearances with reality.

KURRUBI. It is only as a beggar that you are real.

NEBUCHADNEZZAR. It is only as a beggar that I am a sham.

KURRUBI. Come away with me.

NEBUCHADNEZZAR. My dear Kurrubi, I have the world to rule.

NIMROD (*scoffingly*). I have the world to rule.

> (*He tries to get on to the throne, but* NEBUCHADNEZZAR *gets there first.*)

NEBUCHADNEZZAR. Down, you.

> (*He forces* NIMROD *back into the position of a footstool.* KURRUBI *comes close to the two struggling monarchs and flings her arms round* NEBUCHADNEZZAR.)

KURRUBI. Let this horrible dream go. You are no king. Be yourself again, the beggar you always were. I love you. Let us get out of this stone house and this city of stones. I will beg for you and care for you. We will wander across the great plains to the lands the Angel told me about. Crossing the desert we shall not be afraid. At night we will sleep on the ground clasped in each other's arms, sleep under the trees beneath a heaven full of stars.

NEBUCHADNEZZAR. Senior Theologian.

> (UTNAPISHTIM *comes through the door right.*)

UTNAPISHTIM. What is your will?

NEBUCHADNEZZAR. The ex-King almost succeeded just now in getting on to the throne, and this girl demands that I should become a beggar. She will not understand that I never was a beggar. All this knocking around with an Angel and then all those poets has filled her head with nonsense. Talk to her. She doesn't know much about human affairs.

> (*He sits down discontentedly on the throne. The* SENIOR THEOLOGIAN *leads* KURRUBI *to the right, where they both sit down.*)

UTNAPISHTIM (*kindly*). I am Babylon's Senior Theologian, my child.

KURRUBI (*joyful*). Oh, then you think about God?

UTNAPISHTIM. I am always thinking about God.

KURRUBI. Do you know Him well?

UTNAPISHTIM (*somewhat regretfully*). Not nearly so well as you do, my child, since you were close to His countenance. I am but human. And God has hidden Himself from us humans. We may not see Him. We may only seek for Him. Do you love the King, my child?

KURRUBI. I love the beggar the Angel gave me to.

UTNAPISHTIM. The King and this beggar are one and the same. Therefore you also love the King.

KURRUBI (*sinking her head*). I can only love the beggar.

UTNAPISHTIM (*smiling*). And so you want the King to become a beggar?

KURRUBI. I only want to do what the Angel told me.

UTNAPISHTIM. Who brought you to a beggar who is a King. I can understand that you are confused. You can't make up your mind now whether you ought to be a Queen or the King a beggar. Is not that so, my child?

KURRUBI. It is so, reverend Father.

UTNAPISHTIM. You see, my child, how much easier everything is when we just talk it over quietly. What we have to find out now is what Heaven really intended, haven't we?

KURRUBI. Yes, reverend Father.

(*Two* POETS *totter in with tankards and large mutton bones, but are caught by* AKKI *and thrown out before the others notice them. Only* NEBUCHADNEZZAR *makes an impatient move in their direction, when the noise disturbs him, but without taking his eyes off* UTNAPISHTIM *and* KURRUBI, *to whom he listens, bending forward.*)

UTNAPISHTIM. When I was young, at the time of the Flood, I used to think that Heaven demanded absolute obedience from us, as we theologians put it in the curious language we talk.

The older I get, the more clearly I can see that this conception is not entirely correct. Heaven demands from man above all what is possible. It knows that it cannot bring us to our perfect stature at a single stroke; that to try would be merely to destroy us. So Heaven loves us in our very imperfection. It is patient with us and is content always to lead us lovingly back to the right way, as a father does with his small son, and so gradually to educate us over thousands of years.

KURRUBI. Yes, reverend Father.

UTNAPISHTIM. Therefore we men make a mistake if we see Heaven as a strict master who makes impossible demands upon us which would only create confusion and do widespread mischief. Do you understand me, my child?

KURRUBI. You are very good to me, reverend Father.

(*The* PRIME MINISTER *appears in the screen door.*)

PRIME MINISTER. May one congratulate?

NEBUCHADNEZZAR. We are just talking it over.

(PRIME MINISTER *goes. At a sign from* UTNAPISHTIM, NEBUCHADNEZZAR *comes down from the throne and across to the other two, who have stood up.*)

UTNAPISHTIM. So it is now with you and the King. If you interpret Heaven's commandment literally and demand that the King, because he received you as a beggar, must now become a beggar again, all human order will be thrown into confusion. Men want to see grace bestowed on their Kings, not on their beggars. They want to see you as Queen, and not as a poor thing huddled in rags. And you can be a help to men, my child, for they need your help. You can lead the King in the right ways, and he will do good with your help. Marry him, so that our prayers for peace and righteousness may be heard.

(*He is about to join their hands when the* PRIME MINISTER *bursts in.*)

PRIME MINISTER. We shall have to negotiate. They are throwing stones at the giant statue of His Majesty with the changeable head.

UTNAPISHTIM. And my statue?

PRIME MINISTER. Unharmed, and covered with roses.

UTNAPISHTIM. Thank God. Conversions to the Established Church will continue.

(NIMROD *has taken the chance to slip on to the throne.*)

NIMROD. The army will attack at once.

PRIME MINISTER. How can it? It has marched off against the villages beyond the Lebanon and only fifty men of the Palace Guard remain.

UTNAPISHTIM. So Babylon falls victim to the everlasting desire for world conquest.

NEBUCHADNEZZAR (*who has taken* NIMROD's *place, sadly*). I had hardly become a King and here I am, a footstool again. There has never been so swift a change in the order of things. Clearly, there is a universal catastrophe impending.

PRIME MINISTER. Your Majesty exaggerates a little. People like ourselves will always come out on top somehow.

NIMROD AND NEBUCHADNEZZAR. What is to be done, Prime Minister?

PRIME MINISTER. We must ask ourselves first, Your Majesties, what the fundamental cause of this rebellion is.

NIMROD AND NEBUCHADNEZZAR. Ask yourself, Prime Minister.

PRIME MINISTER. Is it simply the wish to see Kurrubi as Queen which has brought the Babylonians out on the streets? Though the shouts of the people would seem to suggest this, the experienced politician takes a different view. The real reason lies elsewhere. It is simply the appearance of the Angel which has undermined the authority of the State.

UTNAPISHTIM. I must protest. Not only will it be possible, with a little careful interpretation, to make the Angel's utterances, which I have collected, theologically acceptable, but there is nothing harmful to the State in them and nothing revolutionary.

PRIME MINISTER. Your Eminence misunderstands. I am not criticizing the Angel, but his appearance on earth. It is pure poison. At this moment, for example, he is hovering over the Hanging Gardens and diving southwards head first into the sea. I ask the question: Is this a way to behave? A State and sound government are only possible if earth remains earth and Heaven Heaven; since earth presents reality which has to be dealt with by politicians, and Heaven is a charming theory of the theologians about which nobody else needs to bother very much. If, however, Heaven becomes a reality, as now through the appearance of the Angel, human order collapses, since, faced by a visible Heaven, the State is inevitably reduced to a farce. And here we have before us the result of this cosmic carelessness: the people have risen against us. Why? Because the marriage was not solemnized quickly enough. It only needs an Angel to flutter round and all respect for us vanishes.

NIMROD AND NEBUCHADNEZZAR. We are greatly enlightened.

PRIME MINISTER. The best thing, therefore, is to deny the Angel officially.

(*Consternation.*)

UTNAPISHTIM. Impossible. He has been publicly seen.

PRIME MINISTER. We will give out that it was the actor, Urshnabi, from the Court Theatre.

NEBUCHADNEZZAR. What a contradiction! Just now you were pleased with the appearance of the Angel.

NIMROD. You were going to use religion to stabilize the political structure and stamp out Republicanism.

PRIME MINISTER (*bowing*). The more often a politician contradicts himself, the greater he is.

UTNAPISHTIM. I'm not very happy theologically about the Angel, either. But the Established Church owes its revival to him.

PRIME MINISTER. We will forbid anyone to leave it again on pain of death.

UTNAPISHTIM. Though I have nothing against making certain

concessions to the atheists, I'd rather have half the national revenue.

PRIME MINISTER. Impossible, Eminence.

UTNAPISHTIM. In that case I refuse to deny the Angel.

PRIME MINISTER. The revolution threatens us all.

UTNAPISHTIM. Not me, Prime Minister. It is a rebellion against the monarchy, not against the Church. I am at the moment the most popular politician in Babylon. Half the national revenue, or I set up a Church State.

PRIME MINISTER. A third.

UTNAPISHTIM. Half.

PRIME MINISTER. In that case I should have to demand the most strenuous denial, your Eminence.

UTNAPISHTIM. It will be given out from every pulpit.

NEBUCHADNEZZAR (*still hesitating*). But I wanted to make my peace with Heaven.

UTNAPISHTIM. It shall be done, Majesty. That is privately perfectly possible. Just get married. Nothing could be more pleasing to Heaven than a happy marriage.

PRIME MINISTER. I have nothing whatever against this reconciliation, so long as it takes place genuinely in private. But I must insist that in future the appearance of Angels must be properly organized.

NIMROD AND NEBUCHADNEZZAR. Then all we have to agree about is where Kurrubi came from.

PRIME MINISTER. We announce her as the lost daughter of the Duke of Lamash.

NIMROD AND NEBUCHADNEZZAR. Have the necessary documents prepared immediately.

PRIME MINISTER (*producing a parchment*). My office has already prepared them.

NIMROD AND NEBUCHADNEZZAR. Let the proper steps be taken at once.

(*The* CAPTAIN OF THE GUARD *appears at the screen door, badly cut about.*)

CAPTAIN. We are beaten. The Guards are going over to the people. They're attacking the doors with a battering ram.

(*The first blows of the battering ram can be heard.*)

NIMROD. We are lost.

(*He runs from the throne, but is stopped by the* PRIME MINISTER *and the* SENIOR THEOLOGIAN.)

PRIME MINISTER AND UTNAPISHTIM (*together*). Steadiness, Majesty, coolness. So long as we are in a position to plan official action, nothing is lost.

(*They lead* NIMROD *back to the throne which* NEBUCHAD-NEZZAR *has meanwhile occupied.*)

NEBUCHADNEZZAR (*delighted*). Now *I*'m on top again.

PRIME MINISTER (*formally, to* KURRUBI). My dear child. To do you honour and to give expression to his love for you, His Majesty nominates you the lost daughter of the Duke of Lamash; the daughter, that is, of a somewhat unfortunate but highly honoured politician who last year – er – passed on. He put you out – and this explains your present poverty – on the bank of the Euphrates in a basket, in circumstances which the historians still have to work out. This is an official document, there can be no further doubt about your origin. We beg, therefore, that you will confirm this to the people.

KURRUBI (*horrified*). To all the people?

PRIME MINISTER. This formality is essential. We will go on to the balcony with ten trumpeters immediately.

KURRUBI. I am to deny that God created me?

UTNAPISHTIM. Naturally not, my dear child.

KURRUBI. That the Angel brought me down to Earth?

UTNAPISHTIM. But no, my dearest daughter. We know where you came from and are thankful to have experienced this miracle. None of us demands that you should stifle this knowledge in your heart. On the contrary, preserve it in your soul as a secret, as your private, sacred knowledge of the truth, as I myself shall preserve it. What we are asking from you, my child, is merely a paraphrase of the wonderful truth for publication to people who will turn anything out of the ordinary to crude sensationalism.

KURRUBI. Honoured Father, you said you thought always about God. You cannot allow this.

UTNAPISHTIM (*unhappily*). It is better so, my child.

KURRUBI. Then you agree with the Prime Minister?

UTNAPISHTIM. Not at all, my dearest daughter. But it is my duty to save Heaven from injuring itself. The heads of the Babylonians are stuffed with superstitions about spirits with many arms and Gods with wings, and my theology, which teaches one God, is only gradually winning the upper hand. An Angel would confuse them and open the way to immature ideas. God's Messenger has swooped down all too soon on us children.

(KURRUBI *turns to* NEBUCHADNEZZAR.)

KURRUBI. You hear what they are asking of me, my beloved?

NEBUCHADNEZZAR AND NIMROD. We have to make this demand of you.

KURRUBI. Am I to betray Heaven from whose stars I descended – in whose name we love one another?

NEBUCHADNEZZAR AND NIMROD. There are human necessities.

KURRUBI. You will not run away with me?

NEBUCHADNEZZAR AND NIMROD. We must be sensible.

(*A silence. Outside the noise of the battering gets steadily louder and more threatening*.)

KURRUBI. Then let me depart, O King of Babylon.

(*General amazement*.)

NEBUCHADNEZZAR. What do you mean?

UTNAPISHTIM. I don't understand you, my dearest daughter.

PRIME MINISTER. Everything is in perfect order, my dear child.

KURRUBI. I am going to search for the beggar whom I love.

NEBUCHADNEZZAR. But I was that beggar.

KURRUBI. You lie.

UTNAPISHTIM AND PRIME MINISTER (*together*). We confirm it. We confirm it.

KURRUBI. You never tell the truth. You want to deny even the Angel. Let me go. I want to find the beloved whom I have lost.

(*Despairingly,* NEBUCHADNEZZAR *comes down from his throne.*)

NEBUCHADNEZZAR. But I am that beloved.

KURRUBI. I do not know you.

NEBUCHADNEZZAR. But I am Nebuchadnezzar, the King.

NIMROD. You are Nebuchadnezzar, the ex-King.

(*He tries to get on to the throne, but* NEBUCHADNEZZAR *flings himself on him and hurls him down.*)

KURRUBI. Who you are I do not know. You have taken on the figure of my beloved and you are not my beloved. At one moment you are a king – at the next a footstool. You are make-believe: the beggar I seek is the reality. I kissed him. I cannot kiss you. He struck me to the ground. You canot strike me down because you dare not leave your throne for fear of losing it. Your power is weakness ... Your riches are poverty. Your love for me is self-love. You neither live nor are you dead. You exist, but you have no existence. Let me go, King of Babylon, away from you and from this city.

(NEBUCHADNEZZAR *has again seated himself on the throne.*)

NEBUCHADNEZZAR (*softly*). You have seen the basis of my power: my son. He leapt just now through this hall. An idiot is to inherit my empire. I am lost without your love. I cannot touch another woman.

KURRUBI. I love a beggar, and I betray him if I do not leave you.

NEBUCHADNEZZAR (*almost inaudibly*). And yet I love you.

PRIME MINISTER. Confused. I'm getting confused. This all comes of creating girls out of nothing.

NEBUCHADNEZZAR (*quite calm*). I will hear the people's petition.

PRIME MINISTER. Majesty ...

NEBUCHADNEZZAR. Let them come in.

(*The* CAPTAIN *goes backstage.*)

UTNAPISHTIM. The end of the dynasty.

287

PRIME MINISTER. Thank God, I have the Republican Constitution already drawn up.

(*The two of them withdraw to the wall, left. Gradually, behind the screen, the people can be seen. The two* WORKING MEN, GIMMIL, *the* POLICEMAN *who has now also become a revolutionary, the* BANKER, ALI *the wine-merchant, the* WORKING MEN'S WIVES, *the* PROSTITUTE, *and many more ordinary people and soldiers, all armed with stones, cudgels and spears. Slowly they come forward, staring at the girl and the motionless* NEBUCHADNEZZAR.)

NEBUCHADNEZZAR. You have forced your way into my palace. You have broken down my doors with a battering ram. Why?

(*An embarrassed silence.*)

1ST WORKING MAN. We've come …

2ND WORKING MAN. The girl …

(*The banker,* ENGGIBI, *steps forward.*)

ENGGIBI. Your Majesty. Such astonishing things have been coming to pass that we have ventured to appear without first seeking an audience through the proper channels which surround the throne.

(*Laughter in the crowd.*)

A VOICE. Well done, Banker.

ENGGIBI. An Angel came to Babylon. He brought with him a girl whom Your Majesty apparently cannot make up his mind to marry.

A VOICE. That's the way. Give it to him.

ENGGIBI. That we stand armed in this hall, that the Palace Guard has come over to us, that the populace has seized power for itself – these facts do not mean that Your Majesty is being in any way compelled to this marriage. We would, however, make Your Majesty aware that, whereas we wish to have this girl as Queen, we do not absolutely insist on Your Majesty as King.

(*Laughter and tremendous applause.*)

NEBUCHADNEZZAR (*calmly*). I was perfectly ready to marry the girl. But she turned me down.

GIMMIL. She's given the King the brush-off.

ALI. Don't blame her.

(*The crowd boos and whistles and there is loud laughter.*)

1ST WORKING MAN. Down with this King!

2ND WORKING MAN. To the lamp-post with him.

NIMROD (*triumphantly*). Put me in his place. I will inaugurate the true Socialist State.

1ST WORKING MAN. We know these true Socialist States.

GIMMIL. All they do is to enrich kings and officials.

NIMROD. I will conquer the world afresh. I appeal to Babylonian national patriotism. If there are villages beyond the Lebanon there are villages across the sea.

2ND WORKING MAN. He's as big a bloodhound as the other.

1ST WORKING MAN. We want no more world conquests.

1ST WIFE. They have eaten up our children.

ALL. No more kings.

(*As silence falls all look anxiously at* NEBUCHADNEZZAR, *still motionless on his throne.*)

NEBUCHADNEZZAR. I give the maiden back. Let her belong to him who loves her the most.

(*Confused shouts from all the men.*)

MEN'S VOICES. To me. To me. I love her. I love her best.

ENGGIBI. The maiden belongs to me. I alone have the financial means to keep her in a manner worthy of her origin.

NEBUCHADNEZZAR. You are mistaken, Banker. The girl loves a beggar whose name she has forgotten, whom she ran into by accident on the banks of the Euphrates. She demanded that I should become a beggar. She will ask the same from you.

(*The* BANKER *falls back, disillusioned.*)

Do you not want the child? Won't you give them up, your millions? Will you not venture to become the poorest of the poor? Which of you, now, is the beggar the girl is looking for? Who will give his all to transform himself into the beloved one who no longer exists? The wine-merchant? The milkman? The policeman? A soldier? A worker? Let him step forward. (*Silence.*) You are silent? Do you throw Heaven's Grace back in its face?

(*Silence.*)

Perhaps the lovely lady can make use of her? Perhaps she could find something to do in her house? Only, of course, we should have to secure the approval of the Church authorities.

TABTUM. In my brothel? That girl? I keep a respectable house, Your Majesty.

NEBUCHADNEZZAR. Does nobody want the child from Heaven?

1ST WORKING MAN. Let her go to Akki, the beggar.

NEBUCHADNEZZAR. Akki the beggar is dead.

(KURRUBI *looks up, shocked.*)

2ND WORKING MAN. The poets are good enough for her.

CROWD. The poets! The poets!

NEBUCHADNEZZAR. There are no more poets. They died in my dungeons.

1ST WIFE. Hand her over to the Hangman.

GIMMIL. He's the poorest of men.

ALL. The Hangman! Give her to the Hangman!

NEBUCHADNEZZAR. Very well.

(*He signs with his hand.* AKKI *comes forward.*)

KURRUBI (*to the crowd*). Help me!

1ST WORKING MAN. Witch's brat!

POLICEMAN. She bewitched us.

GIMMIL. She brings bad luck.

2ND WORKING MAN. Misery.

VOICE. Death.

VOICES BEHIND. Get out. Away.

OTHERS. Don't touch her.

OTHERS. Ignore her.

KURRUBI (*turning to* UTNAPISHTIM). Help me, reverend Father. Take me with you.

(*The* SENIOR THEOLOGIAN *turns away.*)

(*Turning in despair back to the crowd.*) But help me. Save me! (*The* ANGEL *appears suddenly above Nebuchadnezzer's throne even more fantastically hung about than the last time, having added to the sunflowers, fir-cones, etc. starfish and corals and cuttlefish, mussels and snail-shells. Behind, brilliantly lit, and disappearing when the* ANGEL *does, the Andromeda Galaxy.*)

ANGEL. Kurrubi! Kurrubi, my child!

ALL. The Angel!

KURRUBI. Angel. My Angel.

ANGEL. Don't be frightened, my child. I'm afraid I look a bit odd. I've come straight out of the sea and I'm still hung about with seaweed and dripping with water.

KURRUBI. Save me, Angel.

ANGEL. For the last time I appear to you, my child. For the last time my face reflects the beauty of the Earth, for I have now investigated it completely.

KURRUBI. You have come at the right time, Angel – at the right moment. Take me with you.

ANGEL. All that I have found on this star reflects God's grace and nothing but God's grace:

The unreal miracle amidst the noble deserts of the stars. The blue of Sirius, the whiteness of Vega, the roaring Pleiads in the blackness of night of the universe – so exciting in their form and their strength, winnowing with their breathing great sheaves of light in space, the bellows of the universe,

All these weigh nothing against this tiny grain of matter, this minute ball, chained to its sun, encircled by its little moon, enclosed in ether, breathing amidst the green of its continents and the silver of its seas.

KURRUBI. Take me back with you into your Heaven, Angel – spread your wings before God's mighty countenance. I don't want to die on this Earth. I am afraid. I am deserted by all.

ANGEL.

So now I take flight, now I depart, laden with coloured
stones, hung about with wonders. With starfish and moss
and cuttlefish, with humming birds fluttering round my head,
in my hands
sunflowers, mallows and ears of corn,
with tinkling icicles,
corals in my hair, blackthorn and snail-shells,
my feet red from the sand, the hem of my garment wet
with dew,
Staggering beneath all this grace, beneath all this weight,
as though drunk, with heavy-beating wings.
So I depart, so I take flight,
leaving you, the fortunate one, here on the Earth.
So I go back to my suns,
in the glow of the Andromeda Galaxy in the misty distance.
So I dive back into the dark fires of Antar.

KURRUBI (*in despair*). Take me from this Earth, Angel. Take me
with you.

ANGEL. Farewell, Kurrubi, my child. Farewell for ever (*disappearing*).

NEBUCHADNEZZAR. The Angel is going. He is going back to his
impersonal stars. You are alone. Heaven has forsaken you.
Mankind has rejected you.

KURRUBI (*broken, softly*). Angel. Take me with you, my Angel.
(*A silence.*)

NEBUCHADNEZZAR. Hangman. Take the maiden out into the
desert. Kill her. Bury her in the sand.

(AKKI *carries* KURRUBI *out through the silent throng.*)

(*Tragically.*) I strove after perfection. I created a New Order.
I sought to extinguish poverty. I wanted to inaugurate the age
of reason. Heaven has turned its face from my works. I am
without grace.

(*The* GENERAL *appears in the background surrounded by
soldiers.*)

GENERAL. Your army turned back, King Nebuchadnezzar. News of the rebellion reached us in time. The palace is surrounded and the people are at your mercy.

(*The crowd falls on its knees.*)

ALL. Mercy, great King! Mercy! Mercy!

NEBUCHADNEZZAR. I betrayed the maiden for the sake of my power. The Minister betrayed her for reasons of state, the priest for the sake of his theology, all of you for the sake of your property. So now my power will prevail over your reasons of state, over your theology, and over your property. Seize the Minister and the Theologian, and lead the people into captivity. Out of their bodies I will forge weapons to revenge my shame. Very well, then. Is Heaven so high that my curses cannot reach it? Is it so broad that I cannot hate it? Stronger than my will? Nobler than my spirit? Braver than my courage? I will herd mankind into one great enclosure and in the midst of it I will raise a tower which shall pierce the clouds and, traversing the infinities of space, reach the very heart of my enemy. I will oppose to the Creation out of the void the creation of the spirit of man, and we shall see which is the better: my justice, or the injustice of God.

(*A* COOK *and the* CAPTAIN OF THE GUARD *hurry into the now empty stage.*)

COOK. All the wine casks have been drunk dry and the larders plundered.

CAPTAIN. The dungeons are empty, the doors open, the poets gone.

(*The* FORMAL ONE *rushes in right.*)

FORMAL ONE. My second-hand bookshop. I can't find my second-hand bookshop.

(*The* IDIOT *walks across the stage on a tightrope.* NEBU-CHADNEZZAR *covers his face in helpless rage – in helpless sorrow.*)

NEBUCHADNEZZAR. No! No!

(*Darkness. The scenery vanishes overhead. Vaguely, a measureless*

293

desert can be glimpsed, a vast wilderness through which AKKI
and KURRUBI *are fleeing.*)

AKKI. Farther, my child, farther. In the teeth of the sandstorm
which howls against us more powerfully every minute and
is tearing my hangman's robes to pieces.

KURRUBI. I am seeking my beggar from Nineveh. The beggar
I love. The beggar I have lost.

AKKI. And I love an earth which still exists; an earth of beggars,
lonely in its happiness, and lonely in its dangers, colourful and
wild, wonderful in all its possibilities; an earth which I conquer again and again, maddened by its beauty, entranced by
its face, ever oppressed and never defeated. On, then, gift of
God, given to me once again, and flying now with me from
fate. On, then, maiden, while we still have breath. On, then,
child, given over to death. Behind us, rearing itself endlessly
into the sky, blind and unstable, the steel and stone, challenging downfall, of the tower of Babel, the horseman who races
us, the arrow which chases us. And, in front, what faces us?
Strength behind courage lagging, feet in soft sand flagging,
sandstorms our faces scarring, high cliffs our freedom barring,
and, at the last, a land that forgets the past; a land rising in the
silver light of a new dawning, full of new persecutions, but
full, too, of new promises, and full of the songs of a new
morning.

(*They disappear, followed, it may be, by a few poets leaping
through the sandstorm.*)

THE
PHYSICISTS

Translated from the German by

JAMES KIRKUP

FIRST PUBLISHED IN GREAT BRITAIN 1964
TRANSLATED BY JAMES KIRKUP FROM THE GERMAN

Die Physiker

© 1962 BY PETER SCHIFFERLI, VERLAGS AG 'DIE ARCHE', ZÜRICH
ENGLISH VERSION © 1963 BY JAMES KIRKUP

CHARACTERS

Fräulein Doktor Mathilde von Zahnd	Alienist
Marta Boll	Head Nurse
Monika Stettler	Nurse
Uwe Sievers	Chief Male Attendant
McArthur	Male Attendant
Murillo	Male Attendant
Herbert Georg Beutler ('Newton')	Patient
Ernst Heinrich Ernesti ('Einstein')	Patient
Johann Wilhelm Möbius	Patient
Oskar Rose	A Missionary
Frau Lina Rose	His Wife
Adolf-Friedrich Wilfried-Kaspar Jörg-Lukas	Their Sons
Richard Voss	Inspector of Police
Police Doctors	
Guhl	Policeman
Blocher	Policeman

founder, Fräulein Doktor Mathilde von Zahnd, were housed – decayed aristocrats, arterio-sclerotic politicians (unless still in office), debilitated millionaires, schizophrenic writers, manic-depressive industrial barons and so on: in short, the mentally disturbed elite of half the western world, for the Fräulein Doktor is a very celebrated person, not just because the hunchbacked spinster in her eternal white coat is descended from a great and very ancient family, of which she is the last presentable member, but because she is also a philanthropist and a psychiatrist of enormous repute; one might almost call her world-famous – her correspondence with C. G. Jung has just been published.

But now the distinguished but not always very pleasant patients have been transferred long since to the elegant, light and airy new building, where for terrific fees even the most disastrous past experiences are turned into blissful memories. The new building spreads over the southern section of the extensive park, branching out into various wings and pavilions (stained-glass windows by Erni in the chapel) that descend towards the plain, while the 'villa's' lawns, dotted with gigantic trees, slope down to the lake. There is a stone embankment along the edge of the lake.

Now only three patients at the very most occupy the drawing-room of the sparsely inhabited 'villa': as it happens, they are all three physicists, though this is not entirely due to chance, for humane principles are put into practice here, and it is felt that 'birds of a feather' should 'flock together'. They live for themselves, each one wrapped in the cocoon of his own little world of the imagination; they take their meals together in the drawing-room, from time to time discuss scientific matters or just sit gazing dully before them – harmless, lovable lunatics, amenable, easily handled and unassuming. In fact, they would be model patients were it not that certain serious, nay, hideous events have recently taken place: three months ago, one of them throttled a nurse, and now the very same thing has just happened again. So once more the police are back in the house and the drawing-room is more than usually animated.

The dead nurse is lying on the parquet floor in a tragic and quite unmistakable attitude, somewhat in the background, so as not to distress the public too much. But it is impossible not to see that a struggle has taken place. The furniture is in great disorder. A standard lamp and two chairs have been knocked over, and left downstage a round table has been over-turned so that it presents only its legs to the spectator.

Apart from all this, the transformation into an asylum has left painful traces on the salon. (*The villa was once the Zahnd summer residence.*) The walls have been covered to a height of six feet with hygienic, wash-able, glossy paint: above this, the original plaster emerges, with some remnants of stucco mouldings. The three doors in the background, which lead from a small hall into the physicists' sick-rooms, are upholstered with black leather. Moreover, they are numbered from one to three. To the left of the little hall is an ugly central-heating unit; to the right there is a washbasin with towels on a rail.

The sound of a violin, with piano accompaniment, comes from Room Number 2 (*the middle room*). Beethoven. Kreutzer Sonata. To the left is the wall overlooking the park, with very high windows that reach right down to the linoleum-covered parquet floor. Heavy curtains hang to right and left of the high windows. The glass doors lead on to a terrace, whose stone balustrade is silhouetted against the green of the park and the relatively sunny November light. It is a little after half past four in the afternoon. To the right, over a fireplace which is never used and is covered by a wire guard, there hangs the portrait of an old man with a pointed beard, enclosed in a heavy, gilded frame. Downstage right, a massive oak door. A ponderous chandelier is suspended from the brown, coffered ceiling.

Furniture: beside the round table there stand – when the room is in order – three chairs, all painted white like the table. The remaining fur-niture, with well-worn upholstery, belongs to various periods. Down-stage right, a sofa and a small table flanked by two easy chairs. The standard lamp should really be behind the sofa, when the room should not appear overcrowded. Little is required for the furnishing of a stage on which, contrary to the plays of the ancients, the satire precedes the tragedy. We can begin.

Police officials in plain clothes are busied round the corpse: stolid, good-natured fellows who have already downed a glass or two of white wine: their breaths smell of it. In the centre of the drawing-room stands the INSPECTOR OF POLICE, RICHARD VOSS, wearing coat and hat;

on the left is the head nurse, MARTA BOLL, *looking as resolute as she really is. In the arm-chair on the far right sits a policeman taking everything down in shorthand. The inspector takes a cigar out of a brown leather cigar case.*

INSPECTOR. All right if I smoke?

SISTER BOLL. It's not usual.

INSPECTOR. I beg your pardon.
  (*He puts the cigar back in the case.*)

SISTER BOLL. A cup of tea?

INSPECTOR. No brandy?

SISTER BOLL. You're in a medical establishment.

INSPECTOR. Then nothing. Blocher, you can take the photographs now.

BLOCHER. Yes, sir.
  (*He begins taking photographs. Flashes.*)

INSPECTOR. What was the nurse's name?

SISTER BOLL. Irene Straub.

INSPECTOR. Age?

SISTER BOLL. Twenty-two. From Kohlwang.

INSPECTOR. Relatives?

SISTER BOLL. A brother in Liechentstein.

INSPECTOR. Informed?

SISTER BOLL. By telephone.

INSPECTOR. The murderer?

SISTER BOLL. Please, Inspector – the poor man's ill, you know.

INSPECTOR. Well, the assailant?

SISTER BOLL. Ernst Heinrich Ernesti. We call him Einstein.

INSPECTOR. Why?

SISTER BOLL. Because he thinks he is Einstein.

INSPECTOR (*turns to the police stenographer*). Have you got the statement down, Guhl?

GUHL. Yes, sir.

INSPECTOR. Strangled, doctor?

POLICE DOCTOR. Quite definitely. With the flex of the standard

302

lamp. These madmen often have gigantic reserves of strength. It's phenomenal.

INSPECTOR. Oh. Is that so? In that case I consider it most irresponsible to leave these madmen in the care of female nurses. This is the second murder –

SISTER BOLL. Please, Inspector.

INSPECTOR. – the second accident within three months in the medical establishment known as Les Cerisiers.

(*He takes out a notebook.*)

On the twelfth of August a certain Herbert Georg Beutler, who believes himself to be the great physicist Sir Isaac Newton, strangled Dorothea Moser, a nurse.

(*He puts the notebook back.*)

And in this very room. If they'd had male attendants such a thing would never have happened.

SISTER BOLL. Do you really think so?

INSPECTOR. I do.

SISTER BOLL. Nurse Moser was a member of the League of Lady Wrestlers and Nurse Straub was District Champion of the National Judo Association.

INSPECTOR. And what about you?

SISTER BOLL. Weight-lifter.

INSPECTOR. Now I'd like to see the murderer.

SISTER BOLL. Please, Inspector.

INSPECTOR. I mean – the assailant.

SISTER BOLL. He's playing his fiddle.

INSPECTOR. Doing what?

SISTER BOLL. Can't you hear him?

INSPECTOR. Then kindly request him to stop.

(SISTER BOLL *does not react.*)

I have to ask him some questions.

SISTER BOLL. Definitely not.

INSPECTOR. And why not?

SISTER BOLL. We cannot allow it, on medical grounds. Herr Ernesti has to play his fiddle, and play it now.

INSPECTOR. But damn it, the man's just strangled a nurse!

SISTER BOLL. Inspector. He's not just any man, but a sick man who needs calming down. And because he thinks he is Einstein he can only calm down when he's playing the fiddle.

INSPECTOR. Can I be going mad?

SISTER BOLL. No.

INSPECTOR. I'm getting confused.

(*He wipes the sweat from his forehead.*)

Warm in here.

SISTER BOLL. I don't think so.

INSPECTOR. Sister Boll. Kindly fetch the doctor in charge.

SISTER BOLL. Quite out of the question. The Fräulein Doktor is accompanying Einstein on the piano. Einstein can only calm down when the Fräulein Doktor plays his accompaniments.

INSPECTOR. And three months ago the Fräulein Doktor had to play chess with Sir Isaac Newton, to calm *him* down. We can't have any more of this, Sister. I simply must speak to the doctor in charge.

SISTER BOLL. Certainly –

INSPECTOR. Thank you.

SISTER BOLL. – but you'll have to wait.

INSPECTOR. How long's this fiddling going to last?

SISTER BOLL. Fifteen minutes, an hour. It all depends.

(*The* INSPECTOR *controls his impatience.*)

INSPECTOR. Very well, I'll wait.

(*He roars.*)

I'll wait!

BLOCHER. We're just about finished, sir.

INSPECTOR. So am I.

(*Silence. The* INSPECTOR *wipes his forehead.*)

You can take away the body.

BLOCHER. Very well, sir.

SISTER BOLL. I'll show them the way through the park to the chapel.

(*She opens the french windows. The body is carried out. Equipment also. The* INSPECTOR *takes off his hat and sinks exhaustedly into the easy chair to the left of the sofa. The fiddling continues, with piano accompaniment. Then out of Room Number 3 comes* HERBERT GEORG BEUTLER *in early eighteenth-century costume. He wears a full-bottomed wig.*)

NEWTON. Sir Isaac Newton.

INSPECTOR. Inspector Richard Voss.

(*He remains seated.*)

NEWTON. I'm so glad. Really very glad. Truly. I heard a noise in here, groans and gurglings, and then people coming and going. May I inquire just what has been going on?

INSPECTOR. Nurse Straub was strangled.

NEWTON. The District Champion of the National Judo Association?

INSPECTOR. The District Champion.

NEWTON. Gruesome.

INSPECTOR. By Ernst Heinrich Ernesti.

NEWTON. But he's playing his fiddle.

INSPECTOR. He has to calm himself down.

NEWTON. The tussle must have taken it out of him. He's rather highly-strung, poor boy. How did he – ?

INSPECTOR. With the cord of the standard lamp.

NEWTON. With the cord of the standard lamp. Yes. That's another possibility. Poor Ernesti. I'm sorry for him. Truly sorry. And I'm sorry for the Ladies' Judo Champion too. Now you'll have to excuse me. I must put things straight.

INSPECTOR. Do. We've got everything we want.

(NEWTON *rights the table and chairs.*)

NEWTON. I simply can't stand disorder. Really it was my love of order that made me become a physicist – (*he rights the standard lamp*) – to interpret the apparent disorder of Nature in the light of a more sublime order. (*He lights a cigarette.*) Will it disturb you if I smoke?

INSPECTOR. On the contrary, I was just thinking ...

(*He takes a cigar out of his case.*)

NEWTON. Excuse me, but we were talking about order just now, so I must tell you that the patients are allowed to smoke here but not the visitors. If they did it would stink the place out.

INSPECTOR. I see.

(*He puts the cigar away.*)

NEWTON. Will it disturb you if I have a nip of brandy?

INSPECTOR. No. Not at all.

(*From behind the wire guard in front of the fire* NEWTON *takes a bottle of brandy and a glass.*)

NEWTON. That poor Ernesti. I'm really upset. How on earth could anyone bring himself to strangle a nurse?

(*He sits down on the sofa and pours out a glass of brandy.*)

INSPECTOR. I believe you strangled one yourself.

NEWTON. Did I?

INSPECTOR. Nurse Dorothea Moser.

NEWTON. The lady wrestler?

INSPECTOR. On the twelfth of August. With the curtain cord.

NEWTON. But that was something quite different, Inspector. I'm not mad, you know. Your health.

INSPECTOR. And yours.

(NEWTON *drinks.*)

NEWTON. Dorothea Moser. Let me cast my mind back. Blonde hair. Enormously powerful. Yet, despite her bulk, very flexible. She loved me and I loved her. It was a dilemma that could only be resolved by the use of a curtain cord.

INSPECTOR. Dilemma?

NEWTON. My mission is to devote myself to the problems of gravitation, not the physical requirements of a woman.

INSPECTOR. Quite.

NEWTON. And then there was this tremendous difference in our ages.

INSPECTOR. Granted. You must be well on the wrong side of two hundred.

(NEWTON *stares at him uncomprehendingly.*)

NEWTON. How do you mean?

INSPECTOR. Well, being Sir Isaac Newton –

NEWTON. Are you out of your mind, Inspector, or are you just having me on?

INSPECTOR. Now look –

NEWTON. Do you really think I'm Sir Isaac Newton?

INSPECTOR. Well, don't you?

(NEWTON *looks at him suspiciously*.)

NEWTON. Inspector, may I tell you a secret? In confidence?

INSPECTOR. Of course.

NEWTON. Well, it's this. I am not Sir Isaac Newton. I only pretend to be Sir Isaac Newton.

INSPECTOR. What for?

NEWTON. So as not to confuse poor Ernesti.

INSPECTOR. I don't get it.

NEWTON. You see, unlike me, Ernesti is really sick. He thinks he's Albert Einstein.

INSPECTOR. But what's that got to do with you?

NEWTON. Well, if Ernesti were to find out that *I* am the real Albert Einstein, all hell would be let loose.

INSPECTOR. Do you mean to say –

NEWTON. I do. I am he. The celebrated physicist and discoverer of the theory of relativity, born March 14th, 1879, in the city of Ulm.

(*The* INSPECTOR *rises in some confusion of mind.*)

INSPECTOR. How do you do?

(NEWTON *also rises.*)

NEWTON. Just call me – Albert.

INSPECTOR. And you can call me Richard.

(*They shake hands.*)

NEWTON. I could give you a Kreutzer with a good deal more dash than Ernesti. The way he plays the Andante – simply barbarous! Simply barbarous!

INSPECTOR. I don't understand anything about music.

NEWTON. Let's sit down, shall we?

(*He draws the* INSPECTOR *down beside him on the sofa.* NEWTON *puts his arm around the* INSPECTOR's *shoulders.*)

NEWTON. Richard.

INSPECTOR. Yes, Albert?

NEWTON. You're cross, aren't you, because you can't arrest me?

INSPECTOR: But Albert –

NEWTON. Is it because I strangled the nurse that you want to arrest me, or because it was I who paved the way for the atomic bomb?

INSPECTOR. But Albert –

NEWTON. When you work that switch by the door, what happens, Richard?

INSPECTOR. The light goes on.

NEWTON. You establish an electrical contact. Do you understand anything about electricity, Richard?

INSPECTOR. I am no physicist.

NEWTON. I don't understand much about it either. All I do is to elaborate a theory about it on the basis of natural observation. I write down this theory in the mathematical idiom and obtain several formulae. Then the engineers come along. They don't care about anything except the formulae. They treat electricity as a pimp treats a whore. They simply exploit it. They build machines – and a machine can only be used when it becomes independent of the knowledge that led to its invention. So any fool nowadays can switch on a light or touch off the atomic bomb.

(*He pats the* INSPECTOR's *shoulders.*)

And that's what you want to arrest me for, Richard. It's not fair.

INSPECTOR. But I don't want to arrest you, Albert.

NEWTON. It's all because you think I'm mad. But, if you don't understand anything about electricity, why don't you refuse to turn on the light? It's you who are the criminal, Richard. But I must put my brandy away; if Sister Boll comes there will be wigs on the green.

(NEWTON *hides the bottle of brandy behind the wire guard in front of the fire, but leaves the glass where it is.*)

Well, goodbye.

INSPECTOR. Goodbye, Albert.

NEWTON. Oh, Richard. You're the one who should be arrested.
(*He disappears into Room Number 3.*)

INSPECTOR. Now I *will* have a smoke.
(*He takes a cigar firmly out of his cigar case, lights it and smokes.*
BLOCHER *comes through the french windows.*)

BLOCHER. We're ready to leave, sir.
(*The* INSPECTOR *stamps his foot.*)
Yes, sir.
(*The* INSPECTOR *calms down and growls.*)

INSPECTOR. Go back to town with the men, Blocher. I'll come on
later. I'm waiting for the doctor in charge!

BLOCHER. Very well, sir.
(BLOCHER *goes.*
The INSPECTOR *puffs out great clouds of smoke, stands up, goes
to the chimney-piece and stands looking at the portrait. Meanwhile the violin and piano have stopped. The door to Room Number
2 opens and* FRÄULEIN DOKTOR MATHILDE VON ZAHND
*comes out. She is hunchbacked, about fifty-five, wearing a white
surgical overall-coat and stethoscope.*)

FRL. DOKTOR. My father, August von Zahnd, Privy Councillor.
He used to live in this villa before I turned it into a sanatorium.
He was a great man, a real person. I am his only child. He
hated me like poison; indeed he hated everybody like poison.
And with good reason, for as an expert in economics, he saw,
revealed in human beings, abysses which are for ever hidden
from psychiatrists like myself. We alienists are still hopelessly
romantic philanthropists.

INSPECTOR. Three months ago there was a different portrait hanging here.

FRL. DOKTOR. That was my uncle, the politician. Chancellor
Joachim von Zahnd.
(*She lays the music score on the small table in front of the sofa.*)
Well, Ernesti has calmed down. In the end he just flung him-
self on the bed and fell sound asleep. Like a little boy, not a

309

care in the world. I can breathe again: I was afraid he'd want to fiddle through the entire Brahms G Major Sonata.

(*She sits in the arm-chair left of sofa.*)

INSPECTOR. Excuse me, Fräulein Doktor, for smoking in here. I gather it's prohibited, but –

FRL. DOKTOR. Smoke away as much as you like, Inspector. I badly need a cigarette myself; Sister or no Sister. Give me a light.

(*He lights her cigarette and she smokes.*)

Poor Nurse Straub. Simply frightful. She was such a neat, pretty little thing.

(*She notices the glass.*)

Newton?

INSPECTOR. I had the pleasure of speaking to him.

FRL. DOKTOR. I'd better put it away.

INSPECTOR. Allow me.

(*The* INSPECTOR *forestalls her and puts the glass away.*)

FRL. DOKTOR. On account of Sister Boll, you know.

INSPECTOR. I know.

FRL. DOKTOR. So you had a talk with Sir Isaac?

INSPECTOR. Yes, and I discovered something.

(*He sits on the sofa.*)

FRL. DOKTOR. Congratulations.

INSPECTOR. Newton thinks he is really Einstein.

FRL. DOKTOR. That's what he tells everybody. But in fact he really believes he is Newton.

INSPECTOR (*taken aback*). Are you sure?

FRL. DOKTOR. It is I who decide who my patients think they are. I know them far better than they know themselves.

INSPECTOR. Maybe so. In that case you should co-operate with us, Fräulein Doktor. The authorities are complaining.

FRL. DOKTOR. The public prosecutor?

INSPECTOR. Fuming.

FRL. DOKTOR. As if it were my business, Inspector.

INSPECTOR. But two murders –

FRL. DOKTOR. Please, Inspector.

INSPECTOR. Two accidents in three months. You must admit that the safety precautions in your establishment would seem inadequate.

FRL. DOKTOR. What sort of safety precautions have you in mind, Inspector? I am the director of a medical establishment, not a reformatory. One can't very well lock murderers up *before* they have committed their murders, can one?

INSPECTOR. It's not a question of murderers but of madmen, and they can commit murders at any time.

FRL. DOKTOR. So can the sane; and, significantly, a lot more often. I have only to think of my grandfather, Leonidas von Zahnd, the Field-Marshal who lost every battle he ever fought. What age do you think we're living in? Has medical science made great advances or not? Do we have new resources at our disposal, drugs that can transform raving madmen into the gentlest of lambs? Must we start putting the mentally sick into solitary confinement again, hung up in nets, I shouldn't wonder, with boxing gloves on, as they used to? As if we were still unable to distinguish between dangerous patients and harmless ones.

INSPECTOR. You weren't much good at distinguishing between them in the cases of Beutler and Ernesti.

FRL. DOKTOR. Unfortunately, no. *That's* what disturbs me, not the fuming of your public prosecutor.

(EINSTEIN *comes out of Room Number 2, carrying his violin. He is lean with long, snow-white hair and moustache.*)

EINSTEIN. I just woke up.

FRL. DOKTOR. Oh, Professor !

EINSTEIN. Did I play well?

FRL. DOKTOR. Beautifully, Professor.

EINSTEIN. What about Nurse Irene? Is she –

FRL. DOKTOR. Don't give it another thought, Professor.

EINSTEIN. I'm going back to bed.

FRL. DOKTOR. Yes, do, Professor.

(Einstein *goes back into his room. The* Inspector *has jumped to his feet.*)

INSPECTOR. So that was him!

FRL. DOKTOR. Yes. Ernst Heinrich Ernesti.

INSPECTOR. The murderer –

FRL. DOKTOR. Please, Inspector.

INSPECTOR. I mean, the assailant, the one who thinks he's Einstein. When was he brought in?

FRL. DOKTOR. Two years ago.

INSPECTOR. And Sir Isaac Newton?

FRL. DOKTOR. One year ago. Both incurable. Look here, Voss, I'm no beginner, God knows, at this sort of job. You know that, and so does the public prosecutor; he has always respected my professional opinion. My sanatorium is world-famous and the fees are correspondingly high. Errors of judgment and incidents that bring the police into my house are luxuries I cannot afford. If anything was to blame here, it was medical science, not me. These incidents could not have been foreseen; you or I would be just as likely to strangle a nurse. No – medically speaking there is no explanation for what has happened. Unless –

(*She has taken a fresh cigarette. The* Inspector *lights it for her.*)
Inspector. Haven't you noticed something?

INSPECTOR. What do you mean?

FRL. DOKTOR. Consider these two patients.

INSPECTOR. Yes?

FRL. DOKTOR. They're both physicists. Nuclear physicists.

INSPECTOR. Well?

FRL. DOKTOR. Inspector, you really have a very unsuspecting mind.
(*The* Inspector *ponders.*)

INSPECTOR. Doktor von Zahnd.

FRL. DOKTOR. Well, Voss?

INSPECTOR. You don't think –

FRL. DOKTOR. They were both doing research on radioactive materials.

INSPECTOR. You suppose there was some connection?

FRL. DOKTOR. I suppose nothing. I merely state the facts. Both of them go mad, the conditions of both deteriorate, both become a danger to the public and both of them strangle their nurses.

INSPECTOR. And you think the radioactivity affected their brains?

FRL. DOKTOR. I regret to say that is a possibility I must face up to. —
(*The* INSPECTOR *looks about him.*)

INSPECTOR. What's on the other side of the hall?

FRL. DOKTOR. The green drawing-room and upstairs.

INSPECTOR. How many patients have you got here now?

FRL. DOKTOR. Three.

INSPECTOR. Only three?

FRL. DOKTOR. The rest were transferred to the new wing immediately after the first incident. Fortunately I was able to complete the building just in time. Rich patients contributed to the costs. So did my own relations. They died off one by one, most of them in here. And I was left sole inheritor. Destiny, Voss. I am always sole inheritor. My family is so ancient, it's something of a miracle, in medicine, that I should be relatively normal, I mean, mentally.
(*The* INSPECTOR *thinks a moment.*)

INSPECTOR. What about the third patient?

FRL. DOKTOR. He's also a physicist.

INSPECTOR. Well, that's extraordinary. Don't you think so?

FRL. DOKTOR. Not at all. I put them all together. The writers with the writers, the big industrialists with the big industrialists, the millionairesses with the millionairesses and the physicists with the physicists.

INSPECTOR. What's his name?

FRL. DOKTOR. Johann Wilhelm Möbius.

INSPECTOR. Was he working with radioactive materials as well?

FRL. DOKTOR. No.

INSPECTOR. Mightn't he also perhaps –

FRL. DOKTOR. He's been fifteen years here. He's harmless. His condition has never changed.

INSPECTOR. Doktor von Zahnd, you can't get away with it like
that. The public prosecutor insists that your physicists have
male attendants.

FRL. DOKTOR. They shall have them.

(*The* INSPECTOR *picks up his hat.*)

INSPECTOR. Good. I'm glad you see it that way. This is the second
visit I have paid to Les Cerisiers, Fräulein Doktor. I hope I
shan't have to pay a third. Goodbye.

(*He puts on his hat, goes out left through the french windows on
to the terrace and makes his way across the park.* DOKTOR
MATHILDE VON ZAHND *gazes thoughtfully after him. Enter
right the* SISTER, MARTA BOLL, *who stops short, sniffing the air.
She is carrying a patient's dossier.*)

SISTER BOLL. Please, Fräulein Doktor.

FRL. DOKTOR. Oh, I'm sorry.

(*She stubs out her cigarette.*)

FRL. DOKTOR. Have they laid out Nurse Straub?

SISTER BOLL. Yes, under the organ-loft.

FRL. DOKTOR. Have candles and wreaths put round her.

SISTER BOLL. I've already telephoned the florists about it.

FRL. DOKTOR. How is my Great-Aunt Senta?

SISTER BOLL. Restless.

FRL. DOKTOR. Double her dose. And my Cousin Ulrich?

SISTER BOLL. No change.

FRL. DOKTOR. Fräulein Sister Boll, I regret to say that one of our
traditions here at Les Cerisiers must come to an end. Until
now I have employed female nurses only. From tomorrow the
villa will be in the hands of male attendants.

SISTER BOLL. Fräulein Doktor von Zahnd. I won't let my three
physicists be snatched away from me. They are my most interesting cases.

FRL. DOKTOR. My decision is final.

SISTER BOLL. I'd like to know where you are going to find
three male nurses, what with the demand for them these
days.

314

FRL. DOKTOR. That's my problem. Leave it to me. Has Frau Möbius arrived?

SISTER BOLL. She's waiting in the green drawing-room.

FRL. DOKTOR. Send her in.

SISTER BOLL. Here is Möbius's dossier.

(SISTER BOLL *gives her the dossier and then goes to the door on the right, where she turns.*)

But –

FRL. DOKTOR. Thank you, Sister, thank you.

(SISTER BOLL *goes. The* DOKTOR *opens the dossier and studies it at the round table,* SISTER BOLL *comes in again right leading* FRAU ROSE *and three boys of fourteen, fifteen and sixteen. The eldest is carrying a brief-case.* HERR ROSE, *a missionary, brings up the rear. The* DOKTOR *stands up.*)

My dear Frau Möbius –

FRAU ROSE. Rose. Frau Rose. It must be an awful surprise to you, Fräulein Doktor, but three weeks ago I married Herr Rose, who is a missionary. It was perhaps rather sudden. We met in September at a missionary convention.

(*She blushes and rather awkwardly indicates her new husband.*) Oskar was a widower.

(*The* FRÄULEIN DOKTOR *shakes her by the hand.*)

FRL. DOKTOR. Congratulations, Frau Rose, heartiest congratulations. And my best wishes to you, too, Herr Rose.

(*She gives him a friendly nod.*)

FRAU ROSE. You do understand why we took this step?

FRL. DOKTOR. But of course, Frau Rose. Life must continue to bloom and flourish.

HERR ROSE. How peaceful it is here! What a friendly atmosphere! Truly a divine peace reigns over this house, just as the psalmist says: For the Lord heareth the needy and despiseth not his prisoners.

FRAU ROSE. Oskar is such a good preacher, Fräulein Doktor.

(*She blushes.*)

My boys.

FRL. DOKTOR. Good afternoon, boys.

THREE BOYS. Good afternoon, Fräulein Doktor.

> (*The youngest picks something up from the floor.*)

JÖRG-LUKAS. A piece of electric wire, Fräulein Doktor. It was lying on the floor.

FRL. DOKTOR. Thank you, young man. Grand boys you have, Frau Rose. You can face the future with confidence.

> (*FRAU ROSE sits on the sofa to the right, the DOKTOR at the table left. Behind the sofa the three boys, and on the chair at extreme right, HERR ROSE.*)

FRAU ROSE. Fräulein Doktor, I have brought my boys with me for a very good reason. Oskar is taking over a mission in the Marianas.

HERR ROSE. In the Pacific Ocean.

FRAU ROSE. I thought it only proper that my boys should make their father's acquaintance before their departure. This will be their one and only opportunity. They were still quite small when he fell ill and now, perhaps, they will be saying goodbye for ever.

FRL. DOKTOR. Frau Rose, speaking as a doctor, I would say that there might be objections, but speaking as a human being I can understand your wish and gladly give my consent to a family reunion.

FRAU ROSE. And how is my dear little Johann Wilhelm?

> (*The DOKTOR leafs through the dossier.*)

FRL. DOKTOR. Our dear old Möbius shows signs neither of improvement nor of relapse, Frau Rose. He's spinning his own little cocoon.

FRAU ROSE. Does he still claim to see King Solomon?

FRL. DOKTOR. Yes.

HERR ROSE. A sad and deplorable delusion.

FRL. DOKTOR. Your harsh judgment surprises me a bit, Herr Missionary. Nevertheless, as a theologian you must surely reckon with the possibility of a miracle.

HERR ROSE. Oh, of course – but not in the case of someone mentally sick.

316

FRL. DOKTOR. Whether the manifestations perceived by the mentally sick are real or not is something which psychiatry is not competent to judge. Psychiatry has to concern itself exclusively with states of mind and with the nerves, and in this respect things are in a bad enough way with our dear old Möbius, even though his illness takes rather a mild form. As for helping him, goodness me, another course of insulin shock treatment might be indicated, but as the others have been without success I'm leaving it alone. I can't work miracles, Frau Rose, and I can't pamper our dear old Möbius back to health; but I certainly don't want to make his life a misery either.

FRAU ROSE. Does he know that I've – I mean, does he know about the divorce?

FRL. DOKTOR. He has been told the facts.

FRAU ROSE. Did he understand?

FRL. DOKTOR. He takes hardly any interest in the outside world any more.

FRAU ROSE. Fräulein Doktor. Try to understand my position. I am five years older than Johann Wilhelm. I first met him when he was a fifteen-year-old schoolboy, in my father's house, where he had rented an attic room. He was an orphan and wretchedly poor. I helped him through high school and later made it possible for him to read physics at the university. We got married on his twentieth birthday, against my parents' wishes. We worked day and night. He was writing his dissertation and I took a job with a transport company. Four years later we had our eldest boy, Adolf-Friedrich, and then came the two others. Finally there were prospects of his obtaining a professorship; we thought we could begin to relax at last. But then Johann Wilhelm fell ill and his illness swallowed up immense sums of money. To provide for my family I went to work in a chocolate factory. Tobler's chocolate factory.

(*She silently wipes away a tear.*)

For years I worked my fingers to the bone.

(*They are all moved.*)

317

FRL. DOKTOR. Frau Rose, you are a brave woman.

HERR ROSE. And a good mother.

FRAU ROSE. Fräulein Doktor, until now I have made it possible for Johann Wilhelm to stay in your establishment. The fees are far beyond my means, but God came to my help time and time again. All the same, I am now, financially speaking, at the end of my tether. I simply cannot raise the extra money.

FRL. DOKTOR. That's understandable, Frau Rose.

FRAU ROSE. I'm afraid now you'll think I married Oskar so as to get out of providing for Johann Wilhelm. But that is not so. Things will be even more difficult for me now. Oskar brings me six sons from his previous marriage!

FRL. DOKTOR. Six?

HERR ROSE. Six.

FRAU ROSE. Six. Oskar is a most zealous father. But now there are nine boys to feed and Oskar is by no means robust. And his salary is not high.

(*She weeps.*)

FRL. DOKTOR. Come, now, Frau Rose, you mustn't. Don't cry.

FRAU ROSE. I reproach myself bitterly for having left my poor little Johann Wilhelm in the lurch.

FRL. DOKTOR. Frau Rose! You have no need to reproach yourself.

FRAU ROSE. My poor little Johann Wilhelm will have to go into a state institution now.

FRL. DOKTOR. No he won't, Frau Rose. Our dear old Möbius will stay on here in the villa. You have my word. He's got used to being here and has found some nice, kind colleagues. I'm not a monster, you know!

FRAU ROSE. You're so good to me, Fräulein Doktor.

FRL. DOKTOR. Not at all, Frau Rose, not at all. There are such things as grants and bequests. There's the Oppel Foundation for invalid scientists, there's the Doktor Steinemann Bequest. Money's as thick as muck around here and it's my duty as his doctor to pitchfork some of it in the direction of your dear little Johann Wilhelm. You can steam off to the Marianas with a clear conscience. But now let us have a word with Möbius himself – our dear, good old Möbius.

(*She goes and opens the door Number* 1. FRAU ROSE *rises expectantly.*)

Dear Möbius. You have visitors. Now leave your physicist's lair for a moment and come in here.

(JOHANN WILHELM MÖBIUS *comes out of Room Number* 1. *He is about forty, a rather clumsy man. He looks around him uncertainly, stares at* FRAU ROSE, *then at the boys and finally at the missionary,* HERR ROSE. *He appears not to recognize them and remains silent.*)

FRAU ROSE. Johann Wilhelm!

THREE BOYS. Papa!

(MÖBIUS *remains silent.*)

FRL. DOKTOR. My dear Möbius, you're not going to tell me you don't recognize your own wife?

(MÖBIUS *stares at* FRAU ROSE.)

MÖBIUS. Lina?

FRL. DOKTOR. That's better, Möbius. Of course it's Lina.

MÖBIUS. Hullo, Lina.

FRAU ROSE. My little Johann Wilhelm, my dear, dear little Johann Wilhelm.

FRL. DOKTOR. There we are, now. Frau Rose, Herr Rose, if you have anything else to tell me I shall be at your disposal in the new wing over there.

(*She goes off through door left.*)

FRAU ROSE. These are your sons, Johann Wilhelm.

(MÖBIUS *starts.*)

MÖBIUS. Three?

FRAU ROSE. Of course, Johann Wilhelm. Three.

(*She introduces the boys to him.*)

Adolf-Friedrich, your eldest.

(MÖBIUS *shakes his hand.*)

MÖBIUS. How do you do, Adolf-Friedrich, my eldest.

ADOLF-FRIEDRICH. How do you do, Papi.

MÖBIUS. How old are you, Adolf-Friedrich?

ADOLF-FRIEDRICH. Sixteen, Papi.

MÖBIUS. What do you want to be?

ADOLF-FRIEDRICH. A minister, Papi.

MÖBIUS. I remember now. We were walking across St Joseph's Square. I was holding your hand. The sun was shining brightly and the shadows were just as if they'd been drawn with a compass.

(MÖBIUS *turns to the next boy.*)

And you – you are – ?

WILFRIED-KASPAR. My name is Wilfried-Kaspar, Papi.

MÖBIUS. Fourteen?

WILFRIED-KASPAR. Fifteen. I should like to study philosophy.

MÖBIUS. Philosophy?

FRAU ROSE. He's an exceptionally mature boy for his age.

WILFRIED-KASPAR. I have read Schopenhauer and Nietzsche.

FRAU ROSE. This is your youngest boy, Jörg-Lukas. Fourteen.

JÖRG-LUKAS. How do you do, Papi.

MÖBIUS. How do you do, Jörg-Lukas, my youngest.

FRAU ROSE. He's the one who takes after you most.

JÖRG-LUKAS. I want to be a physicist, Papi.

(MÖBIUS *stares at his youngest in horror.*)

MÖBIUS. A physicist?

JÖRG-LUKAS. Yes, Papi.

MÖBIUS. You mustn't, Jörg-Lukas. Not under any circumstances. You get that idea right out of your head. I – I forbid it!

(JÖRG-LUKAS *looks puzzled.*)

JÖRG-LUKAS. But you became a physicist yourself, Papi –

MÖBIUS. I should never have been one, Jörg-Lukas. Never. I wouldn't be in the madhouse now.

FRAU ROSE. But Johann Wilhelm. That's not right. You are in a sanatorium, not a madhouse. You're having a little trouble with your nerves, that's all.

(MÖBIUS *shakes his head.*)

320

MÖBIUS. No, Lina. People say I am mad. Everybody. Even you. And my boys too. Because King Solomon appears to me.
(*They are all struck dumb with embarrassment. Then* FRAU ROSE *introduces* HERR ROSE.)

FRAU ROSE. Let me introduce Oskar Rose to you, Johann Wilhelm. He is my husband. A missionary.

MÖBIUS. Your husband? But *I'm* your husband.

FRAU ROSE. Not any more, my little Johann Wilhelm.
(*She blushes.*)
We're divorced, you know.

MÖBIUS. Divorced?

FRAU ROSE. Now you know that, surely?

MÖBIUS. No.

FRAU ROSE. Doktor von Zahnd told you. Of course she did.

MÖBIUS. Possibly.

FRAU ROSE. And then I married Oskar. He has six boys of his own. He was a minister at Guttannen and now he has been given a post in the Marianas.

MÖBIUS. In the Marianas?

HERR ROSE. In the Pacific Ocean.

FRAU ROSE. We're joining the ship at Bremen tomorrow.

MÖBIUS. I see.
(*He stares at* HERR ROSE. *They are all embarrassed.*)

FRAU ROSE. Yes, that's right.
(MÖBIUS *nods to* HERR ROSE.)

MÖBIUS. I am glad to make the acquaintance of my boys' new father.

HERR ROSE. I have taken them to my bosom, Herr Möbius, all three of them. God will provide. As the psalmist says: The Lord is my shepherd, I shall not want.

FRAU ROSE. Oskar knows all the psalms off by heart. The Psalms of David, the Psalms of Solomon.

MÖBIUS. I am glad the boys have found such an excellent father. I have not been a satisfactory father to them.
(*The three boys protest at this.*)

THREE BOYS. Ah, no, Papi.

MÖBIUS. And Lina has found a husband more worthy of her.

FRAU ROSE. But my dear little Johann Wilhelm –

MÖBIUS. I congratulate you. Heartiest congratulations.

FRAU ROSE. We must be going soon.

MÖBIUS. To the Marianas.

FRAU ROSE. I mean, we must say goodbye to one another.

MÖBIUS. For ever.

FRAU ROSE. Your sons are remarkably musical, Johann Wilhelm. They are very gifted players on their recorders. Play your papi something, boys, as a parting present.

THREE BOYS. Yes, mama.

(ADOLF-FRIEDRICH *opens the brief-case and distributes recorders.*)

FRAU ROSE. Sit down, my little Johann Wilhelm.

(MÖBIUS *sits down at the round table.* FRAU ROSE *and* HERR ROSE *sit down on the sofa. The boys take their places in the middle of the room.*)

Now. What are you going to play?

JÖRG-LUKAS. A bit of Buxtehude.

FRAU ROSE. Ready – one, two, three.

(*The boys play.*)

More feeling, boys, more expression!

(*The boys play with more expression.* MÖBIUS *jumps up.*)

MÖBIUS. I'd rather they didn't. Please, don't!

(*The boys stop playing, bewildered.*)

Don't play any more. Please. For King Solomon's sake. Don't play any more.

FRAU ROSE. But Johann Wilhelm!

MÖBIUS. Please, don't play any more. Please, don't play any more, please, please.

HERR ROSE. Herr Möbius. King Solomon himself will rejoice to hear the piping of these innocent lads. Just think: Solomon, the Psalmist, Solomon, the singer of the Song of Songs.

MÖBIUS. Herr Missionary. I have met Solomon face to face. He is no longer the great golden king who sang of the Shulamite, and of the two young roes that are twins, which feed among the roses. He has cast away his purple robe!

(MÖBIUS *suddenly dashes past his horrified family to his room and throws open the door.*)

Now here in my room he crouches naked and stinking, the pauper king of truth, and his psalms are horrible. Listen carefully, Herr Missionary. You love the words of the psalms and know them all by heart. Well, you can learn these by heart as well.

(*He has run to the round table left, turned it over, climbed into it and sat down.*)

A Song of Solomon to be sung to the Cosmonauts.

> We shagged off into outer space
> To the deserts of the moon. Foundered in her dust
> Right from the start there were plenty
> That soundlessly shot their bolts out there.
> But most of them cooked
> In the lead fumes of Mercury, were wiped out
> In the oil-swamps of Venus and
> Even on Mars we were wolfed by the sun –
> Thundering, radioactive, yellow.
>
> Jupiter stank
> An arrow-swift rotatory methane mash
> He, the almighty, slung over us
> Till we spewed up our guts over Ganymede.

FRAU ROSE. But, Johann Wilhelm –
MÖBIUS.

> Saturn we greeted with curses
> What came next, a waste of breath
>
> Uranus Neptune
> Greyish-green, frozen to death
> Over Pluto and Transpluto fell the final
> Dirty jokes.

We had long since mistaken the sun for Sirius
Sirius for Canopus
Outcasts we cast out, up into the deep
Towards a few white stars
That we never reached anyhow

Long since mummied in our spacecraft
Caked with filth

In our deathsheads no more memories
Of breathing earth.

SISTER BOLL. But Herr Möbius!

(SISTER BOLL *has entered, right, with* NURSE MONIKA.
MÖBIUS *sits staring blankly, his face like a mask, inside the
overturned table.*)

MÖBIUS. And now get yourselves off to the Marianas!

FRAU ROSE. My little Johann Wilhelm –

THREE BOYS. Papi!

MÖBIUS. Get yourselves away! And quick about it! Off to the
Marianas the whole pack of you!

(*He stands up with a threatening look. The* ROSE *family is non-
plussed.*)

SISTER BOLL. Come, Frau Rose. Come, boys. Herr Rose. He
needs time to calm down.

MÖBIUS. Away with you! Get out!

SISTER BOLL. Just a mild attack. Nurse Monika will stay with
him and calm him down. Just a mild attack.

MÖBIUS. Get out, will you! For good and all! Off to the Pacific
with the lot of you!

JÖRG-LUKAS. Goodbye, Papi! Goodbye!

(SISTER BOLL *leads the overwrought and weeping family off
right.* MÖBIUS *goes on yelling unrestrainedly after them.*)

MÖBIUS. I never want to set eyes on you again! You have insulted King Solomon! May you be damned for ever! May you
and the entire Marianas sink and drown in the Mariana Deep!

Four thousand fathoms down! May you sink and rot in the blackest hole of the sea, forgotten by God and man!

MONIKA. We're alone now. Your family can't hear you any more.

(MÖBIUS *stares wonderingly at* NURSE MONIKA *and finally seems to come to himself.*)

MÖBIUS. Ah, yes, of course.

(NURSE MONIKA *is silent. He is somewhat embarrassed.*)

Was I a bit violent?

MONIKA. Somewhat.

MÖBIUS. I had to speak the truth.

MONIKA. Obviously.

MÖBIUS. I got worked up.

MONIKA. You were putting it on.

MÖBIUS. So you saw through me?

MONIKA. I've been looking after you for two years now.

(*He paces up and down, then stops.*)

MÖBIUS. All right. I admit I was just pretending to be mad.

MONIKA. Why?

MÖBIUS. So that I could say goodbye to my wife and sons for ever.

MONIKA. But why in such a dreadful way?

MÖBIUS. Oh no, it was a humane way. If you're in a madhouse already, the only way to get rid of the past is to behave like a madman. Now they can forget me with a clear conscience. My performance finally cured them of ever wanting to see me again. The consequences for myself are unimportant; life outside this establishment is the only thing that counts. Madness costs money. For fifteen years my Lina has been paying out monstrous sums, and an end had to be put to all that. This was a favourable moment. King Solomon has revealed to me what was to be revealed; the Principle of Universal Discovery is complete, the final pages have been dictated and my wife has found a new husband, a missionary, a good man through and through. You should feel reassured now, nurse. Everything is in order.

(*He is about to go.*)

MONIKA. You had it all planned.

MÖBIUS. I am a physicist.

(*He turns to go to his room.*)

MONIKA. Herr Möbius.

(*He stops.*)

MÖBIUS. Yes, nurse?

MONIKA. I have something to tell you.

MÖBIUS. Well?

MONIKA. It concerns us both.

MÖBIUS. Let's sit down.

(*They sit down: she on the sofa, he in the arm-chair on its left.*)

MONIKA. We must say goodbye to one another too. And for ever.

(*He is frightened.*)

MÖBIUS. Are you leaving me?

MONIKA. Orders.

MÖBIUS. What has happened?

MONIKA. I'm being transferred to the main building. From to-morrow the patients here will be supervised by male attendants. Nurses won't be allowed to enter the villa any more.

MÖBIUS. Because of Newton and Einstein?

MONIKA. At the request of the public prosecutor. Doktor von Zahnd feared there would be difficulties and gave way.

(*Silence. He is dejected.*)

MÖBIUS. Nurse Monika, I don't know what to say. I've forgotten how to express my feelings; talking shop with the two sick men I live with can hardly be called conversation. I am afraid that I may have dried up inside as well. Yet you ought to know that for me everything has been different since I got to know you. It's been more bearable. These were two years during which I was happier than before. Because through you, Nurse Monika, I have found the courage to accept being shut away, to accept the fate of being a madman. Goodbye.

(*He stands, holding out his hand.*)

326

MONIKA. Herr Möbius, I don't think you *are* mad.

(MÖBIUS *laughs and sits down again.*)

MÖBIUS. Neither do I. But that does not alter my position in any way. It's my misfortune that King Solomon keeps appearing to me and in the realm of science there is nothing more repugnant than a miracle.

MONIKA. Herr Möbius, I believe in this miracle.

(MÖBIUS *stares at her, disconcerted.*)

MÖBIUS. You believe in it?

MONIKA. I believe in King Solomon.

MÖBIUS. And that he appears to me?

MONIKA. That he appears to you.

MÖBIUS. Day in, day out?

MONIKA. Day in, day out.

MÖBIUS. And you believe that he dictates the secrets of nature to me? How all things connect? The Principle of Universal Discovery?

MONIKA. I believe all that. And if you were to tell me that King David and all his court appeared before you I should believe it all. I simply know that you are not sick. I can feel it.

(*Silence. Then* MÖBIUS *leaps to his feet.*)

MÖBIUS. Nurse Monika! Get out of here!

(*She remains seated.*)

MONIKA. I'm staying.

MÖBIUS. I never want to see you again.

MONIKA. You need me. Apart from me, you have no one left in all the world. Not one single person.

MÖBIUS. It is fatal to believe in King Solomon.

MONIKA. I love you.

(MÖBIUS *stares perplexed at* MONIKA, *and sits down again. Silence.*)

MÖBIUS. I love you too. (*She stares at him.*) That is why you are in danger. Because we love one another.

(EINSTEIN, *smoking his pipe, comes out of Room Number 2.*)

EINSTEIN. I woke up again. I suddenly remembered.

MONIKA. Now, Herr Professor.

EINSTEIN. I strangled Nurse Irene.

MONIKA. Try not to think about it, Herr Professor.

(*He looks at his hands.*)

EINSTEIN. Shall I ever again be able to touch my violin with these hands?

(MÖBIUS *stands up as if to protect* MONIKA.)

MÖBIUS. You were playing just now.

EINSTEIN. Well, I hope?

MÖBIUS. The Kreutzer Sonata. While the police were here.

EINSTEIN. The Kreutzer! Well, thank God for that!

(*His face, having brightened, clouds over again.*)

All the same, I don't like playing the fiddle and I don't like this pipe either. It's foul.

MÖBIUS. Then give them up.

EINSTEIN. I can't do that, not if I'm Albert Einstein.

(*He gives them both a sharp look.*)

Are you two in love?

MONIKA. We are in love.

(EINSTEIN *proceeds thoughtfully backstage to where the murdered nurse lay.*)

EINSTEIN. Nurse Irene and I were in love too. She would have done anything for me. I warned her. I shouted at her. I treated her like a dog. I implored her to run away before it was too late. In vain. She stayed. She wanted to take me away into the country. To Kohlwang. She wanted to marry me. She even obtained permission for the wedding from Fräulein Doktor von Zahnd herself. Then I strangled her. Poor Nurse Irene. In all the world there's nothing more absurd than a woman's frantic desire for self-sacrifice.

(MONIKA *goes to him.*)

MONIKA. Go and lie down again, Herr Professor.

EINSTEIN. You may call me Albert.

MONIKA. Be sensible, now, Albert.

EINSTEIN. And you be sensible, too, Nurse. Obey the man you love and run away from him; or you're lost.

(*He turns back towards Room Number 2.*)

I'm going back to bed.

(*He disappears into Room Number 2.*)

MONIKA. That poor, confused creature.

MÖBIUS. Well, he must have convinced you finally of the impossibility of remaining in love with me.

MONIKA. But you're not mad.

MÖBIUS. It would be wiser if you were to treat me as if I were. Make your escape now! Go on, run! Clear off! Or I'll treat you like a dog myself.

MONIKA. Why can't you treat me like a woman?

MÖBIUS. Come here, Monika.

(*He leads her to an arm-chair, sits down opposite her and takes her hands.*)

Listen. I have committed a grave mistake. I have not kept King Solomon's appearances to myself. So he is making me atone for it. For life. But you ought not to be punished for what I did. In the eyes of the world, you are in love with a man who is mentally sick. You're simply asking for trouble. Leave this place; forget me: that would be the best thing for us both.

MONIKA. Don't you want me?

MÖBIUS. Why do you talk like that?

MONIKA. I want to sleep with you, I want to have children by you. I know I'm talking quite shamelessly. But why won't you look at me? Don't you find me attractive? I know these nurses' uniforms are hideous.

(*She tears off her nurse's cap.*)

I hate my profession! For five years I've been looking after sick people out of love for my fellow-beings. I never flinched; everyone could count on me: I sacrificed myself. But now I want to sacrifice myself for one person alone, to exist for one person alone, and not for everybody all the time. I want to exist for the man I love. For you. I will do anything you ask, work for you day and night: only you can't send me away! I have no one else in the world! I am as much alone as you.

MÖBIUS. Monika. I must send you away.

MONIKA (*despairing*). But don't you feel any love for me at all?

MÖBIUS. I love you, Monika. Good God, I love you. That's what's mad.

MONIKA. Then why do you betray me? and not only me. You say that King Solomon appears to you. Why do you betray him too?

(MÖBIUS, *terribly worked-up, takes hold of her.*)

MÖBIUS. Monika! You can believe what you like of me. I'm a weakling; all right. I *am* unworthy of your love. But I have always remained faithful to King Solomon. He thrust himself into my life, suddenly, unbidden, he abused me, he destroyed my life, but I have never betrayed him.

MONIKA. Are you sure?

MÖBIUS. Do you doubt it?

MONIKA. You think you have to atone because you have not kept his appearances secret. But perhaps it is because you do not stand up for his revelations.

(*He lets her go.*)

MÖBIUS. I – I don't follow you.

MONIKA. He dictates to you the Principle of Universal Discovery. Why won't you fight for that principle?

MÖBIUS. But after all, people do regard me as a madman.

MONIKA. Why can't you show more spirit?

MÖBIUS. In my case, to show spirit would be a crime.

MONIKA. Johann Wilhelm. I've spoken to Fräulein Doktor von Zahnd.

(MÖBIUS *stares at her.*)

MÖBIUS. You spoke to her?

MONIKA. You are free.

MÖBIUS. Free?

MONIKA. We can get married.

MÖBIUS. God.

MONIKA. Fräulein Doktor von Zahnd has arranged everything. Of course, she still considers you're a sick man, but not dangerous. And it's not a hereditary sickness. She said she was madder than you, and she laughed.

MÖBIUS. That was good of her.

MONIKA. She's a great woman.

MÖBIUS. Indeed.

MONIKA. Johann Wilhelm! I've accepted a post as district nurse in Blumenstein. I've been saving up. We have no need to worry. All we need is to keep our love for each other.

(MÖBIUS *has stood up. It gradually gets darker in the room.*)
Isn't it wonderful?

MÖBIUS. Indeed, yes.

MONIKA. You don't sound very happy.

MÖBIUS. It's all happened so unexpectedly –

MONIKA. I've done something else.

MÖBIUS. What would that be?

MONIKA. I spoke to Professor Schubert.

MÖBIUS. He was my teacher.

MONIKA. He remembered you perfectly. He said you'd been his best pupil.

MÖBIUS. And what did you talk to him about?

MONIKA. He promised he would examine your manuscripts with an open mind.

MÖBIUS. Did you explain that they have been dictated by King Solomon?

MONIKA. Naturally.

MÖBIUS. Well?

MONIKA. He just laughed. He said you'd always been a bit of a joker. Johann Wilhelm! We mustn't think just of ourselves. You are a chosen being. King Solomon appeared to you, revealed himself in all his glory and confided in you the wisdom of the heavens. Now you have to take the way ordained by that miracle, turning neither to left nor right, even if that way

leads through mockery and laughter, through disbelief and
doubt. But the way leads out of this asylum, Johann Wilhelm,
it leads into the outside world, not into loneliness, it leads into
battle. I am here to help you, to fight at your side. Heaven,
that sent you King Solomon, sent me too.

(MÖBIUS *stares out of the window.*)

Dearest.

MÖBIUS. Yes, dear?

MONIKA. Aren't you happy?

MÖBIUS. Very.

MONIKA. Now we must get your bags packed. The train for
Blumenstein leaves at eight twenty.

MÖBIUS. There's not much to pack.

MONIKA. It's got quite dark.

MÖBIUS. The nights are drawing in quickly now.

MONIKA. I'll switch on the light.

MÖBIUS. Wait a moment. Come here.

(*She goes to him. Only their silhouettes are visible.*)

MONIKA. You have tears in your eyes.

MÖBIUS. So have you.

MONIKA. Tears of happiness.

(*He rips down the curtain and flings it over her. A brief struggle.
Their silhouettes are no longer visible. Then silence. The door to
Room Number 3 opens. A shaft of light shines into the darkened
room. In the doorway stands NEWTON in eighteenth-century costume. MÖBIUS rises.*)

NEWTON. What's happened?

MÖBIUS. I've strangled Nurse Monika Stettler.

(*The sound of a fiddle playing comes from Room Number 2.*)

NEWTON. Einstein's off again. Kreisler. Humoresque.

(*He goes to the fireplace and gets the brandy.*)

ACT TWO

One hour later. The same room. It is dark outside. The police are again present, measuring, sketching, photographing. But this time the corpse of MONIKA STETTLER *cannot be seen by the audience and it is assumed to be lying backstage right, below the window. The drawing-room is brightly lit. The chandelier and the standard lamp have been switched on. On the sofa sits* FRÄULEIN DOKTOR MATHILDE VON ZAHND, *looking gloomy and preoccupied. There is a box of cigars on the small table in front of her.* GUHL, *with his stenographer's notebook, is occupying the arm-chair on the extreme right.* INSPECTOR VOSS, *wearing his coat and hat, turns away from where the corpse is presumed to be lying and comes downstage.*

FRL. DOKTOR. Cigar?
INSPECTOR. No, thanks.
FRL. DOKTOR. Brandy?
INSPECTOR. Later.
        (*A silence.*)
INSPECTOR. Blocher, you can take your photographs now.
BLOCHER. Very well, Inspector.
        (*Photographs and flashes.*)
INSPECTOR. What was the nurse's name?
FRL. DOKTOR. Monika Stettler.
INSPECTOR. Age?
FRL. DOKTOR. Twenty-five. From Blumenstein.
INSPECTOR. Any relatives?
FRL. DOKTOR. None.
INSPECTOR. Have you got the statement down, Guhl?
GUHL. Yes, sir.

INSPECTOR. Strangled again, doctor?

POLICE DOCTOR. Quite definitely. And again, tremendous strength was used. But with the curtain cord this time.

INSPECTOR. Just like three months ago.

(*He sits down wearily in the arm-chair downstage right.*)

FRL. DOKTOR. Would you like to have the murderer brought in?

INSPECTOR. Please, Fräulein Doktor.

FRL. DOKTOR. I mean, the assailant.

INSPECTOR. I don't think so.

FRL. DOKTOR. But –

INSPECTOR. Fräulein Doktor von Zahnd. I am doing my duty, taking down evidence, examining the corpse, having it photographed and getting the police doctor's opinion. But I do not wish to examine Möbius. I leave him to you. Along with the other radioactive physicists.

FRL. DOKTOR. And the public prosecutor?

INSPECTOR. He's past being angry now. He's just brooding.

(*The DOKTOR wipes her forehead.*)

FRL. DOKTOR. Warm in here.

INSPECTOR. *I* don't think so.

FRL. DOKTOR. This third murder –

INSPECTOR. Please, Fräulein Doktor.

FRL. DOKTOR. This third accident is the end as far as my work at Les Cerisiers goes. Now I can resign. Monika Stettler was my best nurse. She understood the patients. She could enter into their states of mind. I loved her like a daughter. But her death is not the worst thing that's happened. My reputation as a doctor is ruined.

INSPECTOR. You'll build it up again. Blocher, get another shot from above.

BLOCHER. Very well, Herr Inspektor.

(*Two enormous male attendants enter right pushing a trolley with food, plates and cutlery on it. One of them is a negro. They are accompanied by a chief male attendant who is equally enormous.*)

334

CHIEF ATTNDT. Dinner for the dear good patients, Fräulein Doktor.

(*The* INSPECTOR *jumps up.*)

INSPECTOR. Uwe Sievers.

CHIEF ATTNDT. Correct, Herr Inspektor. Uwe Sievers. Former European heavyweight boxing champion. Now chief male attendant at Les Cerisiers.

INSPECTOR. And these two other bruisers?

CHIEF ATTNDT. Murillo, South American champion, also a heavyweight. And McArthur (*pointing to the negro*), North American middleweight champion. McArthur, the table.

(MCARTHUR *rights the overturned table.*)

Murillo, the tablecloth.

(MURILLO *spreads a white cloth over the table.*)

McArthur, the Meissen.

(MCARTHUR *lays the plates.*)

Murillo, the silver.

(MURILLO *lays out the silver.*)

McArthur, the soup-tureen in the middle.

(MCARTHUR *sets the soup-tureen in the centre of the table.*)

INSPECTOR. And what are the dear good patients having for dinner?

(*He lifts the lid of the tureen.*)

Liver-dumpling soup.

CHIEF ATTNDT. Poulet à la broche. Cordon Bleu.

INSPECTOR. Fantastic.

CHIEF ATTNDT. First class.

INSPECTOR. I am a mere fourteenth-class official. Plain cooking is all we can run to in my home.

CHIEF ATTNDT. Fräulein Doktor. Dinner is served.

FRL. DOKTOR. Thank you, Sievers. You may go. The patients will help themselves.

CHIEF ATTNDT. Herr Inspektor. Glad to have made your acquaintance.

(*The three attendants bow and go out right. The* INSPECTOR *gazes after them.*)

INSPECTOR. Well I'm damned.

FRL. DOKTOR. Satisfied?

INSPECTOR. Envious. If we had them with the police –

FRL. DOKTOR. Their wages are astronomical.

INSPECTOR. With all your industrial barons and multi-million-airesses you can certainly afford such luxuries. Those fellows will finally set the public prosecutor's mind at rest. They wouldn't let anyone slip through their fingers.

(*From Room Number 2 comes the sound of Einstein playing his fiddle.*)

There's Einstein at it again.

FRL. DOKTOR. Kreisler. As usual. Liebesleid. The pangs of love.

BLOCHER. We're finished now, Herr Inspektor.

INSPECTOR. Take the body out. Again.

(*Two policemen lift the corpse. Then* MÖBIUS *rushes out of Room Number 1.*)

MÖBIUS. Monika! My beloved!

(*The two policemen stand still, carrying the corpse.* FRÄULEIN DOKTOR *rises majestically.*)

FRL. DOKTOR. Möbius! How could you do it! You have killed my best nurse, my sweetest nurse!

MÖBIUS. I'm sorry, Fräulein Doktor.

FRL. DOKTOR. Sorry.

MÖBIUS. King Solomon ordained it.

FRL. DOKTOR. King Solomon.

(*She sits down again, heavily. Her face is white.*)

So it was His Majesty who arranged the murder.

MÖBIUS. I was standing at the window staring out into the falling dusk. Then the King came floating up out of the park over the terrace, right up close to me, and whispered his commands to me through the window-pane.

FRL. DOKTOR. Excuse me, Inspector, my nerves.

INSPECTOR. Don't mention it.

FRL. DOKTOR. A place like this wears one out.

INSPECTOR. I can well believe it.

336

FRL. DOKTOR. If you'll excuse me –
  (*She stands up.*)
Herr Inspektor Voss, please express my profound regret to the
public prosecutor for the incidents that have taken place in my
sanatorium. Kindly assure him that everything is now well in
hand again. Doctor, gentlemen, it was a pleasure.
  (*She first of all goes upstage right, bows her head ceremoniously
  before the corpse, looks at* MÖBIUS *and goes off right.*)
INSPECTOR. There. Now you can take the body into the chapel.
  Put her beside Nurse Irene.
MÖBIUS. Monika!
  (*The two policemen carrying the corpse and the others carrying
  their apparatus go out through the doors to the garden. The police
  doctor follows them.*)
Monika, my love.
  (*The* INSPECTOR *walks to the small table beside the sofa.*)
INSPECTOR. Möbius, come and sit down. Now I absolutely must
  have a cigar. I've earned it.
  (*He takes a gigantic cigar out of the box and considers its size.*)
Good grief!
  (*He bites off the end and lights the cigar.*)
My dear Möbius, behind the fire-guard you will find a bottle
of brandy hidden away by Sir Isaac Newton.
MÖBIUS. Certainly, Herr Inspektor.
  (*The* INSPECTOR *blows out clouds of smoke while* MÖBIUS *goes
  and gets the brandy and the glass.*)
May I pour you one?
INSPECTOR. Indeed you may.
  (*He takes the glass and drinks.*)
MÖBIUS. Another?
INSPECTOR. Another.
  (MÖBIUS *pours out another glass.*)
MÖBIUS. Herr Inspektor, I must ask you to arrest me.
INSPECTOR. But what for, my dear Möbius?
MÖBIUS. Well, after all, Nurse Monika –

INSPECTOR. You yourself admitted that you acted under the orders of King Solomon. As long as I'm unable to arrest *him* you are a free man.

MÖBIUS. All the same –

INSPECTOR. There's no question of all the same. Pour me another glass.

MÖBIUS. Certainly, Herr Inspektor.

INSPECTOR. And now hide the brandy bottle away again or the attendants will be getting drunk on it.

MÖBIUS. Very well, Herr Inspektor.

(*He puts the brandy away.*)

INSPECTOR. You see, it's like this. Every year in this small town and the surrounding district, I arrest a few murderers. Not many. A bare half-dozen. Some of these it gives me great pleasure to apprehend; others I feel sorry for. All the same I have to arrest them. Justice is Justice. And then you come along and your two colleagues. At first I felt angry at not being able to proceed with the arrests. But now? All at once I'm enjoying myself. I could shout with joy. I have discovered three murderers whom I can, with an easy conscience, leave unmolested. For the first time justice is on holiday – and it's a terrific feeling. Justice, my friend, is a terrible strain; you wear yourself out in its service, both physically and morally; I need a breathing space, that's all. Thanks to you, my dear Möbius, I've got it. Well, goodbye. Give my kindest regards to Einstein and Newton.

MÖBIUS. Very well, Herr Inspektor.

INSPECTOR. And my respects to King Solomon.

(*The* INSPECTOR *goes.* MÖBIUS *is left alone. He sits down on the sofa and takes his head in his hands.* NEWTON *comes out of Room Number 3.*)

NEWTON. What's cooking?

(MÖBIUS *does not reply.* NEWTON *takes the lid off the tureen.*) Liver-dumpling soup.

(*Lifts the lid off the other dishes on the trolley.*)

Poulet à la broche. Cordon Bleu. Extraordinary. We usually only have a light supper in the evenings. And a very modest one. Ever since the other patients were moved into the new building.

(*He helps himself to soup.*)

Lost your appetite?

(MÖBIUS *remains silent.*)

I quite understand. I lost mine too after my nurse.

(*He sits and begins to drink the soup.* MÖBIUS *rises and is about to go to his room.*)

Stay here.

MÖBIUS. Sir Isaac?

NEWTON. I have something to say to you, Möbius.

(MÖBIUS *remains standing.*)

MÖBIUS. Well?

(NEWTON *gestures at the food.*)

NEWTON. Wouldn't you like to try just a spoonful of the liver-dumpling soup? It's excellent.

MÖBIUS. No.

NEWTON. Möbius, we are no longer lovingly tended by nurses, we are being guarded by male attendants. Great hefty fellows.

MÖBIUS. That's of no consequence.

NEWTON. Perhaps not to you, Möbius. It's obvious you really want to spend the rest of your days in a madhouse. But it is of some consequence to me. The fact is, I want to get out of here.

(*He finishes his plate of soup.*)

Mmm – Now for the poulet à la broche.

(*He helps himself.*)

These new attendants have compelled me to act straight away.

MÖBIUS. That's your affair.

NEWTON. Not altogether. A confession, Möbius. I am not mad.

MÖBIUS. But of course not, Sir Isaac.

NEWTON. I am not Sir Isaac Newton.

MÖBIUS. I know. Albert Einstein.

339

NEWTON. Fiddlesticks. Nor am I Herbert Georg Beutler, as they think here. My real name, dear boy, is Kilton.

(MÖBIUS *stares at him in horror*.)

MÖBIUS. Alec Jaspar Kilton?

NEWTON. Correct.

MÖBIUS. The author of the theory of Equivalents?

NEWTON. The very same.

(MÖBIUS *moves over to the table*.)

MÖBIUS. So you wangled your way in here?

NEWTON. By pretending to be mad.

MÖBIUS. In order to – spy on me?

NEWTON. In order to get to the root of your madness. My impeccable German was acquired in our Intelligence Service. A frightful grind.

MÖBIUS. And because poor Nurse Dorothea stumbled on the truth, you –

NEWTON. – Yes. I am most extraordinarily sorry about the whole thing.

MÖBIUS. I understand.

NEWTON. Orders are orders.

MÖBIUS. Of course.

NEWTON. I couldn't do anything else.

MÖBIUS. Naturally.

NEWTON. My whole mission hung in the balance, the most secret undertaking of our Secret Service. I had to kill, if I wanted to avert suspicion. Nurse Dorothea no longer considered me to be demented; Fräulein Doktor von Zahnd thought I was only slightly touched; to prove my total insanity I had to commit a murder. I say, this poulet à la broche is simply superb.

(*Einstein is fiddling in Room Number 2.*)

MÖBIUS. Einstein's at it again.

NEWTON. That Bach Gavotte.

MÖBIUS. His dinner's getting cold.

NEWTON. Let the old idiot get on with his fiddling.

MÖBIUS. Is that a threat?

NEWTON. I have the most immeasurable respect for you. It would grieve me to have to take violent steps.

MÖBIUS. So your mission is to abduct me?

NEWTON. Yes, if the suspicions of our Intelligence Service prove correct.

MÖBIUS. What would they be?

NEWTON. Our Intelligence Service happens to consider you to be the greatest genius among present-day physicists.

MÖBIUS. I'm a man whose nerves are sick, Kilton, that's all.

NEWTON. Our Intelligence Service has other ideas on the subject.

MÖBIUS. And what is your opinion?

NEWTON. I simply consider you to be the greatest physicist of all time.

MÖBIUS. And how did your Intelligence Service get on my trail?

NEWTON. Through me. Quite by chance I read your dissertation on the foundations of a new concept of physics. At first I thought it was a practical joke. Then the scales seemed to fall from my eyes. I realized I was reading the greatest work of genius in the history of physics. I began to make inquiries about its author but made no progress. Thereupon I informed our Intelligence Service: they got on to you.

EINSTEIN. You were not the only one who read that dissertation, Kilton.

> (*He has entered unnoticed from Room Number 2 with his fiddle and bow under his arm.*)

As a matter of fact, I'm not mad either. May I introduce myself? I too am a physicist. Member of a certain Intelligence Service. A somewhat different one from yours, Kilton. My name is Joseph Eisler.

MÖBIUS. The discoverer of the Eisler-effect?

EINSTEIN. The very same.

NEWTON. 'Disappeared' in 1950.

EINSTEIN. Of my own free will.

> (NEWTON *is suddenly seen to have a revolver in his hand.*)

NEWTON. Eisler, might I trouble you to stand with your face to the wall, please?

EINSTEIN. Why of course.

(*He saunters easily across to the window-seat, lays his fiddle and bow on the mantelpiece, then swiftly turns with a revolver in his hand.*)

My dear Kilton, we both, I suspect, know how to handle these things, so don't you think it would be better if we were to avoid a duel? If possible? I shall gladly lay down my Browning if you will do the same with your Colt.

NEWTON. Agreed.

EINSTEIN. Behind the fire-guard with the brandy. Just in case the attendants come in suddenly.

NEWTON. Good.

(*They both put their revolvers behind the fire-guard.*)

EINSTEIN. You've messed up all my plans, Kilton. I thought you really were mad.

NEWTON. Never mind: I thought you were.

EINSTEIN. Things kept going wrong. That business with Nurse Irene, for example, this afternoon. She was getting suspicious, and so she signed her own death-warrant. I am most extraordinarily sorry about the whole thing.

MÖBIUS. I understand.

EINSTEIN. Orders are orders.

MÖBIUS. Of course.

EINSTEIN. I couldn't do anything else.

MÖBIUS. Naturally.

EINSTEIN. My whole mission hung in the balance; it was the most secret undertaking of our Secret Service. But let's sit down.

NEWTON. Yes, let's sit down.

(*He sits down on the left side of the table*, EINSTEIN *on the right*.)

MÖBIUS. Eisler, I presume that you, too, want to compel me now to –

EINSTEIN. Now Möbius –

342

MÖBIUS. – want to persuade me to visit your country.

EINSTEIN. We also consider you to be the greatest physicist of all time. But just at the moment all I'm interested in is my dinner. It's a real gallows-feast.

(*He ladles soup into his plate.*)

Still no appetite, Möbius?

MÖBIUS. Yes; it's suddenly come back. Now that you've both got to the bottom of things.

(*He sits down between them at the table and helps himself to the soup.*)

NEWTON. Burgundy, Möbius?

MÖBIUS. Go ahead.

(NEWTON *pours out the wine.*)

NEWTON. I'll attack the Cordon Bleu, what?

MÖBIUS. Make yourselves perfectly at home.

NEWTON. Bon appétit.

EINSTEIN. Bon appétit.

MÖBIUS. Bon appétit.

(*They eat. The three male attendants come in right, the chief attendant carrying a notebook.*)

CHIEF ATTNDT. Patient Beutler!

NEWTON. Here.

CHIEF ATTNDT. Patient Ernesti!

EINSTEIN. Here.

CHIEF ATTNDT. Patient Möbius!

MÖBIUS. Here.

CHIEF ATTNDT. Head Nurse Sievers, Nurse Murillo, Nurse Mc-Arthur.

(*He puts the notebook away.*)

On the recommendation of the authorities, certain security measures are to be observed. Murillo. The grille.

(MURILLO *lets down a metal grille over the window. The room now suddenly has the aspect of a prison.*)

McArthur. Lock up.

(MCARTHUR *locks the grille.*)

343

Have the gentlemen any further requests before retiring for the night? Patient Beutler?

NEWTON. No.

CHIEF ATTNDT. Patient Ernesti?

EINSTEIN. No.

CHIEF ATTNDT. Patient Möbius?

MÖBIUS. No.

CHIEF ATTNDT. Gentlemen, we take our leave. Good night.

> (*The three attendants go. Silence.*)

EINSTEIN. Monsters.

NEWTON. They've got more of the brutes lurking in the park. I've been watching them from my window for some time.

> (EINSTEIN *goes up and inspects the grille.*)

EINSTEIN. Solid steel. With a special lock.

> (NEWTON *goes to the door of his room, opens it and looks in.*)

NEWTON. They've put a grille over my window. Quick work.

> (*He opens the other two doors.*)

Same for Eisler. And for Möbius.

> (*He goes to the door right.*)

Locked.

> (*He sits down again. So does* EINSTEIN.)

EINSTEIN. Prisoners.

NEWTON. Only logical. What with our nurses and everything.

EINSTEIN. We'll never get out of this madhouse now unless we act together.

MÖBIUS. I do not wish to escape.

EINSTEIN. Möbius –

MÖBIUS. I see no reason for it at all. On the contrary. I am quite satisfied with my fate.

> (*Silence.*)

NEWTON. But I'm not satisfied with it. That's a fairly decisive element in the case, don't you think? With all respect to your personal feelings, you are a genius and therefore common property. You mapped out new directions in physics. But you haven't a monopoly of knowledge. It is your duty to open the doors for us, the non-geniuses. Come on out: within a year, we'll have you in a top hat, white tie and tails, fly you to Stockholm and give you the Nobel prize.

MÖBIUS. Your Intelligence Service is very altruistic.

NEWTON. I don't mind telling you, Möbius, they have a suspicion that you've solved the problem of gravitation.

MÖBIUS. I have.

(*Silence.*)

EINSTEIN. You say that as if it were nothing.

MÖBIUS. How else should I say it?

EINSTEIN. *Our* Intelligence Service believed you would discover the Unitary Theory of Elementary Particles.

MÖBIUS. Then I can set their minds at rest as well. I have discovered it.

(NEWTON *mops his forehead.*)

NEWTON. The basic formula.

EINSTEIN. It's ludicrous. Here we have hordes of highly-paid physicists in gigantic state-supported laboratories working for years and years and years vainly trying to make some progress in the realm of physics while you do it quite casually at your desk in this madhouse.

(*He too mops his forehead.*)

NEWTON. Möbius. What about the – the Principle of Universal Discovery?

MÖBIUS. Yes, something on those lines, too. I did it out of curiosity, as a practical corollary to my theoretical investigations. Why play the innocent? We have to face the consequences of our scientific thinking. It was my duty to work out the effects that would be produced by my Unitary Theory of Elementary Particles and by my discoveries in the field of gravitation. The result is – devastating. New and inconceivable forces would be unleashed, making possible a technical advance that would transcend the wildest flights of fantasy if my findings were to fall into the hands of mankind.

EINSTEIN. And that can scarcely be avoided.

345

NEWTON. The only question is: who's going to get at them first?
(MÖBIUS *laughs*.)

MÖBIUS. You'd like that for your own Intelligence Service,
wouldn't you, Kilton, and the military machine behind it?

NEWTON. And why not? It seems to me, if it can restore the
greatest physicist of all time to the confraternity of the physical sciences, any military machine is a sacred instrument. It's
nothing more nor less than a question of the freedom of scientific knowledge. It doesn't matter who guarantees that freedom. I give my services to any system, providing that system
leaves me alone. I know there's a lot of talk nowadays about
physicists' moral responsibilities. We suddenly find ourselves
confronted with our own fears and we have a fit of morality.
This is nonsense. We have far-reaching, pioneering work to
do and that's all that should concern us. Whether or not
humanity has the wit to follow the new trails we are blazing
is its own look-out, not ours.

EINSTEIN. Admittedly we have pioneer work to do. I believe that
too. But all the same we cannot escape our responsibilities.
We are providing humanity with colossal sources of power.
That gives us the right to impose conditions. If we are physicists, then we must become power politicians. We must decide in whose favour we shall apply our knowledge, and I for
one have made my decision. Whereas you, Kilton, are nothing but a lamentable aesthete. If you feel so strongly about
the freedom of knowledge why don't you come over to our
side? We too for some time now have found it impossible to
dictate to our physicists. We too need results. Our political
system too must eat out of the scientist's hand.

NEWTON. Both our political systems, Eisler, must now eat out of
Möbius's hand.

EINSTEIN. On the contrary. He must do what we tell him. We
have finally got him in check.

NEWTON. You think so? It looks more like stalemate to me. Our
Intelligence Services, unfortunately, both hit upon the same

346

idea. So don't let's delude ourselves. Let's face the impossible situation we've got ourselves into. If Möbius goes with you, I can't do anything about it because you would stop me. And similarly you would be helpless if Möbius decided in my favour. It isn't we who have the choice, it's him.

(EINSTEIN *rises ceremoniously.*)

EINSTEIN. Let us retrieve our revolvers.

(NEWTON *rises likewise.*)

NEWTON. Let us do battle.

(NEWTON *brings the two revolvers and hands* EINSTEIN *his weapon.*)

EINSTEIN. I'm sorry this affair is moving to a bloody conclusion. But we must fight it out, between us and then with the attendants. If need be with Möbius himself. He may well be the most important man in the world, but his manuscripts are more important still.

MÖBIUS. My manuscripts? I've burnt them.

(*Dead silence.*)

EINSTEIN. Burnt them?

MÖBIUS (*embarrassed*). I had to. Before the police came back. So as not to be found out.

(EINSTEIN *bursts into despairing laughter.*)

EINSTEIN. Burnt.

(NEWTON *screams with rage.*)

NEWTON. Fifteen years' work.

EINSTEIN. I shall go mad.

NEWTON. Officially, you already are.

(*They put their revolvers in their pockets and sit down, utterly crushed, on the sofa.*)

EINSTEIN. We've played right into your hands, Möbius.

NEWTON. And to think that for this I had to strangle a nurse and learn German!

EINSTEIN. And I had to learn to play the fiddle. It was torture for someone like me with no ear for music.

MÖBIUS. Shall we go on with dinner?

NEWTON. I've lost my appetite.

EINSTEIN. Pity about the Cordon Bleu.

(MÖBIUS *stands*.)

MÖBIUS. Here we are, three physicists. The decision we have to make is one that we must make as physicists; we must go about it therefore in a scientific manner. We must not let ourselves be influenced by personal feelings but by logical processes. We must endeavour to find a rational solution. We cannot afford to make mistakes in our thinking, because a false conclusion would lead to catastrophe. The basic facts are clear. All three of us have the same end in view, but our tactics differ. Our aim is the advancement of physics. You, Kilton, want to preserve the freedom of that science, and argue that it has no responsibility but to itself. On the other hand you, Eisler, see physics as responsible to the power politics of one particular country. What is the real position now? That's what I must know if I have to make a decision.

NEWTON. Some of the world's most famous physicists are waiting to welcome you. Remuneration and accommodation could not be better. The climate is murderous, but the air-conditioning is excellent.

MÖBIUS. But are these physicists free men?

NEWTON. My dear Möbius, these physicists declare they are ready to solve scientific problems which are decisive for the defence of the country. Therefore, you must understand –

MÖBIUS. So they are not free.

(*He turns to* EINSTEIN.)

Joseph Eisler, your line is power politics. But that requires power. Have you got it?

EINSTEIN. You misunderstand me, Möbius. My political power, to be precise, lies in the fact that I have renounced my own power in favour of a political party.

MÖBIUS. Would you be able to persuade that party to take on your responsibility, or is there a risk of the party persuading you?

ACT TWO

EINSTEIN. Möbius, that's ridiculous. I can only hope that the
party will follow my recommendations, nothing more. In
any case, without hope, all political systems are untenable.

MÖBIUS. Are your physicists free at least?

EINSTEIN. Well, naturally, they too are needed for the defence of
the country –

MÖBIUS. Extraordinary. Each of you is trying to palm off a different theory, yet the reality you offer me is the same in both
cases: a prison. I'd prefer the madhouse. Here at least I feel
safe from the exactions of power politicians.

EINSTEIN. But after all, one must take certain risks.

MÖBIUS. There are certain risks that one may not take: the destruction of humanity is one. We know what the world has
done with the weapons it already possesses; we can imagine
what it would do with those that my researches make possible, and it is these considerations that have governed my conduct. I was poor. I had a wife and three children. Fame
beckoned from the university; industry tempted me with
money. Both courses were too dangerous. I should have had
to publish the result of my researches, and the consequences
would have been the overthrow of all scientific knowledge
and the breakdown of the economic structure of our society. A
sense of responsibility compelled me to choose another course.
I threw up my academic career, said no to industry and aban-
doned my family to its fate. I took on the fool's cap and
bells. I let it be known that King Solomon kept appearing to
me, and before long, I was clapped into a madhouse.

NEWTON. But that couldn't solve anything.

MÖBIUS. Reason demanded the taking of this step. In the realm
of knowledge we have reached the farthest frontiers of per-
ception. We know a few precisely calculable laws, a few basic
connections between incomprehensible phenomena and that
is all. The rest is mystery closed to the rational mind. We have
reached the end of our journey. But humanity has not yet got
as far as that. We have battled onwards, but now no one is

349

following in our footsteps; we have encountered a void. Our knowledge has become a frightening burden. Our researches are perilous, our discoveries are lethal. For us physicists there is nothing left but to surrender to reality. It has not kept up with us. It disintegrates on touching us. We have to take back our knowledge and I have taken it back. There is no other way out, and that goes for you as well.

EINSTEIN. What do you mean by that?

MÖBIUS. You must stay with me here in the madhouse.

NEWTON. What! Us?

MÖBIUS. Both of you.

> (*Silence.*)

NEWTON. But Möbius, surely you can't expect us to – for the rest of our days to –

MÖBIUS. I expect you have secret radio transmitters.

EINSTEIN. Well?

MÖBIUS. You inform your superior that you have made a mistake, that I really am mad.

EINSTEIN. Then we'd be stuck here for the rest of our lives. Nobody's going to lose any sleep over a broken-down spy.

MÖBIUS. But it's the one chance I have to remain undetected. Only in the madhouse can we be free. Only in the madhouse can we think our own thoughts. Outside they would be dynamite.

NEWTON. But damn it all, we're not mad.

MÖBIUS. But we *are* murderers.

> (*They stare at him in perplexity.*)

NEWTON. I resent that!

EINSTEIN. You shouldn't have said that, Möbius!

MÖBIUS. Anyone who takes life is a murderer, and we have taken life. Each of us came to this establishment for a definite purpose. Each of us killed his nurse, again for a definite purpose. You two did it so as not to endanger the outcome of your secret mission; and I, because Nurse Monika believed in me. She thought I was an unrecognized genius. She did not realize

350

that today it's the duty of a genius to remain unrecognized. Killing is a terrible thing. I killed in order to avoid an even more dreadful murder. Then you come along. I can't do away with you, but perhaps I can bring you round to my way of thinking. Are those murders we committed to stand for nothing? Either they were sacrificial killings, or just plain murders. Either we stay in this madhouse or the world becomes one. Either we wipe ourselves out of the memory of mankind or mankind wipes out itself.

(*Silence.*)

NEWTON. Möbius!

MÖBIUS. Kilton.

NEWTON. This place. These ghastly male attendants. That hunchback of a doctor!

MÖBIUS. Well?

EINSTEIN. We're caged in, like wild beasts!

MÖBIUS. We are wild beasts. We ought not to be let loose on humanity.

(*Silence.*)

NEWTON. Is there really no other way out?

MÖBIUS. None.

(*Silence.*)

EINSTEIN. Johann Wilhelm Möbius, I am a man of integrity. I'm staying.

(*Silence.*)

NEWTON. I'm staying too, for ever.

(*Silence.*)

MÖBIUS. Thank you. Thank you for leaving the world this faint chance of survival.

(*He raises his glass.*)

To our nurses!

(*They have gravely risen to their feet.*)

NEWTON. I drink to Dorothea Moser.

THE OTHERS. Nurse Dorothea!

NEWTON. Dorothea! You had to be sacrificed. In return for your love, I gave you death! Now I want to prove myself worthy of you.

EINSTEIN. I drink to Irene Straub!

THE OTHERS. Nurse Irene!

EINSTEIN. Irene! You had to be sacrificed. As a tribute to your memory and your devotion, I am now going to behave like a rational human being.

MÖBIUS. I drink to Monika Stettler.

THE OTHERS. Nurse Monika!

MÖBIUS. Monika! You had to be sacrificed. May your love bless the friendship which we three have formed in your name. Give us the strength to be fools, that we may guard faithfully the secrets of our knowledge.

(*They drink and put the glasses on the table.*)

NEWTON. Let us be changed to madmen once again. Let us put on the shade of Newton.

EINSTEIN. Let us once again scrape away at Kreisler and Beethoven.

MÖBIUS. Let us have King Solomon appear before us once again.

NEWTON. Let us be mad, but wise.

EINSTEIN. Prisoners but free.

MÖBIUS. Physicists but innocent.

(*The three of them wave to each other and go back to their rooms. The drawing-room stands empty. Then enter right* McArthur *and* Murillo. *They are now wearing black uniforms, peaked caps and pistols. They clear the table.* McArthur *wheels the trolley with the china and cutlery off right.* Murillo *places the round table in front of the window right, and puts on it the upturned chairs, as if the place were a restaurant closing for the night. Then* Murillo *goes off right. The room stands empty again. Then enters right* Fräulein Doktor Mathilde von Zahnd. *As usual she is wearing a white surgical coat. Stethoscope. She looks about her. Finally* Sievers *comes in, also wearing a black uniform.*)

SIEVERS. Yes, boss?

FRL. DOKTOR. Sievers, the portrait.

> (McARTHUR *and* MURILLO *carry in a large oil-painting, a portrait in a heavy gilded frame. It represents a general.* SIEVERS *takes down the old portrait and hangs up the new one.*)

It's better for General Leonidas von Zahnd to be hung in here than among the women patients. He still looks a great man, the old war-horse, despite his goitre. He loved heroic deaths and that is what there have been in this house.

> (*She gazes at her father's portrait.*)

And so the Privy Councillor must go into the women's section among the millionairesses. Put him in the corridor for the time being.

> (McARTHUR *and* MURILLO *carry out the picture right.*)

Has my general administrator arrived with his minions?

CHIEF ATTNDT. They are waiting in the green drawing-room. Shall I serve champagne and caviare?

FRL. DOKTOR. That gang's here to work, not stuff its guts.

> (*She sits down on the sofa.*)

Have Möbius brought in, Sievers.

CHIEF ATTNDT. Sure, boss.

> (*He goes to Room Number* 1. *Opens door.*)

Möbius, out!

> (MÖBIUS *appears. He is exalted.*)

MÖBIUS. A night of prayer. Deep blue and holy. The night of the mighty king. His white shadow is loosed from the wall; his eyes are shining.

> (*Silence.*)

FRL. DOKTOR. Möbius, on the orders of the public prosecutor I may speak to you only in the presence of an attendant.

MÖBIUS. I understand, Fräulein Doktor.

FRL. DOKTOR. What I have to say to you applies also to your colleagues.

> (McARTHUR *and* MURILLO *have returned.*)

McArthur and Murillo. Fetch the other two.

> (McARTHUR *and* MURILLO *open doors Numbers* 2 *and* 3.)

MURILLO AND MCARTHUR. Out!

> (NEWTON *and* EINSTEIN *come out, also in a state of exaltation.*)

NEWTON. A night of secrets. Unending and sublime. Through the bars of my window glitter Jupiter and Saturn unveiling the laws of the infinite.

EINSTEIN. A blessed night. Comforting and good. Riddles fall silent, questions are dumb. I should like to play on for ever.

FRL. DOKTOR. Alec Jaspar Kilton and Joseph Eisler –

> (*They both stare at her in amazement.*)

I have something to say to you.

> (*They both draw their revolvers but are disarmed by* MURILLO *and* MCARTHUR.)

Gentlemen, your conversation was overheard; I had had my suspicions for a long time. McArthur and Murillo, bring in their secret radio transmitters.

CHIEF ATTNDT. Hands behind your heads!

> (MÖBIUS, EINSTEIN *and* NEWTON *put their hands behind their heads while* MCARTHUR *and* MURILLO *go into rooms Numbers 2 and 3.*)

NEWTON. It's funny!

> (*He laughs. The others do not. Spooky.*)

EINSTEIN. I don't know.

NEWTON. Too funny!

> (*He laughs again, then falls silent.* MCARTHUR *and* MURILLO *come in with the transmitters.*)

CHIEF ATTNDT. Hands down.

> (*The physicists obey. Silence.*)

FRL. DOKTOR. Sievers. The searchlights.

CHIEF ATTNDT. Okay, boss.

> (*He raises his hand. Searchlights blaze in from outside, bathing the physicists in a blinding light. At the same time,* SIEVERS *switches off the lights in the room.*)

FRL. DOKTOR. The villa is surrounded by guards. Any attempt to escape would be useless.

> (*To the attendants.*)

You three, get out!

(*The three attendants leave the room, carrying the revolvers and radio apparatus. Silence.*)

You alone shall hear my secret. You alone among men. Because it doesn't matter any longer whether you know or not.

(*Silence.*)

(*Grandly*) He has appeared before me also. Solomon, the golden king.

(*All three stare at her in perplexity.*)

MÖBIUS. Solomon?

FRL. DOKTOR. This many a long year.

(NEWTON *softly giggles.*)

(*Unconcerned*) The first time was in my study. One summer evening. Outside, the sun was still shining, and a woodpecker was hammering away somewhere in the park. Then suddenly the golden king came floating towards me like a tremendous angel.

EINSTEIN. She's gone mad.

FRL. DOKTOR. His gaze came to rest upon me. His lips parted. He began to converse with his handmaiden. He had arisen from the dead, he desired to take upon himself again the power that once belonged to him here below, he had unveiled his wisdom, that Möbius might reign on earth, in his name.

EINSTEIN. She must be locked up. She should be in a madhouse.

FRL. DOKTOR. But Möbius betrayed him. He tried to keep secret what could not be kept secret. For what was revealed to him was no secret. Because it could be thought. Everything that can be thought is thought at some time or another. Now or in the future. What Solomon had found could be found by anyone, but he wanted it to belong to himself alone, his means towards the establishment of his holy dominion over all the world. And so he did seek me out, his unworthy handmaiden.

EINSTEIN (*insistently*). You – are – mad. D'you hear, you – are – mad.

FRL. DOKTOR. He did command me to cast down Möbius, and reign in his place. I hearkened unto his command. I was a doctor and Möbius was my patient. I could do with him whatever I wished. Year in, year out, I fogged his brain and made photocopies of the golden king's proclamations, down to the last page.

NEWTON. You're raving mad! Absolutely! Get this clear once and for all! (*Softly*) We're all mad.

FRL. DOKTOR. I went cautiously about my work. At first I exploited only two or three discoveries, in order to rake in the necessary capital. Then I founded enormous plants and factories, one after the other. I've created a giant cartel. I shall exploit to the full, gentlemen, the Principle of Universal Discovery.

MÖBIUS (*insistent*). Fräulein Doktor Mathilde von Zahnd, yóu are sick. Solomon does not exist. He never appeared to me.

FRL. DOKTOR. Liar.

MÖBIUS. I only pretended to see him in order to keep my discoveries secret.

FRL. DOKTOR. You deny him.

MÖBIUS. Do be reasonable. Don't you see you're mad?

FRL. DOKTOR. I'm no more mad than you.

MÖBIUS. Then I must shout the truth to the whole world. You sucked me dry all these years, without shame. You even let my poor wife go on paying for me.

FRL. DOKTOR. You are powerless, Möbius. Even if your voice were to reach the outside world, nobody would believe you. Because to the public at large you are nothing but a dangerous lunatic. By the murder you committed.

(*The truth dawns on the three men.*)

MÖBIUS. Monika –

EINSTEIN. Irene –

NEWTON. Dorothea –

FRL. DOKTOR. I simply seized my opportunity. The wisdom of Solomon had to be safeguarded and your treachery punished.

I had to render all three of you harmless. By the murders you committed. I drove those three nurses into your arms. I could count upon your reactions. You were as predictable as automata. You murdered like professionals.

(MÖBIUS *is about to throw himself upon her but is restrained by* EINSTEIN.)

There's no point in attacking me, Möbius. Just as there was no point in burning manuscripts which I already possess in duplicate.

(MÖBIUS *turns away.*)

What you see around you are no longer the walls of an asylum. This is the strong room of my trust. It contains three physicists, the only human beings apart from myself to know the truth. Those who keep watch over you are not medical attendants. Sievers is the head of my works police. You have taken refuge in a prison you built for yourselves. Solomon thought through you. He acted through you. And now he destroys you, through me.

(*Silence.*)

But I'm taking his power upon myself. I have no fears. My sanatorium is full of my own lunatic relatives, all of them loaded with jewels and medals. I am the last normal member of my family. No more. The last one. I am barren. I can love no one. Only humanity. And so King Solomon took pity on me. He, with his thousand brides, chose me. Now I shall be mightier than my forefathers. My cartel will dictate in each country, each continent; it will ransack the solar system and thrust out beyond the great nebula in Andromeda. It all adds up, and the answer comes out in favour, not of the world, but of an old hunchbacked spinster.

(*She rings a little bell and the* CHIEF ATTENDANT *comes in right.*)

CHIEF ATTNDT. Yes, boss?

FRL. DOKTOR. I must go, Sievers. The board of trustees is waiting. Today we go into world-wide operation. The assembly lines are rolling.

(*She goes out right with* CHIEF ATTENDANT. *The three physicists are alone. Silence. It is all over. Stillness.*)

NEWTON. It is all over.

(*He sits down on the sofa.*)

EINSTEIN. The world has fallen into the hands of an insane, female psychiatrist.

(*He sits down beside* NEWTON.)

MÖBIUS. What was once thought can never be unthought.

(MÖBIUS *sits down in the arm-chair on the left of the sofa. Silence. The three stare before them. Then each speaks in turn, quite calmly and naturally, simply introducing themselves to the audience.*)

NEWTON. I am Newton. Sir Isaac Newton. Born the 4th of January, 1643, at Woolsthorpe, near Grantham. I am president of the Royal Society. But there's no need to get up on my behalf. I wrote the Mathematical Principles of Natural Philosophy. I said: Hypotheses non fingo – I do not invent hypotheses. In the fields of experimental optics, theoretical mechanics and higher mathematics my achievements are not without importance; but I had to leave unresolved certain problems concerning the nature of gravitational force. I also wrote theological works. Commentaries on the Prophet Daniel and on the Revelation of St John the Divine. I am Newton, Sir Isaac Newton. I am the president of the Royal Society.

(*He rises and goes into his room.*)

EINSTEIN. I am Einstein. Professor Albert Einstein. Born the 14th of March, 1879, at Ulm. In 1902 I started work testing inventions at the Federal Patent Office in Berne. It was there that I propounded my special theory of relativity which changed our whole concept of physics. Then I became a member of the Prussian Academy of Science. Later I became a refugee. Because I am a Jew. It was I who evolved the Formula $E = mc^2$, the key to the transformation of matter into energy. I love my fellow-men and I love my violin, but it was on my recommendation that they built the atomic bomb. I am Einstein. Professor Albert Einstein, born the 14th of March, 1879, at Ulm.

(*He rises and goes into his room. He is heard fiddling. Kreisler. Liebesleid.*)

MÖBIUS. I am Solomon. I am poor King Solomon. Once I was immeasurably rich, wise and God-fearing. The mighty trembled at my word. I was a Prince of Peace, a Prince of Justice. But my wisdom destroyed the fear of God, and when I no longer feared God my wisdom destroyed my wealth. Now the cities over which I ruled are dead, the Kingdom that was given unto my keeping is deserted: only a blue shimmering wilderness. And somewhere round a small, yellow, nameless star there circles, pointlessly, everlastingly, the radioactive earth. I am Solomon. I am Solomon. I am Solomon. I am poor King Solomon.

(*He goes into his room. Now the drawing-room is empty. Only Einstein's fiddle is heard.*)